THE REAL
ANTI-SEMITISM
IN AMERICA

THE REAL ANTI-SEMITISM IN AMERICA

BY

Nathan Perlmutter and Ruth Ann Perlmutter

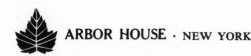 ARBOR HOUSE · NEW YORK

Library of Congress Catalogue Card Number: 81-71672

ISBN: 0-87795-378-3

Manufactured in the United States of America

10 9 8 7 6 5 4 3 2 1

Acknowledgments

The following page constitutes an extension of the copyright page.

Grateful acknowledgment is made for permission to reprint the following selections:

Excerpt from "Concerning the Jews" from *In Defense of Harriet Shelley and Other Essays* by Mark Twain. Reprinted by permission of Harper & Row Publishers, Inc.

Charts of surveys conducted by Yankelovich, Skelly and White, Inc. Reprinted by permission of Yankelovich, Skelly and White, Inc.

Tenth version of the table in the Comparative Survey of Freedom, published by Freedom House, January-February 1981 edition of *Freedom at Issue*. Copyright © 1981 by Freedom House. Reprinted by permission of the publisher.

Excerpt from "The Harlem Ghetto" from *Notes of a Native Son* by James Baldwin. Copyright © 1955 by James Baldwin. Reprinted by permission of Beacon Press.

Contents

Foreword

ESSENTIALLY, THIS BOOK'S thesis is that today the interests of Jews are not so much threatened by their familiar nemesis, crude anti-Semitism, as by a-Semitic governmental policies, the proponents of which may be free of anti-Semitism and indeed may well—literally—count Jews among some of their best friends. Oil dependency, the thirst of Western economics for recycled petrodollars, the shading of individual rights by compensatory group rights, neo-isolationism in the guise of peace, the depreciation of military preparedness are all illustrations.

To be sure, old-fashioned anti-Semitism is anything but a vestigial remainder. Here it appears *in cognito* as anti-Zionism; there it prowls naked; in one place it is indulged without passion but is politically utilitarian; in another place, its political utility nil, its passion nevertheless smolders.

Some of the views we express are not popularly shared. We hope, however, that they are provocative of reasoned discussion. Some are popular wisdoms. We hope we have provided these with fresh relevancy. In either event, our views, though surely influenced by our associations, are attributable solely to ourselves and not to our associations.

9

The manuscript was read in whole or in part by Abraham
Foxman, Theodore Freedman, Philip Perlmutter and Joseph
Rosner. For their thoughtful suggestions, we are warmly grateful and lastingly indebted. Rochelle Amera was of invaluable
assistance in the preparation of the manuscript.

—Nathan Perlmutter and Ruth Ann Perlmutter

I have set before you life and
death, blessing and cursing; therefore
choose life, that both thou and thy
seed may live.

Deuteronomy XXX:19

1

Nazis I Have Known

IN MY LIFETIME I have experienced two Nazis—that I know of. Each introduced me to a stranger in myself. Together, but individually, they dispelled my stereotype of Nazis. Nazis, it seems, are not as monolithic as our haunted memory casts them. In short, the beasts are human.

I met my first Nazi in a chance encounter. I was in my early forties, robust. He was in his mid-fifties, a relatively older man. I beat him up, severely.

It was a Sunday, about 7:30 in the morning, in the Yorkville section of Manhattan and I was going for a *Times.* Our news dealer was closed, so I continued walking. On the next block, the man, who in minutes I would be pummeling, was coming toward me, carrying the Sunday *Times.*

"Where'd you get the paper?"

He stopped despite it being very cold: "You go down two blocks, and on the corner . . ."

I thanked him, he said I was welcome, and repeated the directions. I remember thinking, "Polite man." He had a thick German accent. He jaywalked across the street and I continued, but in a moment I saw an open candy store across the street. It sold papers and I started toward it.

Now it began happening. The man, who had already crossed the street, turned and as our eyes met, I felt prompted to explain why I wasn't following his patiently given directions. "This place is open," pointing to the candy store. His raised-voice answer was, or incredulously I thought it was, "Don't go in there. It's Yiddish. Jews own it."

In real life, at least in mine, tense moments have not been distinguished by inspired prose. What I said was, "What was that?" and heart pounding, I changed course to walk toward him. "It's a Judische store. Jews own it. Stinking Jews. Don't go in there." Facial expressions italicized his maledictions.

Early Sunday morning in Manhattan is always unreal. But this! My own neighborhood, once resonant with the oratory and marching bands of the German-American Bund, a loud Jew hater replete with German accent and me, whose career had been spent in the employ of the Anti-Defamation League of B'nai B'rith. My shock ebbed quickly—as quickly, hate gorged me. "You sonofabitch. I'm Jewish, damn you, and if you weren't older than me, I'd punch you in the nose." I was still controlled, my threat's condition, his immunity.

I'm not precisely sure what he answered. It's not that I have now forgotten; that same night I wasn't word-for-word sure. But what it added up to was crystal clear. He asserted that Jews are filth and also retorted that no Jew would or could lay a hand on him, and if I thought I could, to try it.

What followed will read like, and indeed was, pure Street-and-Smith pulp. I mean that "the next thing I knew," his hands were up to his face and my right fist was withdrawing from his suddenly red-running nostrils. Conscious now that I had actually punched him, I became conscious too that my head, my heart, even my arms and legs were one furious furnace of hate and that I would consume him in it. "I followed with a left" and "he started going down." The helplessness of his crumbling fueled rather than appeased me and I pummeled more punches onto his head. Suddenly in the morning quiet, like an off-stage chorus on cue, there sounded shouts of "Stop him!", but no one did.

They should have stopped me. All that they knew was that a younger man was beating up an older man, but this is New York City, where Kitty Genovese lived privately and was murdered publicly. Now he lay before me, hands covering his head. I kicked his legs aside, stepped over him and started toward the nearby candy store.

The "chorus," some six, maybe eight, early risers, was grouped in front of the store. As a kind of rationale in response to their cries moments ago of "Stop him!" and also, I remember thinking, to allay the fear of me in their eyes, I boomed, "He's an anti-Semite. Called me a stinking Jew." They said nothing, and as in a scene from a Western movie when the bad guy moves toward the barroom's swinging doors, they parted to make way for me as I strode into the candy store.

Inside were the two owners and a young man who seemed to be the son of one of them. I said *"Times"* to the youth; he handed one to me and looked, I remember imagining, sympathetic. Again my voice, in explanation rather than reportage: "He called you all stinking Jews. He's turning people away from you—because you're Jewish." The owner, on my, the customer's side of the counter, answered in a half whisper, "Shh, lower it." I recall thinking, not contemptuously, but just thinking, that he didn't want the chorus, now reformed at the door, to know that they were Jews! Then as I was paying the owner behind the counter, he spoke. In a voice too loud, a voice pitched for hearing by the chorus behind me, he more declared than said, "We're not Jews!"

An hour or so later, back in my apartment I received a long-distance call from my brother. We must have talked for ten minutes and I never once mentioned what had happened. As best I can reconstruct it, I didn't mention it because the experience was in hiding from my consciousness, waiting to sort out its heaving confusions of mugged dignity and brawler's pride, waiting for composure of breath as well as some orderliness of meaning, before reentering my consciousness.

Of course, later that day and for days thereafter, my wife and I hashed and rehashed, analyzed and dissected my wild morning minutes.

Were the candy-store people really not Jewish? I didn't give a damn. It was irrelevant. If they were and were hiding it, I also didn't care. They were merely props, not *dramatis personae* in the happening.

Something else. I knew that very afternoon that had I been walking a street in Greenwich Village, or in Brooklyn Heights, or anywhere other than in German Yorkville, and the same man said the same thing in the same accent, I'd never have responded as I did. Under such circumstances, it somehow wouldn't have mattered, not all that much. And even in Yorkville, had the same man said the same thing in a French or an English accent, it also would never have exploded as it did. The combustibles, the *only* combustibles, were a German-accented anti-Semite in Germantown.

I also thought about his age. I said mid-fifties, but for all that I actually knew, he might have been sixty. What of the morality of a forty-four-year-old beating up a man nearly eligible for Social Security? I thought about it, but I had no problem with it. This is the way my mind ran, and indeed runs: Why should his age have been his shield? Did sixty-year-old Nazis disqualify themselves from acting against Jews? Or for that matter, were eighteen-year-old Nazis to be absolved of their crimes because they were "too young to understand"? And thirty-five-year-old Nazis, should they have been fought with a turned cheek because they were breadwinners for warm and loving families? No, I had no problem with what I had done and in a satisfied, almost peaceful frame of mind conjectured that I'd have beaten him senseless if he were seventy!

The question begs itself in the writing of this as it did in the thinking of it. What if he had been a burly, younger man? Would I have reacted as I did? I think I would have. More candidly, less "modestly," I know I would have.

But there are less academic questions, questions of chilling realism. When in two minutes I left the candy store, he had already gone. What if he had still been there, unconscious or dead? What if in falling he had hit his head and been killed? I thought about that and about my career and about my family. The end line of my ruminations, however, was that had I ignored the man, his hating face and hating words, I'd have been shamed longer than I have been ambivalent about my Sunday morning stroll.

I was a houseguest of the Nazi I liked. In the early 1960s I spent a month as a consultant on anti-Semitism to the West German government. One night in Cologne, my host and hostess invited a Count and Countess "Somebody" to a dinner party in my honor. The evening was progressing pleasantly enough and I suppose that's precisely what prompted me to say what I said. I mean, the small talk and each of us being charmingly clever, as if it were any one of fifty thousand Saturday-night parties back home, itched me, stirred guilt in me, made me mean, and so I said it.

I told them that I wanted to confess something. That earlier that day, I afternoon-walked with Father von Sohmer through the town cemetery; that we had paused before a stone that read, "Hans Schmidt, 18 years old, Stalingrad"; that notwithstanding the boy's age, I felt no compassion, but instead, not without bitterness, found myself thinking, "Who invited him there?"

I continued, telling them of Father von Sohmer's comment while I was thinking my private thoughts; that he knew the family and that they were fine people. Knowing the priest well by now and liking him, I knew that his estimate, "fine people," was one, had I known them, I'd likely have shared. But his words did not dissipate my indifference to the dead boy, and that I still was, was my confession.

I suppose the ungracious candor of my remarks, the cognac —to be sure, the cognac—changed the character of the party. The count revealed that he had been "an enthusiastic Hitler youth leader," and my host, withered arm though he had, offered that he had been a Hitler youth leader too, and later, a member of the party.

Somehow I wasn't surprised by the count's having been an enthusiastic young Nazi. He shot enthusiastically, played croquet enthusiastically, and was now an enthusiastic member of an organization dedicated to peace. What's more, I'm sure that he enthusiastically cultivated Jewish friends. I suspect that there's more than one enthusiastic ex-Nazi who today is an enthusiastic good guy while the indifferent-to-Nazism Deutschlander, as a consequence of his personal chemistry, is today indifferent about German democracy.

But it's my host that I want to tell about. During the thirties his closest friend, in appearance more Aryan than he, was Jewish. "I knew, we all knew, Hitler's views on Jews, but we told ourselves that nothing would happen to the Jews we knew. After all, we told ourselves, our Jewish friends were not the kind that Hitler was talking about. At the end of the war, I went home to the Sudetenland to look for my friend, and as if to confirm what subconsciously I knew all along, but which I'd refused to think about, I went directly from the train to the Jewish cemetery." Was it sentimental slobbery? The cognac? Simple sincerity? His voice choked as he murmured, "I found him there."

I asked, softly, conscious of and surprised by the casualness of my tone, "What made you a Nazi?"

His answer: "I was an idealist."

He explained Hitler's platform, its planks, cleanliness of mind and body, honesty in government, purging the nation of social and political decadence. "About Jews," he continued, "we have a faculty—man, that is—to block out on things we don't want to believe. And when in the closing years of the war, rumors reached us about the extermination camps, rumors we had every reason to believe, we still would not see. By now we had our own families to think about, virtually every German family suffered losses, our own lives to somehow salvage in the bombing wreckage, and so we continued to block out on the genocide in our midst."

"And how did you become an ex-Nazi?"

"In the late forties I was applying for a visa to the United States where an international conference to which I was a delegate was being held. An American sergeant, the bureaucrat in charge, routinely asked me if I had ever been a Nazi. I don't know what prompted me to tell the truth. It would have been so easy to simply say no. But I said yes. The sergeant's cigar almost dropped out of his mouth. When he recovered from my answer, he asked me if I was still a Nazi. I mumbled no, I wasn't. He said, prove it. And now I was speechless. How does one prove a negative? Proof that I was a Nazi was simple; that I wasn't a Nazi, impossible. But at that point, an inspiration hit me. I held up this useless, deformed arm. I said to him, when I was young I had polio. I can't have it again. He gave the visa."

All of this, quietly, so quietly we could hear each other's breath.

After a short, thick silence, I half whispered a question to both my host and the count. "What about your idealism (that word in that context had startled me, and now, twenty years later, still intrigues me) in 1938? After all, the German press was full of Crystal Night, of the violence and the humiliation visited upon Jews. What of your idealism then? Had you done anything, said anything?"

The hour was late, the cognac and the naked conversation softened and hushed the room, and in a kind of oral slow motion my host whispered, "We were cowards."

In the Nazi's home, as his honored guest, soon to bed down in his guest room, pleasant days spent together, in truth liking him, I was without feeling for his "idealism," was unmoved by his mea culpa, felt neither hate, nor hostility, felt only a vague pity, a warmthless pity, not for the victims, not for the survivors, but for my newfound Nazi friend.

My two Nazis and my two selves. Nazi number one is from central casting. Emotionally programmed, I became John Wayne. Nazi number two is a complex of hurting idealism, and now rationally programmed, I became Hamlet. In the one instance, enervating hatred made me strong. In the other, nourishing reason disarmed me. It was so for me: does it hold for other people? Well, sometimes.

My Yorkville microproblem and a Jewish macroproblem is how to nurture our hate as an antibody against the lingering, lethal hatred of us, but to do so without succumbing to toxemia.

And in Cologne too, the conundrum was as Jewish as it was personal. I was civil to the count and to my host, no matter both were Nazis when it mattered, no longer Nazis when it didn't matter. Why? Why was I so measured in Cologne, so primeval in Yorkville? I suspect it's because in Yorkville the enemy was recognizable. I remembered him from long-ago imaginings, or was it from a late-night TV movie? In Cologne, the enemy was camouflaged in manners and education, the arrived Jew's very own wardrobe. But which Nazi bore the greater responsibility for the Holocaust? The oaf, a cog, a classic follower, or my educated friends?

Perhaps my tolerance in Cologne suggests social balance. But Jewishly, understanding can also be a soporific.

2

Discovering Anti-Semitism and Together Growing Older

NAZIS, AS THE opening chapter of this book that is part memoir, part candid view of contemporary anti-Semitism, is a fitting anachronism. An anachronism because Nazism is dead and our vengeance is our good life. Fitting because the Jewish gut has ears, and real or imagined, in it we still hear Nazism's heartbeat. It is fitting too because Jews and Nazis share something in common that is so totally, so exclusively their own, so intimately theirs and theirs alone, that no one, absolutely no one, can fully comprehend it. The Nazi sympathizer wasn't so close to the Nazi, the Christian martyr dying protecting Jews wasn't so close to Jews, as the Nazi and the Jew are close to each other. Ours, only ours, is the oneness, the hysterical oneness of that frozen moment when the wide, wild eyes of the rapist and the wide, wild eyes of the raped lock, when the defiler voraciously defiles and the defiled is haplessly defiled. The moment eternally frozen, endlessly we shame and pain and die in our nightmare without end, in our endlessly anguishing togetherness.

Most American Jews become aware of and responsive to anti-Semitism, its various forms and its varied carriers, incrementally. Our awareness begins in the heritage of parent-passed-on stories, and it swells as psychically we bank our grievances accumulated in the gentile outside. Still, when I was a boy in Brooklyn, in the 1930s, our neighborhood was virtually all Jewish, and our neighborhood being our world, I assumed that the world was all Jewish, or just about. To be sure, we were aware that there were gentiles, President Hoover for instance, and in our history books George Washington (we suspected that Lincoln was one of us), and we knew that there were many Christians, mostly hard-drinking and Jew-tormenting in "the old country," far beyond the ocean's horizon at Coney Island. I said, "or just about." We did have Christians in our neighborhood, and they seemed to be distributed one family to a tenement house, and they all being janitors, I assumed that all Christians were janitors, and the Stanleys and Annas of them all being Polish, Christians, it followed, were Polish janitors. I sometimes wondered at the fallen state of George Washington's descendants.

It wasn't until 1941 when I graduated high school and job hunting, charted my days by the help-wanted classified ads in the *New York Times,* that being Jewish began to pinch.

Column after page-long column, each packed tight with employment agency advertisements, stipulated "Chr only." "Chr" I quickly gathered meant Christian, not in code, but in the economics of per line ad rates. At eighteen I was sufficiently experienced to know that after several days of fringing scarves, I had had it with factory work, so these were office-job ads I was handicapping. What eighteen years had not taught me, however, was that Perlmutter was a dead giveaway that I wasn't a Chr. Upon learning that one's name could be like one's color, a freely offered confession of guilt, I experimented with pronouncing my name as Perl-mutere, hoping that this imagined Frenchification of Perlmutter would permit me to pass. It didn't. I went further. In an interview with one employment agency I not only allowed my name to be Perl-mutere but introduced myself as Nathaniel Perl-mutere. I didn't realize it then, but by calling myself Nathaniel I was, in a manner of speaking, changing my "Christian" name.

Over the years I've grown accustomed to Nathan Perlmutter. In part, because coarse anti-Semitism has ebbed; in part, because Israel no longer suggests huddled losers, Menasha Skulnicks cloned a million times, survivors thanks to their wiles and to the world's pity, but today projects the image of Charlton Heston, a winner—and dare I say it?—the image of the strong, the tall, the intimidatingly confident *goy.* And something else. Being comfortably Jewish in a gentile world, while being of both worlds, takes aging, time in which gentiles accommodate to Perlmutter, time in which Perlmutter trims to the diaspora, and all the contemporaneous while, time in which one grows accustomed to oneself, as Jew, as American, as self.

Incrementally. The growing older, the adolescent's wondrous explorations of other neighborhoods, and the Jewish adolescent's discovery of "restricted" neighborhoods, "restricted" apartment buildings. The teenager's awakening to books and to music, and the teenage Jew's realization that Jack Armstrong, the All-American Boy, likely went to a school with a quota system limiting Jewish enrollment, restricted against Jewish professors. Older still, traveling, discovering secular America, but as a Jew discovering, too, hotels which excluded Jews . . . and dogs.

Incrementally. You of course were familiar since childhood with the phrase *Christ killer,* memory associated with mother-told stories of Lodz, Poland, but now you yourself are a young parent, and your six-year-old daughter asks her mother, "Mommy, why did we kill the little baby Jesus?" *We!* The legacy of anti-Semitism handed down in suburbia as it had been in Lodz, a legacy too of the victim's self-doubt, probated in Denver as it had been in Kiev.

Incrementally. I am fifty-nine years old. My children are older by far than I was when I enlisted in World War II to "fight anti-Semitism." Older than I was when I was discharged, mission presumably accomplished. But still, I am accumulating grievances. The Anti-Defamation League surveys anti-Semitic vandalisms in the United States, finds a co-relationship between the frequency of the vandalisms and the density of Jewish population. The higher the Jewish population, the greater the number of depredations. And even as these findings are being studied, Poland features an anti-Semitic rally and West German polling reveals high levels of anti-Semitism amongst Germans fifty years and older. But there are virtually no Jews in Poland, a smattering in Germany.

It's almost as if the presence of Jews and the absence of Jews have in common that both are stimulants to anti-Semites. Or conversely, that it's really irrelevant to anti-Semites whether we stay or we leave. Their only requirement of us is either the image or the memory of us.

Incrementally. The mannered but insensitive anti-Semite. I met my first prototype of the bigot whose definition of a kike is the Jewish gentleman who just left the room, in 1941 as a student at Georgetown University's School of Foreign Service. It was hardly a momentous experience, rather an extracurricular credit of sorts. The course was titled "The Far East," and for reasons that still elude me, one morning Professor Carpenter opened the class with an expression of annoyed wonderment. "What Henry Wallace and a bunch of Jews know about agriculture is totally beyond me!" He then proceeded with the morning's lecture on Japan. I recall flushing with shame and the overly warm eternity of the ensuing forty-five minutes; I recall, too, opting to just sit there, hoping to shrink, to fade into my desk-seat, become invisible rather than rising, proudly stalking out or resonantly challenging him. The lecture over, I lingered, and when we were alone, I mumbled that I was Jewish, and what did he mean, would he please tell me, by what he had said. I was at least as apologetic for challenging him as I was offended. In truth, I am not now certain that at the moment of confrontation, I wasn't more reluctant to hurt his feelings—a jovial, entertaining teacher—than I was intent upon assuaging my own. His response was to ask me to sit down; I complied. He then patted my head, literally, and told me he meant nothing personal, and that I was different, not like the Jews in the Agriculture Department whom, he asked me to admit, he knew better than I did.

The course's credit? My "Far East" professor's pat on my head made a tougher Jew of me than my dry-as-dust Talmud Torah teacher had.

Mannered insensitivity is still around. Jews, however, have changed. At least, many of us have.

In 1981, the White House proposed one Warren Richardson for the post of assistant secretary for legislation of the Department of Health and Human Services, a cabinet department requiring Senate confirmation. Richardson had been general counsel and chief lobbyist for the Liberty Lobby, a notorious multimillion-dollar organization obsessed with hallucinations of Zionist conspiracies. Its founder, Willis Carto, whom Richardson had served for four faithful years, had written:

> Hitler's defeat was the defeat of Europe. And of America. How could we have been so blind? The blame, it seems, must be laid at the door of the international Jews. It was their propaganda, lies and demands which blinded the West. If Satan himself, with all of the super-human genius and diabolical ingenuity at his

command, had tried to create a permanent disintegration and force for the destruction of the nations, he could have done no better than to invent the Jews.

President Reagan's aides who recommended Richardson were, I am confident, originally ignorant of the true nature of Liberty Lobby. Among letterheads quickly scanned, theirs has the appearance of just another far-out, right wing organization. But immediately that the proposed nomination was made public, the Anti-Defamation League edified the White House—in documented detail. To no avail. Weeks transpired without withdrawal of the nomination. Finally, surfacing evidence suggestive that the nomination would proceed, Richardson's and Liberty Lobby's records were released to the press. Now, quickly, Richardson's name was withdrawn. Because of sensitivity to anti-Semitism? Perhaps. In view, however, of the silence in response to our privately—one might say, considerately—communicated facts, and the prompt action responsive to the publicity, I attribute the withdrawal as much to bureaucratic self-defense warding off political embarrassment as to sensitivity to Jewish outrage.

The story of the rabbi and his devoted disciple is often told. The disciple avows his love for the rabbi. The rabbi inquires, "How do you know you love me?" The disciple responds that he knows what pleases the rabbi and consequently tries always to please him. The rabbi asks, "Do you know what hurts me?" The young man replies that he does not. Finally, the point of the story is made in the rabbi's comment, "How can you say you love me if you don't know what it is that brings me pain?"

My Nazi host loved his Jewish friend, my "Far East" professor gave me good grades, and the White House staff, I am satisfied, harbors amicable feelings for Jews. But day and night, though the differences are among them, what they have in common is insensitivity to what it is that pains us.

There have been, nonetheless, significant changes. Alone and innocent in 1941, I lost my voice. Older now, our innocence gone up in smoke, our voice has changed. American Jews today are resonant. Or, as I was saying, many of us are.

Incrementally. Words, I learned early on, words as neutral as a dictionary, can be demeaning, can be bland yet bristle with hate. Their dictionary meaning is their camouflage, cloaking the user in innocence, suggesting that the offended Jew is overly sensitive. "Churches nearby," "congenial clientele," no matter Funk and Wagnalls, no matter Webster, no matter Oxford and its abridged and unabridged assurances, soon after leaving Brooklyn I learned meant Stay Out, Jew. These terms were euphemisms of exclusion. There were euphemisms of opprobrium too. To this day when evil is attributed to Wall Street or to international bankers, I wait for the other shoe, Jew, to drop. It was as if the word *Jew* were a hyphenated, integral part of the dark side of the world of finance. The noun *Bolshevik,* the adjective *alien,* still have faintly audible, possibly threatening resonance for Jews of my generation. Indeed, during the war quartermaster jokes were flashing caution lights to many of us.

In 1918 the Anti-Defamation League then five years old, our "melting pot" fully one hundred and forty two years old, was prompted to issue guidelines, not on euphemisms for *Jew* but for the use of the very word itself. After defining Jew as one who professes the Jewish religion, or as a person who believes himself descended from biblical Jews, the tract continued:

> There is, however, a third use of the word "Jew," owing to the deliberate policy of the medieval church which purposely shut out all reputable callings to Jews so as to impress upon Christians the superiority of the true faith. Hence, a certain touch of opprobrium and contempt has attached to the very name "Jew," which has lasted to some extent down to the present day among the common people, and even among some of the educated, not one of whom could probably trace the real origin of his prejudice.

However unjustified and obsolete the prejudice thus attached
to the word "Jew" may be, it exists in many minds and has to
be reckoned with by the molders of public opinion. Jews are
naturally and deservedly more sensible to this unconscious prejudice, and have at times attempted to introduce instead of the
word "Jew" other terms such as "Hebrew" or "Israelite" in
order to obviate it. But these have failed to replace the more
familiar nomenclature, and of recent years the better class of
Jews have adopted the policy of boldly identifying themselves
with the term "Jew" with the hope of thus wearing down the
medieval associations connected with it.

With a view to meeting this sentiment among Jews and to
avoid catering to the prejudice which all fair-minded persons,
whatever their creed, would like to see disappear, rules are offered for guidance as to the proper use of the words "Jew" and
"Jewish" in public print:

Note the archaic reference to "the better class of Jews" made
by appellants for verbal fair treatment, themselves, ironically,
Jewish. Not yet archaic, still discernible in our ages-conditioned
plaintiffs' manners, is the low, sweeping, deferential bow as we
speak in earshot of our judges and defendants, the gentiles.
Their prejudice is "unconscious" and is something "which all
fair-minded persons, whatever their creed, would like to see
disappear." Flattery, the accustomed loser's long-shot bet.

The "Rules for Guidance" included assurances that the
words *Jews* and *Jewish* were properly used when describing
Jewish wives, "Jewish children, Jewish young men, and the like.
However, "The word 'Jew' is a noun, and should never be used
as an adjective or verb. To speak of 'Jew girls' or 'Jew stores'
is both objectionable and vulgar . . . "

The most detailed of the rules for the guidance of gentiles was
directed at the press. It urged the avoidance of the use of the
word *Jew* or *Jewish* to describe an individual "unless from the
context it is necessary to call attention to his religion . . . Thus
if a Jew is convicted of a crime he should not be called a 'Jewish

criminal'; and on the other hand, if a Jew makes a great medical or other scientific discovery, he should not be called a great 'Jewish physician' or an eminent 'Jewish scientist.' "

In this time, in the perspective from our now place in American society, this business of words, the correct and the undesirable usage of *Jewish* may seem a small thing. It wasn't and it isn't. We, than whom there are few more inspired weavers of words, remain on guard, remain suspicious of words' capacity to cut and maim us. To be sure, the cutting edge of *Jew* as a pejorative has, in this country, grown dull, taken its rote place along *Catholic* and *Protestant.* But as styles of language and syntax have changed over the years, so have word camouflages concealing deprecation of us.

In the Beginning was the Word . . .

Lewis Carroll was absorbed by words too. He had Humpty Dumpty declare that words meant what Humpty meant them to mean. And so it is today. In the United Nations, words mean what a majority of the General Assembly means them to mean. Ergo, Zionism means racism. And as another wordsmith, Casey Stengel, might have said, "You can look it up"—in the widely reported, published and distributed accounts in print, over radio and by television tube, of United Nations' proceedings. Jews know who the Zionists really are. Anti-Semites know who the Zionists really are. And new generations of Europeans, Americans, Africans and Asians are learning who the racist Zionists are as surely as their parents learned who the Christ killers were.

George Orwell had a fascination with words, too. In *1984* he invented Newspeak. There, words meant the opposite of what they mean. Orwell wasn't dead a figurative moment when life imitating art further proved his genius. The Communist dictatorships of Eastern Europe dubbed themselves the Peoples' *democracies.* Mao Tse-tung's cultural revolution happened not in the world's largest gulag, but in the world's largest *republic,* the People's Republic of China. And today, Zionism, the Jewish people's liberation movement, is, in one more obeisance to Newspeak, another face of "imperialism" and of "racism."

Words. Fidel Castro: "There is nothing in recent history that parallels (the Holocaust) more than the dispossession, persecution and genocide that Zionism is currently practicing against the Palestinian people."

The so-called nonaligned nations, fully two-thirds of the nations of the world, in formal session in Havana charged Zionism with "crimes against humanity." Crimes against humanity! The phrase has been used formally but once before—at the Nuremberg Trials to describe Nazism's crimes.

On the one hand, perhaps it's all only a matter of words. After all, as children we sang, "Sticks and stones will break my bones, but names will never harm me." But we are no longer children, we are of age, and we have the experienced wisdom of Rabbi Heschel:

> . . . death and life are in the power of the tongue. Of all the organs with which the body is endowed, none is as dangerous as the tongue . . . the tongue is a sharper weapon than the sword . . . the holocaust did not begin with building crematoria; it began with uttering evil words, it began with defamation.

In the United States, whatever the forms of manifested anti-Semitism I have described or have glancingly mentioned, by and large they have been expressions of persons, both individual and corporate, expressions of old ways and handed-down mores, and almost never codified, institutionalized or propagated by the state. Unlike the church of old, unlike the Third Reich, unlike the Soviet Union, in all of which anti-Semitism was in the warp and woof of government looms, anti-Semitism in the United States has been plied by prejudice's free-enterprisers.

Further, notwithstanding the long-time neutrality of the state toward discrimination, a neutrality which functionally aided and abetted practicing bigots, and which was finally shaken by the Johnson Administration's civil-rights laws, our national rhetoric, rhetoric though it was, served Jews and other discriminated-against minorities well. The ideals of that rhetoric and its constitutional source provided accommodating context and legal support for the struggle against racial and religious discrimination. Also, no matter these ideals were late in being translated into law, so long as they were official American rhetoric, the bigot's "un-American" practices were in the dock, and his victim's brief was an echo of the Bill of Rights and of the Fourth of July.

Today, for all the significant progress Jews have made in the United States, for all that we have never, in all the millenia of our wanderings, enjoyed a safer harbor than here in the United States, Jews are nonetheless uneasy. Not because of a sensed personal danger, like Tevya's in czarist Anatevka; nor is the unease attributable to lingering resentment from boyhood frustration with patterns of discrimination; it is not because of father-experienced humiliating stereotypes; it is not because of neo-Nazis, stirring again, for we know their shadows are longer by far than their hulk; curiously, more ominously, it isn't even due to anti-Semitism.

Rather is it a fear of Jewish endangerment coiled in state policies, themselves free of anti-Semitism, which in plausible scenarios spring free, jeopardizing Jewish security. The dominant anti-Semitism in the haunting of Jews today is without familiar anti-Semitism. It is nothing personal . . . as yet.

Oil, for instance, is not anti-Semitic. It is a-Semitic. The parching thirst for it, however, has changed the world's Middle East foreign policy, and in the process has compromised Israel's international standing, and has contributed to the sure-footedness of Israel's implacable enemies. Jews worry about that and worriedly ruminate . . . What if a Middle East war were to deprive the world of oil? Would a darkened world, a world ground to a halt, scapegoat Israel? Scapegoat Jews, Israel's advocates?

Soviet-American trade is détente's carrot. Its earned dollars and pounds, its yens, francs and marks now placate capitalists who only yesteryear vowed unyielding hostility to the *red menace,* to *red fascism,* terms preferred to *communism* because more lurid, they more accurately described capitalist views. Détente's acquired technology and supplementary food correspondingly soothes Communists who only yesteryear swore undying contempt for capitalists. For many Jews, however, to say nothing, in this context, of the millions of gentile captives in the Soviet cage, contributions to the stabilization of the Soviet system are a helping hand to the one major power in the world today that has institutionalized anti-Semitism.

Peace, sweet peace, yearned for universally, prayed for in a thousand languages, everyman's shared icon, the effectuation of which is a statesman's passageway to immortality, can in our time, in the Middle East, sour Jewishly shared longings for it. Jews are anxious about a Middle Eastern peace that is imposed and that, though it results in the absence of war, and renders oil safe, makes being Jewish in Israel hazardous. Being accustomed to worrying, the Jewish psyche's tolerance for apprehension is ample. So Jews worry, too, about the fallout of world disapproval and animus, as they continue to press for support of Israel's security and consequently, gradually, increasingly, are perceived by a peace-minded society as intransigently indifferent to "peace."

It seems like only yesterday that my major Jewish concern was to find an unrestricted office job.

3

The Stamp of Anti-Semitism

WHY? WHY THE persistent continuity of anti-Semitism, from ancient and agricultural Egypt to splendorous and militaristic Rome on to classless and scientifically Marxist Moscow? And in all the way stations in between, in time and space, like some perennial poison flower? In our time, studies have abounded. Authoritarian personalities, it has been suggested, are the carriers of bigotry and anti-Semitism. Alas, however, I have known too many authoritarian personalities who, politically speaking, wore white hats, their authoritarianism compromising, but nonetheless furthering do-good causes. Among them have been Jews. Other studies have traced anti-Semitism to the crucifixion story, and while indubitably the crucifixion of Jesus has played a horrific part in the rationalization of anti-Semitism, from John to Torquemada and from Torquemada to Father Coughlin and beyond, I wonder. To be sure, the Christian-professing

czars scorned Jews as Christ killers. But the incredibly long
wandering, forty-year march from Egypt was an escape by Jews
from the jurisdiction of pharaohs who preceded Jesus by centuries. Romans persecuted Jews before taking note of Christians,
and couldn't have cared less about the crucifixion. Voltaire
scorned Christianity yet poured his venom on Jews. Books,
tracts, doctoral theses, sermons, colloquia, workshops, confer-
ences, seminars have attributed anti-Semitism to capitalism and
to communism, to political opportunists, to xenophobia, to
father-hatred, to Jews for being too passive and to Jews for
being too aggressive. But for all that these and dozens of other
explanations may each contain seeds for the sowing of anti-
Semitism by given people in given places at given times, the
question remains, Why is anti-Semitism so ubiquitous and perennial? Why did Egyptians along the Nile, Americans along the
Mississippi, dimeless thugs in Berlin and fat cats in posh country clubs, rich, poor and middle classes, Black and white, male
and female, children and grandparents, churchgoers and atheists, the lettered and the unlettered, the Left and the Right, not
infrequently have in common one thing?—their amenability to
anti-Semitism?

When I was a young man, I knew. After all, young people
tend to knowing, and with certitude. As I have grown older, I
am less certain. Younger, I was certain that if only people
understood the irrationalism of prejudice, they would enlist
with the good guys, vote for fair employment practices laws, be
repelled by rather than giggle at anti-Jewish stereotypes, ride off
into a benignly red setting sun, ecumenizing all the way. So we
threw facts at bigotry, as if our facts were baseballs and prejudice a bottle on a shelf in a tent at a country fair. Hit, surely
it would topple. Well, the antidiscrimination laws have been
passed, anti-Jewish stereotypes, at least those purveyed by non-
Jews have lost fashionableness, and we are awash in ecumenical
rhetoric, but just as with the hit bottle at the country fair,

anti-Semitism is still standing. Survey after survey suggests that some 30% of the American public continues to harbor incipiently unfriendly views of Jews.

In 1898, Mark Twain explored the causes of anti-Semitism in an essay titled, "Concerning the Jews." With candor as innocent of sociologeze as Huck and Jim were of Brotherhood Week, Twain attributed anti-Semitism in significant part to gentile jealousy and resentment of the Jews' besting Christians in the marketplace. In his paper, a philo-Semitic tract, he confesses that he once believed that anti-Semitism was due to "fanaticism," but that he now considers this reasoning to be in error. Twain's thesis is absent from contemporary literary analyses of anti-Semitism, and where approached, ironically, is found in anti-Semitic tracts charging Jews with financial manipulation. But let Twain speak for himself:

> We have all thoughtfully—or unthoughtfully—read the pathetic story of the years of plenty and the years of famine in Egypt, and how Joseph, with that opportunity, made a corner in broken hearts, and the crusts of the poor, and human liberty—a corner whereby he took a nation's money all away, to the last penny; took a nation's live-stock all away, to the last hoof; took a nation's land away, to the last acre; then took the nation itself, buying it for bread, man by man, woman by woman, child by child, till all were slaves; a corner which took everything, left nothing; a corner so stupendous that, by comparison with it, the most gigantic corners in subsequent history are but baby things, for it dealt in hundreds of millions of bushels, and its profits were reckonable by hundreds of millions of dollars . . .
>
> Is it presumable that the eye of Egypt was upon Joseph, the foreign Jew, all this time? I think it likely. Was it friendly? We must doubt it. Was Joseph establishing a character for his race which would survive long in Egypt? And in time would his name come to be familiarly used to express that character—like Shylock's? It is hardly to be doubted. Let us remember that this was *centuries before the crucifixion.*
>
> . . . When I was a boy, in the back settlements of the Mississippi

Valley, where a gracious and beautiful Sunday School simplicity and unpracticality prevailed, the 'Yankee' was hated with a splendid energy. But religion had nothing to do with it. In a trade, the Yankee was held to be about five times the match of the Westerner. His shrewdness, his insight, his judgment, his knowledge, his enterprise, and his formidable cleverness in applying these forces were frankly confessed, and most competently cursed.

In the cotton States, after the war, the simple and ignorant Negroes made the crops for the white planter on shares. The Jew came down in force, set up shop on the plantation, supplied all the Negro's wants on credit, and at the end of the season was the proprietor of the Negro's share of the present crop and of part of his share of the next one. Before long, the whites detested the Jew, and it is doubtful if the Negro loved him.

The Jew is being legislated out of Russia. The reason is not concealed. The movement was instituted because the Christian peasant and villager stood no chance against his commercial abilities. He was always ready to lend money on a crop, and sell vodka and other necessaries of life on credit while the crop was growing. When settlement day came he owned the crop; and next year or year after he owned the farm, like Joseph.

In the dull and ignorant England of John's time everybody got into debt to the Jew. He gathered all lucrative enterprises into his hands; he was the king of commerce; he was ready to be helpful in all profitable ways; he even financed crusades for the rescue of the Sepulchre. To wipe out his account with the nation and restore business to its natural and incompetent channels he had to be banished from the realm.

For the like reasons Spain had to banish him four hundred years ago, and Austria about a couple of centuries later.

In all the ages Christian Europe has been obliged to curtail his activities. If he entered upon a mechanical trade, the Christian had to retire from it. If he set up as a doctor, he was the best one, and he took the business. If he exploited agriculture, the other farmers had to get at something else. Since there was no way to successfully compete with him in any vocation, the law had to step in and save the Christian from the poorhouse. Trade after trade was taken away from the Jew by statute till practically none was left. He was forbidden to engage in agriculture; he was forbidden to practice law; he was forbidden to practice medicine, except among Jews; he was forbidden the handicrafts. Even the seats of learning and the schools of science had to be closed against this tremendous antagonist. Still almost bereft of employments, he found ways to make money, even ways to get rich. Also ways to invest his takings well, for usury was not denied him. In the hard conditions suggested, the Jew with brains had to keep them in good training and well sharpened up, or starve. Ages of restriction to the one tool which the law was not able to take from him—his brain—have made that tool singularly competent.

Protestants have persecuted Catholics, but they did not take their livelihoods away from them. The Catholics have persecuted the Protestants with bloody and awful bitterness, but they never closed agriculture and the handicrafts against them. Why was that? That has the candid look of genuine religious persecution, not a trade-union boycott in a religious disguise.

The Jews are harried and obstructed in Austria and Germany, and lately in France . . . I am persuaded that in Russia, Austria, and Germany nine-tenths of the hostility to the Jew comes from the average Christian's inability to compete successfully with the average Jew in business—in either straight business or the questionable sort.

In Berlin, a few years ago, I read a speech which frankly urged the expulsion of Jews from Germany; and the agitator's reason was as frank as his proposition. It was this: *that eighty-five per cent* of the successful lawyers of Berlin were Jews, and that about the same percentage of the great and lucrative businesses of all sorts in Germany were in the hands of the Jewish race! Isn't it an amazing confession? It was but another way of saying that in a population of 48,000,000, of whom only 500,000 were registered as Jews, eighty-five per cent of the brains and honesty of the whole was lodged in the Jews. I must insist upon the honesty—it is an essential of successful business, taken by and large . . . The speaker's figures may have been inexact, but the *motive of persecution* stands out as clear as day.

The man claimed that in Berlin the banks, the newspapers, the theaters, the great mercantile, shipping, mining, and manufacturing interests, the big army and city contracts, the tramways, and pretty much all other properties of high value, and *also* the small businesses—were in the hands of Jews. He said the Jew was pushing the Christian to the wall all along the line; that it was all a Christian could do to scrape together a living and that the Jew *must* be banished, and soon—there was no other way of saving the Christian. Here in Vienna (Twain was visiting Austria), last autumn, an agitator said that all these disastrous details were true of Austria-Hungary also; and in fierce language he demanded the expulsion of the Jews. When politicians come out without a blush and read the baby act in this frank way, *unrebuked,* it is a very good indication that they have a market back of them, and know where to fish for votes.

You note the crucial point of the mentioned agitation; the argument is that the Christian cannot *compete* with the Jews, and that hence his very bread is in peril. To human beings this is a much more hate-inspiring thing than is any detail connected with religion. With most people, of a necessity, bread and meat take first rank, religion second. I am convinced that the persecution of the Jew is not due in any large degree to religious prejudice.

Four score years later, following untold studies of Why Anti-Semitism?, the total pages of which, laid end to end, would extend from Nuremberg to Jerusalem and back, several law enforcement officials, sociologists, psychologists and educators met in New York City to study data on school-age culprits responsible for anti-Semitic graffiti, vandalisms, synagogue desecrations and assaults. Interestingly, the popular wisdom which ascribes anti-Semitism to the educationally and economically wanting, did not—in these instances—prove out. The apprehended culprits came from sections of the country whose school systems are relatively good and from neighborhoods that are middle class. The experts' conclusion echoed the musings of Mark Twain. The young culprits, they concluded, resented their Jewish classmates because the Jewish children are patently more accomplished. Also that no matter both the Jewish and the gentile teenagers were middle class, the former tended to come from the relatively better, or at least more impressive, homes.

One participant, a non-Jew, likely unfamiliar with if aware

at all of Mark Twain's essay, wondered aloud, "What's a Jewish mother, packing her kid off to school, to do? Tell him: 'Don't excel. Be average!'?"

What Mark Twain, writing in Austria as the nineteenth century was winding down, and what these New-York-area police officers and educators in the twilight of the twentieth century were saying in harmony is a simple proposition encasing a seemingly insoluble conundrum. The proposition: That large numbers of less accomplished gentiles resent smaller numbers of more accomplished Jews. Further, that inasmuch as their relative numbers determine their respective raw strength, they deem their right to be in their might. The age-old conundrum: What's a Jew to do? Be average?

To be sure, Jews have been persecuted where and when they have not been well off. In the ghettoes of Europe, and in their tenement hovels in New York. They have been despised where they have been generations departed. Poland and Germany, referred to earlier. They have even been feared and jeered where they have never been. During World War II, a GI confessed to me that he had never met a Jew but always imagined we had horns.

Still, whatever the anti-Semite's rationalization for his resentment, our propensity for financial success or the squalor of the ghettoes in which we were bred, our cosmopolitanism or our clannishness, our international bankers or our Communists, our religious difference or our indifference to religion, on and on through the ages-old adaptive span of damned-if-you-do, damned-if-you-don't rationalizations for anti-Semitism, the ironic truth is that we have been heedful of our tormentors' charges. The anti-Semites and their false bills of particulars have not only influenced our personalities, they have conditioned our behavior.

To avoid, deflect, blunt, escape, hurdle and shield themselves from anti-Semitism, Jews have tried conversion, pretended in-

visibility, adapted to the cultures of their persecutors, as-
similated, deepened their Jewish commitment, hunkered down
in self-ghettoization, fought back, passed, championed social
and political panaceas, have self-hated and self-loved, made
alliances with other discriminated-against groups, with the rich
and powerful and the poor and powerless, with radicals and
with reactionaries, courted Christians and atheists, have dispatched emissaries to monarchs, tyrants, popes and presidents,
have paid bribes, showered philanthropy, have bloc-voted and
bullet-voted, contributed to political parties, churches, civil liberties organizations, and have supported a plenitude of Jewish
defense organizations.

Joseph the monopolist and his brethren in Egypt, those rich
Jews in Twain's Austria, the overachieving Jewish youths in
New York schools: their visibility was and is their vulnerability.
And so some Jews have sought invisibility. Sometimes to con-
found the legendary Evil Eye, but often to hide from the envi-
ous gentile.

Max Gelberg had been a peddler in the 1920s and for all that
he was a young man, he was tiring of the road and so he settled
down in Smalltown, Florida, opened a dry goods store, and
when I knew him in the late 1950s he owned Downtown. Smalltown had a population then of approximately ten thousand, or
as they like to say in the rural south, ten thousand souls. Everyone knew Max and Max knew most everyone. He was more an
integrated member of the social life of Smalltown, its club, its
service organizations, its Chamber of Commerce, than the
scions of Our Crowd in Fifth Avenue's Harmonie Club.

On the particular day I have in mind, a relentlessly hot
August afternoon, Max was chauffeuring me down the four-
block length of Main Street, stopping and parking his long
black Cadillac, starting again, stopping and parking again, so
that he might introduce me to the four Jewish merchants on the
street. Max was a member of B'nai B'rith, I was with its Florida

ADL office and the introductions were for fund raising purposes. At each store, I'd engage in conversation with Max's fellow townsman and because the parking meter sold time by the minutes, Max was periodically leaving us to pay it its pennies. Finally, on the third stop, seeing that the back-and-forth walks in the blazing sun were tiring him I remonstrated, "Why are you running back and forth so much? To hell with the dollar fine, and take it easy, Max, it's much too hot." His answer is my point. "It's all right, I don't want them to think that the Jew has so much money he doesn't give a damn. Why should they think I'm different."

Max taught Bible class in the Smalltown Baptist Church's Sunday School. Live. Direct from a long run in the Old Testament. Christian acceptance enough, and Max was pleased with it, almost boastful of it. But no matter, after a lifetime in Smalltown, the running meter was still "theirs," and Max, no matter his Cadillac and his Downtown, played at being "average."

For many years, the public relations efforts of Jewish "defense" organizations reflected Max's nervous self-consciousness. Jews were soothingly portrayed as butchers, bakers, candlestick makers, average Joes like you and me whose only difference was that, "by the way," they pray in synagogues rather than in churches. Camouflaged as Everyman, we might, we hoped, escape hostile notice. In the process a few of us anglicized our names and our noses, and some of us began to ourselves believe what we saw in the mirror reflecting not ourselves, but our camouflage. Acting upon what we saw, chameleonlike, we took on the coloration of our costume clothes. If crude anti-Semitism has abated, as demonstrably it has, perhaps it's not so much because our public relations was effective, and gentiles changing, have accepted us, as it is because the change is in us. My immigrant father's angst was that my Jewishness was a diluted version of his. In turn myself a father, my foreboding is that my children are not the Jew I have been.

If they, my more-acculturated-than-I-am children, are not experiencing the degree of anti-Semitism that I have, and my experiences pale as compared to my father's, is the ebbing of anti-Semitism in some measure not attributable to our continuing acculturation? Or said less sociologically, more provocatively, is it not due to our having performed penance for the otherness of our forebears?

The American Way has been our deponent to the truth-in-advertising of our Jewish advertisements for ourselves. Democracy's catechism that All Men Are Created Equal; our legal precept that individuals not groups are responsible before the law; the idealization of the individual in America's passion play, The Western; the reality as well as the romance of Pioneer America; Horatio Alger and capitalism itself have all borne witness to the credibility of Jewish public-relations themes stressing that persons should be judged for what as individuals they are rather than by the natal accident of race, color or creed. Outsiders, defined as such by anti-Jewish prejudice, we sought to deflect attention from our social handicap, our group identity. In its place, Jewish organizations, corporately so to speak, instead stressed the centrality of the individual to the American Way. In a sense Jews, the oldest and still champion master practitioners of ethnicity, actually argued the irrelevancy of ethnicity. And it worked. It worked because the resonance of All Men Are Created Equal, the nostalgic affection and longing for the frontier's individualism, and the very dynamics of rugged capitalism are stronger influences on Americans than their prejudices.

This is not to say that Jews cynically wrapped themselves in the flag in order to gain acceptance. Rather was it a case of a people who had deliberately chosen to come to America in quest of promised freedom and finding that in part at least it was being withheld, determined to hold its promisor to his word. In the process and far from incidentally, our celebration of the American ideal of individual worth, self-serving though it has been, gave sinew and vitality to the ideal itself. Our civil-rights briefs in state courts and in the Supreme Court, our activist role vis-à-vis state legislatures and the United States Congress, our scholarly papers, our propaganda for, refuge in, and spear-carrying in behalf of All Men Are Created Equal and its panoply of accompanying democratic clichés not only worked well for us, it worked well for others looking in but also barred from entry, and it made of the Statue of Liberty a respectable woman.

While most Jews found in their petitioning of the United States to practice its preachments easy compatibility with their participation in Jewish communal life, some responsive to the same anti-Semitic stimuli took and take another course. These have melded, in fact or fancy, into the gentile world, the distance traveled by them from their escaped, restrictive environment the cushion of their imagined safety. The degree of their penetration of the gentile mass, their safety's imagined insurance. It's nothing new. Historically, Jews have Russified themselves, have prided in being Warsawers, preened in being Berliners, not as a Chicago Jew might refer to himself as a Chicagoan and mean nothing more than the statement literally means, but as testimony to hostile jurors that the ways of the mass of Jews were not their ways, and that they were of a preferable, more sophisticated culture, were, in short, really more like their gentile peers than the offending Jews.

These Jews, the rate and velocity of their assimilation related to the levels of prevailing anti-Semitism, are dropouts more than they are turncoats. They have always sought, and seek, personal acceptance, and acceptance they believed would be facilitated by changing their clothes of manners and of speech. In separating themselves from those Jews whose social characteristics gave substance to the gentile's pejorative stereotypes they sought passes into the mainstream. And if in the privacy of their real intentions they were opting to merely Dress British, Think Yiddish, we know too that their personal ruse served as a decompression chamber in which their children often became hothouse *goyim*. Alas, by now we know how tentative a pass it was in Berlin, in Moscow, in Warsaw. And we know more.

Jan Masaryk once deplored the low key of patriotism in pre–World War II Czechoslovakia. "Czechs are for the Czechs and Slavs for the Slavs. No one is for Czechoslovakia—except for the Jews. They are our only Czechoslovakians."

Acculturating Jews used to repeat that quotation boastfully and, I suspect, propagandistically. The intended-to-please nervous chatter of an unpacked guest hoping to stay. He's more Roman than the Romans, more Communist than the Communists. Understandable, but today there are still Czechs in Czechoslovakia, and still Slavs in Czechoslovakia, but there aren't many Jews left.

In the United States the decompression chamber of assimilation has produced scions of notable accomplishment—Senator Barry Goldwater, former Secretary of Defense James Schlesinger, former Secretary of Commerce W. Michael Blumenthal, Secretary of Defense Caspar Weinberger—all now Christians. But in some instances name changing has been a round-trip ticket. Irving Wallace's successful son is a Wallachinsky.

Whereas assimilation is Jewishly deplored, acculturation is natural. Indeed, in the United States some homogenization has served as an insurance against the Balkanization of our land. As the Amish are drops in the bucket of German immigration to America, so are the *Hasidim* but a tiny minority of Eastern European Jewish immigrants. These are peripheral Americans, but significantly, by their own choice. For the mass of us, without some measure of acculturation, European minorities, and particularly the socially shunned Jews, Italians and not so

long ago the Irish would not have made it here. For most
second and beyond generations of American Jews, emptied of
the sentimental memories of our immigrant forebears, acculturation's upside—acceptance and participation in our own
homeland—when weighed against its downside—the watering
of Jewish identity—has made for a personal net plus. But acculturation, while natural, has not been easy. It has changed us in
ways undreamed by yesteryear's sociologists, produced surprises to gentiles as well as to ourselves, has even, where Jews
are small minorities, developed Jewish survival commitment
stronger than the self-confident New York Jew's.

Driving through another Smalltown, Florida, in the 1960s I
saw a dry goods store called Cohen's and thought I'd introduce
myself to Cohen, maybe learn something of the town, maybe
even make a friend for the ADL, so I stopped in. I asked the
man for Mr. Cohen and he said, "My name's Johnson. Bill
Johnson. Help you?"

"I'm looking for Mr. Cohen."

"Mr. Cohen's gone, lives in Jacksonville, I think. This is my
place. Bought it from Mr. Cohen eight years ago. Help you?"

My face must have registered my puzzlement because he
picked up again. "The sign's still 'Cohen's' 'cause I bought the
store with Mr. Cohen's good will." (Mark Twain: "I must insist
upon the honesty—it is an essential of successful business . . .")

Not far from Smalltown there's a sun-drenched town much
like it. I had a friend there—ready-to-wear clothes—with
whom I discussed the then wonder, to me, of a Johnson in a
Smalltown calling his place Cohen's, and for business reasons!
My friend explained, "We get along fine here. No trouble. Oh,
once in a while you hear something, but if we mind our own
business they leave us alone. We get along fine."

In the small towns of the South, Jews do get along fine.
They've prospered, prided in being "accepted," raised families,
sent their children to college, and importantly for them, their

sons and daughters, by and large, know who they are—Jews.

But they've paid a price for getting along fine. It's been minding their own business, not being like, or seeming to be like, those New York Jews, social critics, political naysayers, "troublemakers." For their children who have been off to college—virtually all of them—this asking price has been too high and so they aren't returning to Smalltown; settling instead in the big city, Miami, Atlanta or maybe up North. Even for himself, Cohen never intended to stay, or more accurately, to die, in Smalltown. He viewed the price he paid for his acceptance—"minding our own business"—as rent, and when the kids moved and began raising their own families, he left his rental, his club, his Kiwanis, his Chamber, and moved to Atlanta to be near his grandchildren and to die among Jews.

That price he paid, conformity, seems dearer to intellectual Jews than likely it was to Cohen. But intellectuals didn't settle in Smalltown. The towns and villages of the South were settled in by security-minded Jews, loners, men who wanted to be their own boss and so became storekeepers. They stopped in New York or in Philadelphia en route from Russia and finding economic gall rather than gold in the streets, they moved on to the West, the Southwest, the Rocky Mountain States, the Midwest, the Northeast, throughout all of America, the proverbial packs on their backs, seeking and searching for a place "to make a living." Theirs was a Diaspora within the Diaspora. Ironically, these strange soils preserved them as identifying and identifiable Jews.

Life in small towns where Jews number a score, a *minyan*, sometimes less, makes for being consciously Jewish in a way unknown to many New Yorkers, to many residents of Miami Beach, to many Jews in the Jewish sections of big cities. For all that they are more integrated, they are correspondingly more consciously Jewish because in Smalltown your total environment is Christian. Point and counterpoint, with customers in the Jew store, with Christian friends who look to you as an authority on the Old Testament, and on Sundays, walking Sunday-dressed Main Street. Some days you are consciously Jewish because of overheard anti-Semitic language. Nothing new there. But some days you are consciously Jewish because of philo-Semitism. Baptist: "We don't abuse our Jewish folks. Oughtn't nobody abuse them 'cause they're here to save us."

And sometimes in Smalltown your day-in, day-out awareness that you are Jewish is buoyed by neither hostility nor friendship, but innocence: "Mr. Goldman, you a Protestant Jew or a Catholic Jew?" Or the question not asked hostilely, asked for information of a Jewish teacher at a junior college in Central Florida: "Can you be Jewish *and* an American too?" Or the Sunday school teacher who asked her class, "Who killed Jesus?" and the six-year-old who answered brightly, "Mr. Silverman."

In rural America, the Jew's visibility to Christians has caused him to become visible to himself. His Christian neighbors knowing who they were, he had to know—in order to have peerage—who he was. Besides, they expected it of him. In a way, then, it was necessary to remain Jewish for their sake, to meet their expectations. As a result, his reading in Jewish history, his indoctrination of his children with a sense of the tradition into which they had been born, his sense of his Jewish identity, like a used muscle, grew while his unused self—the secular man in all of us, the part of us that wants to dissent from stifling or insensitive conformity—atrophied.

But walk down New York's Fifth Avenue, Miami Beach's Lincoln Road, Chicago's Michigan Avenue, and your awareness of your Jewishness is as distant from your consciousness as the color of your eyes. The walk is your strolling self's rather than your Jewish self's, the purchase you make is a transaction of strangers, your Jewishness, her gentileness dormant, even as your eyes meet. And when you are in a Jewish neighborhood, because all of your world is Jewish, none of you are. So it is that in New York one's Jewishness is often an unexercised muscle while one's secularity, for being in free use, grows.

I sometimes think that it's been Christianity that's preserved us, albeit as a people apart. But something is happening. Young gentiles today aren't as anti-Semitic as their parents were. They aren't as Christian either, and the connection is to wonder. And it poses a problem too. It's been easier to be Jewish for Christians than for ourselves. We must wish them well, else what will become of us?

A popular folk wisdom in the ghettoes of pre-Hitler Eastern Europe was, Scratch a *goy,* you'll find an anti-Semite. It meant the gentile with whom you were relating may seem like a decent sort, but Proceed with Caution. Like so many folk adages it was more a gut-wisdom than a finding of controlled surveys, more an expression of the apprehensions of insular Jews than the actual experience of integrated Jews. We are no longer ghetto-enclosed, are in our integrated life-styles light-years free of its compacting walls, but if my mother wasn't statistically right, she wasn't all wrong either.

I enjoy country music. I've been "into" country music since 1944 when on Guam as a marine the rec hut's record players featured not so much Bing Crosby, not so much Frank Sinatra or Ella Fitzgerald as seemingly incessant Roy Acuff renditions. For me, it was no island summer romance. To this day I still find the off-key whinings and lamentations of country, its ballads of romantic love unrequited and of requited love in Jesus, soothing, enjoyable. So it is that in the early seventies, during the years of student radicalism, of hippies, of Black-student threats and white-administration capitulations, a time in which I was associated with Brandeis, the Jewish-founded Boston-area university, my wife and I attended a country music "Shower of Stars." The featured entertainer was Merle Haggard, whose repertoire consisted of songs recalling the poverty and the small satisfactions of hard-time country life. His hits also included "I'm an Okie from Muskogee" and "When You're Runnin' Down My Country, Hoss, You're Walking on the Fightin' Side of Me." Simplistic songs of patriotism. The audience in the Boston Symphony Hall was New England "country" and it was poor; you could tell that by the large number of starch-dieted overweights, and when they smiled by their dental work, or their lack of it. They loved Haggard. We did too.

At one point, following a combatively patriotic song, the MC quieted the dinning applause and called out, "How many here from Boston University?" Puzzled silence. "How many here from Harvard?" Now the Boston audience was catching on to the joke, the ridiculing of, to this audience, cultural aliens. Laughter. "How many here from Brandeis?" Uproarious laughter. "You uneducated dopes!" Laughter again, superior, smug. Cambridge's unwashed, shoeless Street People; the area's student demonstrators, the murderer or murderers of a local policeman attempting to quell a student disorder; all of those college types were absent presences in Symphony Hall and these unschooled hardworking clerks, laborers and their housewives were laughing at them, and in their laughter congratulating themselves for being gainfully employed and for loving their country. I was laughing too, and for much the same reasons, when suddenly I felt my wife finger-stabbing me. "What are *you* laughing at!"

It took a moment for me to understand. I had forgotten. I had been asail in Haggard's sounds, I had become one with the audience, my Noble Savages, I suppose, and so had forgotten that both as Jew and university vice-president, I was to them twice villainous.

It would not have been the discreet or wise thing to do, scratching them.

If my mistaken sense of communion was an innocent illusion, misread communion can at times be a miasmic delusion.

One's acculturation to a particular environment, be it real or imagined, can have implications far more ominous to the individual Jew and to the Jewish people than the brush with it at a Shower of Stars in the Symphony Hall of, after all, the Athens of America. Assimilation, the excessive indulgence of acculturation, is spurred by the presence of anti-Semitism and the concurrent absence of Jewish moorings of education and its offshoots of pride and commitment. Absent knowing one's self, present that self's calumniation, one can easily step out of one's identity, disrobe the hair shirt. Furthermore, it can be done without self-debasement, without joining the anti-Semites. Consciously, that is.

In *Jews of Argentina,* its author Robert Weisbrot tells of Juan Peron, then still exiled in Madrid, warning his fellow Argentinians to beware of international conspiracies including Jewish conspiracies. Shortly thereafter Weisbrot attended a film on Peron's life shown in Buenos Aires at which "several young Jewish companions joined the audience in wildly cheering the ex-dictator. Turning aghast to one of my friends, I asked how he and other Jews could applaud such a dangerous man. 'Oh, he doesn't mean us,' my companion reassured me—'just the Zionists.' "

In the 1981 Israeli elections, four Communists were elected to the 120-seat Knesset. Three of the four Communists were elected by Arab votes. So much for the well-worn anti-Semitic old saw linking Jews and Communists. But a whole-cloth lie it isn't.

In countries, the governments or cultures of which persecuted or held Jews at arm's length, small but clearly evident numbers of Jews hitched their wagon to Communist or Socialist or populist or any one of fifty-seven varieties of left-revolutionary stars. Even in the United States as late as in the 1970s Nathan Glazer reported that only a tiny fraction of the Jewish student body of our campuses were radicals, but that among radical students the percentage of Jews was higher proportionately than the percentage of non-Jews. I suspect that a like study in the depression-ridden 1930s, when anti-Jewish discrimination was rife, would have revealed that the percentage of Jews who were Communists and Socialists made for a sparse platoon, but that the small Communist Party nonetheless had a decided Yiddish accent. Indeed, one Jewish organization, disturbed, as well it might be, by canards linking Jews and Communists, sponsored an expensive survey with which to counter the mischievously broadcast stereotype. When it was concluded, the study was buried.

As peripheral men, Jews have viewed political activism as their Open Sesame to otherwise closed societies. However, peripheral Jews, rejected by gentile society and themselves rejecting their Jewish milieu, often enlisted in activism's left-most flanks. Where the dominant establishment was not only closed to them but insensitive as well to its own masses, these Jews struck alliances with indigenous radicals. Themselves on intimate terms with rejection, they empathized readily with these others, no matter their allies of opportunity reflected the state's prevailing mores of anti-Semitism. The radical Jew explained away the peasants' or the workers' anti-Semitism as a derivative of the system. Change the system and anti-Semitism will sere and like an autumn leaf, fall. In its place comradeship would blossom regardless of arid religion. The radical Jewish youths on Glazer's surveyed campuses, well-to-do, well educated, raised middle class and middlebrow, identified with the poor—political noblesse oblige—and prescribed for their unknowingly adopted clients the revolutionary fist. Rarely, if ever, did these radical young Jews identify with the Jewish community. After all, how can one sympathize with what Philip Roth—no anti-

Semite, he—has so fearlessly laid bare? In this twentieth century radical universalism, they were continuing a long, if not honored, tradition. One Aaron Lieberman, the memory of him retrieved from nineteenth-century Russia by Lucy Dawidowicz in her *The Golden Tradition,* is the archetype of the universalist Jew without quarter for Jews. Lieberman, a dedicated populist, was aggressively hostile to everything Jewish. In seeking approbation from a populist publication's editor, he explained himself: "You know well that I abhor Jewry just as I abhor all other national isms . . . You know just as well that I am an internationalist, but I am not ashamed of my Jewish origin and, like all oppressed people, I love that segment of humanity which current national and religious principles designate as Jews. And indeed I do not love them all, but only the suffering masses and those fit to join us. Otherwise I would not be worthy of the name socialist."

Shortly after presenting these credentials, Lieberman committed suicide. As my mother might have observed, Better he didn't live to see what his socialism brought.

The radical Jew now as then affirms his abhorrence of anti-Semitism. Curiously, however, when he declares his Jewishness to be *de minimus* in order to gain acceptance by the radical cadre whose victory he believes to be the condition precedent to political justice, he accepts the premises of the system's anti-Semitism. By declaring his love "only (for) the suffering masses and those fit to join us," but in the same breath as "abhor(ring) Jewry," he distances himself from the mass of Jews, a distinction his revolutionary comrades do not make.

In 1981, Professor Noam Chomsky, patron *rebbe* of the expired but still faintly respiring New Left, authored an introduction for a French book, *Treatise in Defense Against Those Who Accuse Me of Falsifying History.* Its author, Robert Fourisson, propounds the theory that the Holocaust never happened. The Holocaust, it seems, is a Zionist fiction. Chomsky's introduction, he has assured listeners, is not intended as an affirmation of Fourisson's macabre and cruel anti-Semitism. Rather is he, in gifting his name and presence to the book, affirming the Nazi apologist's freedom of speech, freedom to stoke the embers of Jew hatred.

In an ironic way, the radical or revolutionary Jew is among anti-Semitism's more pathetic victims. His God has failed him so often.

Even the Jew's relationship with God has been shaped by anti-Semitism. A dissertation on the Jew's influence on an Episcopalian's or a Christian Scientist's or a Moslem's relationship to his church would, no matter the doctoral candidate's earnestness of purpose, be amusedly viewed as theological busywork. The converse—the gentile's influence on the Jew toward his faith—has been a fact of Jewish life for the forevers of our ancestral memories and continues to condition us right up to this evening's meeting of the Moonies.

As an afflicted faith group we have dug in; we have converted; we have populated homogenized, Universalist faiths; we have made a faith of atheism. Sometimes I have even thought that being Jewish is a stage which agnostics have outgrown.

In times when Christian zeal was more fevered than it is today, we tended more to digging into our faith, pulling it over us to protect and warm us, nearer my God to Thee. In Christendom's first century, Josephus observed of Jews, ". . . they have a passion for liberty that is almost unconquerable, since they are convinced that God alone is their leader and master. They think little of submitting to death in unusual forms and permitting vengeance to fall on kinsmen and friends, if only they may avoid calling any man master."

Fifteen centuries later, in one of those pre-dross Golden Eras that have way-stationed Jewish wanderings, the Spain of Isabella and Ferdinand, many Jews chose that time's version of better red than dead; they converted. To no avail. The Inquisition proceeded to try the converts for the crime of religious subversion, appropriated the worldly goods they thought their newly adopted Catholicism would shield, and finally both Jews and converts whose lives had been spared were expelled.

The passage from slavery to Masada to pogroms to forced conversions, and finally to opportunistic conversions and to the voluntary abandonment of faith identity, suggests an applicable apocryphal Sam Goldwyn story. The movie mogul is said to have convened his writers, instructed them to script a movie which should open with a volcanic eruption, and "after that, build up the drama."

The volcano—the Inquisition—was long cooled, and seventeenth-century England compared to Torquemada's Spain was Eden. But the drama of garden variety anti-Semitism was scripting gentile animus for, and Jewish shame in, being Jewish. Volcanic lava it wasn't, but even cooled ashes have a bitter taste. Alexander Pope in "The Rape of the Lock":

> On her white breast a sparkling cross she wore
> Which Jews might kiss and Infidels adore.

Isaac Watts:

> Lord, I ascribe it to thy grace,
> And not to chance as others do,
> That I was born of Christian race,
> And not a Heathen or a Jew.

John Dryden:

> The Jews, a headstrong, moody, murmuring race,
> As ever tried the extent and stretch of grace,
> God's pampered people, whom, debauched with ease,
> No king would govern nor no God could please.

Popular literature is no less expert a witness to the attitudes of anti-Semites than is recorded history. It affords insights as well into the burdens of having been Jewish in societies that were beginning to open up, to abate their murderous hate and though contemning Jews, were nonetheless also questioning the church. The Inquisition was receding into history and while anti-Semitism persisted, the sentence for being Jewish was scorn, admittedly severe, but hardly lethal. Rationalism was on the march, spreading across Western Europe, and in its wake, "passing" became an increasingly available option for Jews discomfited by their despised faith.

Across the channel, Voltaire was scorning Jews. But Voltaire's anti-Semitism provided his prey with a way out. Bitterly critical of religion and of intellectual backwardness, a literate champion of enlightenment, of the budding sciences, of literature, he was actually embraced by many Jews who selectively heard his railings against all religions, but turned down the volume of his railings against themselves. Says Lucy Dawidowicz: "They even internalized his savage hostility toward Jews, for in their eyes Western culture and humanism were rational, enlightened, progressive, *ergo* good; whereas Judaism was irrational, superstitious, backward, separatist, *ergo* bad." One was no longer obliged to accept the or-else cross in order to escape the constrictions of the Star of David. One could "convert" to rationalism and thereby depart Jewishness walking tall.

Milton Himmelfarb tells the story of Moses Mendelssohn:

At the beginning of Jewish modernity, Moses Mendelssohn, its representative figure, was caught up in an experience neatly paradigmatic for all modern Jews since his time. Mendelssohn wished to live in Berlin—the city, the center of enlightenment and culture. Since Jews needed special permission to live there, he asked a friend to intercede for him with Frederick the Great. The Marquis d'Argens, a French intellectual who was what we would call today a cultural advisor to Frederick, wrote his Francophile (and Judeophobe) master a letter that is a fine example of eighteenth century *esprit:*

An intellectual who is a bad Catholic begs an intellectual who is a bad Protestant to grant the privilege (of residence in Berlin) to an intellectual who is a bad Jew. There is too much *philosophie* in all this for reason not to be on the side of the request.

Now Mendelssohn was not really so bad a Jew as that, but to be allowed—grudgingly—to live in Berlin, he had to be thought a bad Jew. This then, was the first lesson that modern Jews learned: If you want to be admitted to the delights and excitements of modern culture, do not be a good Jew. The second lesson was that the only people who were willing to let you live in Berlin were the bad Christians; good Christians would not have you whether you were a good Jew or a bad one. The third lesson, which was learned later than the first two, was that while Jews had to be bad to live in Berlin, Christians could be good or bad as they chose.

But the chief lesson was that reason was the modern Jew's ally; from this lesson it was only a small step to a reverence for Reason. Christians had less reason to revere Reason, since they could live in Berlin without it. Enthusiasm for modernity and secularism was, therefore, unevenly distributed between Jews and Christians.

In the sense that there are men stories and women stories, stories exchanged by Blacks with Blacks, whites with whites, intended not so much to deprecate the Other, as to smugly compliment themselves, Himmelfarb's is a Jewish story. Its point being not so much the outwitting of the Judeophobe, as the victory of the outweighed, outnumbered, but cleverer underdog. And indeed it was a victory. Mendelssohn hacked a narrow path that soon became a high-speed highway over which Jews streamed into the figurative Berlins of the times. Not incidentally, and more to the point of Jewish faith-identity responses to anti-Semitism, he also set off an explosion of voluntary conversions more powerful than any previously experienced in all of Jewish history. A generation after Mendelssohn's death fully half of Berlin's Jews had voluntarily converted. Where the Inquisition captured reluctant Jews, Jews gladly defected to Rationalism.

Heinrich Heine was soon, as history goes, to observe that "the baptismal certificate is the admission ticket into European civilization." Heine, who converted and presumably confessionally wrote "Liberty is a new religion, the religion of our age," nonetheless continued to identify with the Jewish community. His contemporary Benjamin Disraeli also owned an admission ticket, and like Heine remained an identifying Jew. But alas, there are no transmittable genes for religion, for faith-identity.

The under-pressure converts in England and in Prussia, having lived lives as Jews, could, despite *pro forma* acceptance of Christianity, continue as ethnic Jews in a community of shared roots. In effect winking at their coreligionists, and as alien achievers in the outside world, they enjoyed the best and the worst of both worlds. But the converts' children, reared in the new religion of liberty, were without their forebears' life experience as Jews, were consequently without the conditioned reflexes necessary to the defense of a Jewish heritage that was their fathers' but not their own.

Nowhere has liberty blossomed as gaudily, sunk deeper roots, proven as hardy a perennial as in the United States. Virulent anti-Semitism is minimal here. Correspondingly, so is Jewish apostasy. The *Journal for the Scientific Study of Religion* reports that in surveys conducted during the 1970s, for every million born Jews, a scant 24,000 had become apostates. Significant Jewish losses, however, have been to the more voracious, wilier plunderer, genteel secularism. For every Jewish apostate, there are an estimated four or five Jews who in polls probing religious affiliation allow that they are "Nones," faith-identity mulattoes.

As with radical political movements which while attracting small percentages of the Jewish community nonetheless are disproportionately Jewish, so has it been with Ethical Culture, Universalist, and "love"-propounding religious groupings. The Hare Krishna people, the Moonies, whose Jewish membership has been estimated as high as 30%, and a variety of cults boast percentages of Jewish membership in excess of our less than 3% of the American population. The numbers are low, but why the relatively high percentage?

Rabbi Allen Maller writing in *Judaism* maintains that the hardiness of cults "would indicate that the absence of traditional, conservative religious organizations provides an opening and indeed may even stimulate the growth of cults. Since Jews, especially those with good general educations and poor Jewish ones, are highly secular, we must expect that they will continue to be involved in cults." Heine's admission ticket, well over a century old, an ocean traveled, would seem still to be valid, and in churches undreamed by him.

An American generation of Jews, their fought-for acceptance realized but in a struggle the scars of which were cuts of rejection, had gained entry under cover of ascendant democratic liberality. Themselves rationalists, their children became "Nones," or in some instances without taught answers to childhood questions about the why, the whence and the whither of Judaism, their thirst for answers unslaked, they became cultists.

There is evolving still another faith-identity factor, a new one, in part reactive to how *goyim* view Jews. Israel. If for centuries acculturated Jews have shamed, then weakened in their Jewish identity because of their countrymen's contempt for Jews, Israel has provided modern Jewry with a role-model of pride, with the image of the winner, albeit an embattled one. If there is any one subject on which the Jewish consensus approaches unanimity, it is the security of the state of Israel. And so, ironically, Jews who have with good and sad reason eschewed chauvinistic nationalism, today find strength in their proxy nationalism, in Israel's being. Compounded irony: Judaism is a religion, but anti-Semites have ever stipulated that their charges are based on our nation's failing. For their part, Jews insisted that we were but a faith, were in fact French, German, American, whatever, rather than a nation apart. Indeed, as we have seen, many of us protested our "innocence" by claiming that as individuals we hadn't even kept the faith. But today our attachment to the nation of Israel has sparked new life into our identity as Jews. The wearing of the *yarmulke* may signal orthodoxy in religion, but the recently evident ubiquitousness of the *yarmulke* on campuses, at concerts, in ball parks, in streets far removed from Brooklyn, suggests that the combination of an open America and an Israel that casts a positive nation-image is serving to bolster our long beseiged identification as Jews, to bolster the nationality we protested and the faith we neglected.

We have been discussing Jewish reactions to anti-Semitism, some of which have been compromises, often life-serving, sometimes lifesaving compromises, but compromises nonetheless with societies they fled, fought, hid from or joined. For what but a compromise is our dilution, abandonment or apostasy from beseiged Jewishness? Our adaptability has been our success; the anti-Semite's too.

Contemporary Jewish response to the Holocaust is of another order, another dimension. No compromises here. With each passing year the memory of it has grown fresher, our mourning grief sustained, and our "never again" resolve grown stronger. Surely in this we are not so much reacting to gentiles as to the gnawing apprehensions in ourselves, and our fears for Israel. If gentiles in earshot overhear our communal Kaddish with flagging empathy for our nagging memories and the bellicosity of our "never again," so be it. Our memorial marches commemorating the Holocaust have grown longer, our temple services of remembrance, larger. This, no matter that the very word *Holocaust,* embodying anguish so bottomless, horror so unsurpassed, so unimaginable, that failing the capacity of victim, witness or artist to adequately describe what purposeful men devised and my idealist Nazi friend executed, is only faintly suggestive of what happened, and for having become part of our everyday language its resonance grows fainter with rote usage. But we know. Without adequate words, we know.

Why? Two generations later, why does the memory of the Holocaust loom larger for Jews? So that we may mourn; mourning is our emotional compensation for our anguishing loss. So that we may remember. In remembering, maybe this time we will be alert, on guard for the next time. And for another reason too.

So that our children will know who they really are, so that they will not mistake the comfortable facts of their acculturation for the uncomfortable truth of their vulnerability.

In the early 1970s, a Boston underground newspaper carried a photograph of President Nixon, doctored to resemble Adolf Hitler. It was done ably. So ably that both Nixon and Hitler were simultaneously recognizable in the single visage. Upon observing to the student journalist whose copy I was seeing, a fine and intelligent Jewish collegian, that whatever one might think of Richard Nixon, a Hitler he isn't, and continuing, "My god, think for a moment of all that Hitler represents," the answer I got was: "Come off it, Mr. Perlmutter," and smiling amiably, "For all that it matters, Hitler might as well be Attila the Hun."

In a wink of time Adolf Hitler is ancient history, becomes a celluloid Anthony Quinn. The accessories of Nazism—its posters, swastikas, military caps—become valued memorabilia. The Holocaust itself is denied and even the *New York Times* writes that "most historians" agree it happened, as if there were a minority report somewhere, submitted by historians affirming the contrary.

And we have stoked the embers of the memory of the Holocaust for still another reason, one not devoid of a grotesque quality. That the long nightmare not be forgotten. That this nightmare, no matter we are now awake, not be relegated to our subsconscious, but be consciously remembered so as to cause us continued pain, pain validating that the nightmare really happened.

In 1980 the United States Supreme Court agreed to hear the case of *United States of America* v. *Feodor Federenko*. A Ukrainian who entered the United States in 1949, Federenko was charged with deliberate mass atrocities during World War II. Crimes in 1980 thirty-eight years old, their depersonalized statistics standing in the stead of once living Jews, old ones, young ones. His case—its transcripts obese with words, the droning words of law, the jargon words of procedure, words nonetheless as hot and molten as the memory of their testifying witnesses—was then seven years old.

The Anti-Defamation League issued a press release approving of the Court's action. But even as I dictated the predictable welcoming language for the release, it was not of Federenko or death by brutish murder that I was thinking. Rather I was visited by a thought as unexpected as a vagrant in my home. The press item reporting the Court's decision had routinely reported Federenko's age as seventy-three and that he had been living in a Jewish neighborhood in south Florida.

Seventy-three! His age, the years of grandfathers, the amassed years which clichés associate with terms like *venerable,* suggested human frailties, infirmities of the eyes and teeth, arthritic pain, hardly the rampant sadism of an accused Nazi collaborator. It was almost as if the seventy-three-year-old sundrenched Floridian and the thirty-five-year-old accused

Ukrainian were two different men, and well they might be, in one aging human.

And that Federenko had been living among Jews—again intrusive, irreverent thoughts: Were they "some of his best friends?" Had he picked up Yiddishisms, developed a taste for *gefilte* fish, on and on in an infinite variety of irony.

The elasped years since the Holocaust are years actually longer than the snipped life spans of untold numbers of its victims. And so another thought—about justice and what it is that we seek when trying its defilers so many years after the savagery.

Are we seeking retribution? How does one find retribution for mass murder in the deportation or even in the execution now of septuagenarians? Do we seek in prosecuting those accused of being Nazi war criminals to assure ourselves that the villains will not again commit like crimes? Recidivism is companionable with the young; the old tire of its promptings.

No, what is important about bringing the guilty to justice is the symbolism of their continued freedom, the balm it is for the aching impotence of our own memories. To forgive or to forget the Holocaust, admittedly now two score years old, may have a certain humanistic appeal. But, to my mind it speaks not so much of human charity as of the trivialization of genocide.

And so, huddled, mourning, remembering, donning our own sewn yellow Star of David, in self-segregation we actually strengthen from our debilitation, strengthen our tomorrows from yesteryear's Holocaust.

Jewish responses to anti-Semitism, palpable anti-Semitism, subtle anti-Semitism, imagined anti-Semitism, nonexistent anti-Semitism, are as varied as Jews themselves, and that's as wide and multinuanced a spectrum as Freud and Max Weber, their disciples and their schools have dreamed. It's a case of the old saw about Jews being like everyone else, only more so.

In 1978 Chicago's Nazi Party was prominently featured in hours of prime-time television and in endless copy in newspapers and magazines. The handful of Nazis roused the impassioned indignation of Jews, the protective instincts of civil libertarians, and soberly concentrated the judiciary's brows. The focal point of it all was the planned Nazi march in Skokie, Illinois, a heavily Jewish suburb, substantial numbers of whose residents are concentration-camp survivors. The Nazis' leader? One Frank Collins. Religion? Jewish. Or more accurately, Collins is the son of a Jewish survivor of the infamous Dachau concentration camp. Thirteen years earlier, the King Kleagle of the New York Ku Klux Klan, one Daniel Burros, committed suicide. The cause: exposure by the *New York Times* of his dirty little secret. He was Jewish.

In the book *Christians and Jews,* psychiatrist Rudolf H. Loewenstein wrote: "At some point in the course of analytic treatment almost all non-Jewish patients will manifest varying degrees of anti-Semitism." I have long suspected that his observation would be deepened by the recognition that the same is likely true for many Jewish patients.

Elsewhere on the spectrum of responses, distantly removed from this polar extreme of conditioned self-hate, are those of us who, protesting love of Judaism, will not venture beyond the threshold of our self-circumscribed ghetto. To avoid hearing the gentile's siren song? To be true to our faith, our bride, by resolutely spurning the lures of liaison with Christendom? Perhaps. Perhaps too, for reasons of reciprocated prejudice, and for reasons of fear of "them" rather than of love of "ours." The fear that opts for being anchored in parochialism because it is the known, the prejudice that shuns foreign waters certain that they are contaminating.

I had an aunt who owned a shoe store in a gentile neighborhood. Whereas at day's end a mailman's feet are sore, an ath-

lete's muscles hard-used, an office worker's back tired, my
aunt's lips and facial muscles, I was certain, ached. All that
smiling, all day long, at all those customers she stroked but
feared. Like the Southland's plantation and its *yas-suh!* cotton-
tops, the Diaspora too has produced Jews who please and jest
by day, and at night, exhausted from smiling, at long last relax.

Dr. Abram Sachar, a former president of Brandeis University, the Jewish-sponsored school of higher learning, once received a call from a colleague, a Jesuit university president, who
enthusiastically told him of an opportunity to secure microfilms
of rare Hebrew writings in the Vatican Library. Inasmuch as
the collection was a treasure trove of Judaica and would be
housed at his Jesuit institution, the priest allowed as how he felt
emboldened to ask Sachar if Brandeis's Jewish patrons might
provide the umpty-ump thousand dollars necessary to seize the
opportunity. If they were forthcoming, Brandeis would receive
a copy of the microfilms too.

Sachar, as clever a Jesuit as the priest was a Jewish fund
raiser, said he'd look into it and would report back. His first
move was to the late Cardinal Cushing. He told the cardinal of
the microfilm, its cost, and ventured that inasmuch as the Boston Jewish community had been so very generous to the cardinal's Catholic charities, "Perhaps Your Eminence would appeal, in the spirit of Pope John XXIII's ecumenism, to your
supporters to underwrite the project? It would be so fitting that
the Brandeis-housed copies of ancient Judaica be made possible
by benefactors of Catholic causes."

The Cardinal readily agreed and then and there pledged the
necessary funds. Elated, Sachar called his friend back and
elated him. When the priest asked where he got so much
money, Sachar enjoyed answering in measure matching the
priest's surprise, "Oh, I asked Cardinal Cushing."

Several days later the Cardinal redeemed his pledge. The
amount not being inconsequential and the two men being old

friends as well as mutually admiring fund raisers, Sachar felt free to ask the Cardinal, "Tell me, who gave you so princely a gift and so quickly?"

The Cardinal's eye-twinkling answer: "Some of my Jewish friends."

Jewish philanthropy to Jewish causes is well-known. However, Jewish philanthropy to secular and to Christian causes is also prodigious. In part because we are raised in the spirit and in the practice of charity. In part too, whether the cause is establishment political parties or a Christian charity, because like my aunt, we feel safer being agreeable, grinning.

Jews are familiar with the story they tell on themselves of the stammerer who is refused a job as a radio announcer. His explanation for not getting the position is that the interviewer was an anti-Semite. We have on more than one occasion seen anti-Semitism where it wasn't. But why not? So often we have failed to see it where it was. We're entitled. Still, it does suggest that the long affliction of discrimination, no matter the patient seems well, has left us with a lingering touch of paranoia. That's all right too. It serves as an antibody.

We have Jews too who insist that anti-Semitism does not exist, just as their attitudinal ancestors have in subsequently bloodied times and bloodied places throughout our history. And we have Jews who seem to need the assurance that anti-Semitism is the motor force propelling world events. As there are anti-Semites who attribute the ills of the world to Jewish conspiracies, or at least to Jewish puppeteers, so are there those amongst us who seem disappointed, politely distrustful, when told, No, there is no evidence that President X or Senator Y is an anti-Semite; he just differs with us. The tendency to view the world as responsive to malevolent conspirators is not a gentile monopoly. It rains on Jews too. To be sure, indulged by lever-

aged officials or talented demagogues it has banefully affected
Jews. However, the wounds inflicted by conspiracy-obsessed
Jews are self-inflicted.

Our unremitting consciousness of gentiles—the very words
minority, ghetto, Diaspora, words descriptive of the Jewish condition, resonate with that consciousness—has even influenced
our intramural communication. The Yiddish expressions of our
old-country parents: "Shh, speak softly, gentiles will hear you"
and, descriptive of a self-serving braggart, "He only speaks that
way for the *goyim*" are illustrative examples. Even today, Jews
mute felt criticism of specific Israeli actions for fear that if
"overheard" by non-Jews, larger Jewish concerns for Israel's
well-being will be forfeit. Periodically, ultraorthodox splinter
groups in Israel apply their political influence (greatly inflated
by the dependency of Israel's major political parties on splinter
parties for a parliamentary majority with which to rule) in
order to gain special favor. Automobiles driven on the Sabbath
have been stoned by them, public projects they deem potential
Sabbath nuisances have been frustrated, the civic standing of
Conservative and Reform branches of Judaism has been dimin-
ished by their religious intolerance. Our protests, however, have
been relatively private communications and in decibel count,
whispered protests. As remembering losers, we still regulate our
audio even on warranted self-criticism, lest we be overheard
and Israel's punishment in the court of gentile opinion exceed
its faults. Do we say this critically? Yes, but softly.

Particular Jewish responses to anti-Semitism or to being
treated hostilely or condescendingly or at arm's length fashion
my aunt's, the Jewish chauvinist's, the self-hater's, the Universalist's, etc., individual personality. This, no matter that the
reactive individuals are as triflingly numbered as Collins and
Burros, or as substantially numbered as those who make do of

their marginality by drinking deeply of their heritage, their Jewish identity. It is the organizations which Jews have formed, the seemingly myriad organizations to fight anti-Semitism, to raise funds for worthy Jewish causes, or simply, shelteringly, to be together that have impacted on us in our group interests. Through the unity of organization we have enhanced our group rights and group station, benefiting individually from rewards which as embattled loners would have eluded us. It's the nascent labor movement's one-word slogan—"Organize!"

For years the authors lived in the South, and the social similarities of Jews and Southerners is to be remarked.

Southerners consider themselves as Southerners, and northerners view them that way too, but not the other way around. I mean while Southerners consider northerners Northerners, northerners don't think of themselves as Northerners. New Englanders, yes, Midwesterners, yes, but not Northerners. The difference in outlook, or maybe it's inlook, has more to do with mind than with maps. Southerners have been losers, and what losers share in common knits them tighter together than what winners share in common. Alabamans feel closer to Mississippians than do New Yorkers to Pennsylvanians. Or consider the word *Yankee*. When Southerners use it they are remembering the Civil War, sour-tasting its regurgitations. When a Bay Stater or a Vermonter says *Yankee,* he is invoking, not experiencing, a memory, and even then it's of another war, the Revolutionary War, book-taught rather than grandfather-taled. In the South, history is for the masses, for their study and their handing down. In the North it's for history buffs and for commercial touristic nostalgia. It's like in poker. Winners tell jokes; losers say, Deal.

Southerners suggest Jews and northerners gentiles. For all that Jews see gentiles as gentiles, gentiles are not aware of themselves as gentiles, but rather as Baptists or Lutherans, Catholics or whatever.

More. In the South there are Sons of the Confederacy, Daughters of the Confederacy, Societies for the Preservation of Southern Traditions, Louisiana variations on the themes, Mississippi variations, Florida variations, on and on and on. But has anyone yet found one organization designed to preserve the Northern Way of Life?

And so with Jews. B'nai B'rith, Hadassah, Mizrachi, National Council of Jewish Women, Jewish War Veterans, American Jewish Committee, American Jewish Congress, National Jewish Community Relations Council—and there are so few Jews! I sometimes think as I visit from organization to organization and as often as not see the same faces that we Jews invented interlocking directorates—how else would there be enough of us to go around?

And I have noticed, too, that when a northerner travels South, he's touristing, but when a Southerner travels North, he enters *his* Diaspora.

But Jewish organizations play a very serious, a very significant role in the lives of their members, to be sure, but in the lives as well of the unaffiliated who notwithstanding are perceived by their gentile neighbors as Jews, counted by pollsters as Jews, wooed as Jews by political officeholders. The leverage provided by organizations on the fulcrum that is American democracy has helped Jews all the way from finally-getting-that-office-job-denied-me to the federal government's assistance to harassed Soviet Jews. In a sense our organizations have served as a sectarian government (albeit not elected by popular Jewish vote) within a secular government, that of the popularly elected legislative and executive branches of the American government. In a context concerned with the flow of Jewish history, Albert Memmi held that what really counts for Jews is political sovereignty. He maintained that the Diaspora-rooted Jewish tradition was essentially the product of Jews having been colonialized. Our evolving Jewish behavior, indeed our philosophy for survival, was crafted as a weapon of defense, used by us to survive as colonials. In the unique American democracy it has been our organizations which have converted our individual "colonial" status and made of us a "bloc," a "lobby," no longer the lonely and the powerless, pitied but unheeded.

4

What the Studies Reveal and What They Don't

WE HAVE BEEN speaking subjectively, our views molded, perhaps biased, by our experiences, our perspective seen as wide-angled or narrow by readers reacting from their own experiences out of their own reference frames. But what are the measurements of the acceptance or rejection of Jews, as taken, sorted and tabulated by social scientists and pollsters?

Jews are addicted to the taking of their own temperature. Why not? Their figurative sniffles can, and have, developed into pneumonia. After World War II we traded up our heirloom thermometer "Is it good for the Jews?" for the instruments of the social scientists. Organizations like the American Jewish Committee and the Anti-Defamation League of B'nai B'rith spent small fortunes underwriting studies by sociologists and psychologists designed to tell us how we're doin' with the gentiles. Of course, the prompting was more than the nervous patient's pulse-taking. Apart from hoped-for good news, and always half-expectant, feared bad news, it was and continues to be motivated by the hope that the germs of anti-Semitism being identified, diagnosis and prescription will hurry the cure.

In 1979 Charles Glock and Harold Quinley published *Anti-Semitism in America,* capping a fifteen-year, ten-book, project funded by the Anti-Defamation League, a landmark in research into anti-Semitism. They concluded that although anti-Semitism in the United States "was once virulent," today "very few non-Jews . . . favor discriminating against Jews in public areas such as employment, housing, college admissions, and hotels." Elsewhere the study found that "Christianity fosters anti-Semitism when it teaches that there is no path to salvation except through Christ and where such teachings are interpreted as subjecting all non-believers to damnation."

When the latter finding appeared in the project's publication, *Christian Beliefs and Anti-Semitism,* it attracted wide media attention. One day visiting with my mother, the radio playing, a talk program quite by coincidence featured a discussion of the book's findings. My Yiddish-speaking mother, English not a mastered subject, caught the words "Anti-Defamation League study" and that it cost "$500,000." Proud of her son's association with the ADL, curious about the discussion, and impressed by the imposing figure, she asked me in her mother's tongue, "Nathan, for half a million dollars, what did you learn?" Preoccupied with the radio conversation, I responded in shorthand. I said that the study showed that the more orthodox a Christian is, the more likely he will not like us.

My mother's response was a stiletto in the heart of pollsters. "For that price, Nathan, why didn't you ask me?"

But of course, educators, opinion molders, clergymen pay little heed to their own, let alone my mother. And so social-science findings, if only because of the influence their authors wield, serve a useful purpose no matter they often reveal what was not really hidden.

The project's flagship book was Stephen Steinberg and Gertrude Selznick's *The Tenacity of Prejudice,* published in 1969. In this study anti-Semitic attitudes in various groupings of Americans was measured by the answers to given questions by the survey's respondents. The survey, conducted under the auspices of the Survey Research Center of the University of California, posed interviewees such questions as their view about whether Jews had too much power in the United States, whether Jews care only about their own kind, are they as honest as other businessmen, do they have too much power in the business world, are they more loyal to Israel than to the United States, do they control international banking, and a list of related questions designed to probe the nature and the hold of stereotypical thinking about Jews.

In 1981 the American Jewish Committee, piggy-backing the ADL study, employed Yankelovich, Skelly and White, the polling firm, to sample American opinion on the questions posed a decade and a half earlier by Steinberg and Selznick. A sort of *Son of How We Doin'?*

The respective results of the two surveys read well for temperature takers. The gentile fever seems to be subsiding, but gone it isn't.

In 1964 58% of the country believed that Jews stick together too much. In 1981 our "clannishness" was an annoyance to 53% of our neighbors. A 5% improvement, but we still itch a majority of Americans.

In 1964 one-third of our population believed that Jews don't care what happens to anyone but their own kind. In 1981, the dimunition of this view was 8%, but still held by more than one in every four Americans.

The stereotype about Jewish businessmen and their dishonesty was accepted by one-third of 1964's respondents. In 1981 the persistent stereotype retreated, but is still bothering more than a fifth of the nation. When the word "shady" is coupled with the image of the Jewish businessman, almost half of 1964's population accepted it. In 1981 the image, though receding, is nonetheless clearly imagined by one-third of the nation.

In 1964 almost half the public felt that Jews have a lot of irritating faults. In 1981, a 19% improvement scored, we still see fully 29% of our countrymen answering affirmatively to this hostile impression.

In 1964 some 55% accepted the notion of a Jewish son-in-law or Jewish daughter-in-law. By 1981, field practice apparently working well, acceptance rose to 66% by prospective gentile parents-in-law. While pollsters may view these figures as evidencing declining anti-Semitic attitudes, it is hardly good news for Jews concerned with communal seepage through intermarriage. Accelerating intermarriage, the fact of it not all that far behind the disposition for it, suggests that gentiles may have an increasingly shrinking Jewish pool from which to select a mate.

But the improvements in attitudes toward Jews have not been uniform.

In 1964 only 13% in the *Tenacity of Prejudice* study felt that Jews have too much power in the United States. In 1981 a 10% increase in concern with "Jewish power" disturbs almost one in every four Americans.

Correspondingly, the 1964 finding that 39% of the surveyed sample believed Jews are more loyal to Israel than to America rose to 48% in 1981.

The deterioration in attitudes toward Jews as a political entity, in the very context of bettering views of Jews as individuals, is clearly attributable to the escalation of awareness and concern with the Middle East, and the association of the highly visible American Jewish community with Israel.

The following charts are from the Yankelovich, Skelly and White study.

SOCIAL ACCEPTANCE OF GROUPS

	Jews %	Italian Americans %	Black Americans %	Japanese Americans %
		Group Being Asked About		
Acceptance of members of group in neighborhood	92	91	66	86
Acceptance of member of group for nomination for President	73	76	61	61
Acceptance of member of group as marriage partner for own child	66	72	48	51

TRENDS IN THE SOCIAL ACCEPTANCE OF JEWS

	1964 %	1981 %	Net Difference 1981–1964 %
Acceptance of Jews in neighborhood	92	92	—
Acceptance of Jew for nomination for President	69	73	+4
Acceptance of Jew as marriage partner for own child	55	66	+11

TRENDS IN NEGATIVE BELIEFS ABOUT JEWS

Probably True	1964 %	1981 %	Net Difference: 1981–1964 %
Jews today are trying to push in where they are not wanted	21	19	−2
Jewish employers go out of their way to hire other Jews	60	57	−3
Jews stick together too much	58	53	−5
Jews don't care what happens to anyone but their own kind	30	22	−8
Jews should stop complaining about what happened to them in Nazi Germany	51	40	−11
Jews always like to be at the head of things	63	52	−11
International banking is pretty much controlled by Jews	55	43	−12
Jews are (not) just as honest as other businessmen	34	22	−12

Probably True	1964 %	1981 %	Net Difference: 1981–1964 %
The trouble with Jewish businessmen is that they are so shrewd and tricky that other people don't have a fair chance in competition	40	27	−13
Jews are more willing than others to use shady practices to get what they want	48	33	−15
Jews have a lot of irritating faults	48	29	−19
The movie and television industries are pretty much controlled by Jews	70	46	−24
Jews have too much power in the United States	13	23	+10
Jews are more loyal to Israel than to America	39	48	+9
Jews have too much power in the business world	33	37	+4
Jews are always stirring up trouble with their ideas	13	14	+1

An interesting question in 1981 of both Jews and non-Jews elicited responses revealing beyond their yes or no boundaries. Asked if they believed that an increase in anti-Semitism is possible in (a) their community, or (b) elsewhere in the country, 7% of the non-Jews thought it possible in their own geographic area, while 40% of the Jewish sample felt the same way. The possibility of increasing anti-Semitism elsewhere in the country was viewed as possible by 21% of the non-Jews, three times as many as sensed it possible in their own backyard, and by a hefty 67% of the Jews polled. This tendency to project upon "others," "elsewhere," a readiness to rock intergroup boats, presumably even-keeled in one's own community is reminiscent of the widespread Southern view during the racially turbulent 1950s and 1960s that civil rights workers and Klansmen both were "outsiders," and that "we get along fine." The substantial difference in views of Jews and non-Jews is not surprising. The testimony of victims and of passersby are often divergent.

In both studies, and in periodic polling by Gallup and Harris in the interval between 1964 and 1981, the population forest microscoped, its trees too were studied in order to more precisely locate the problem and to locate as well the uncontaminated areas. So it is that we have a plethora of statistics on attitudes toward Jews held by groups separated according to their educational attainments, their occupation, their religious identification, their race, etc.

A finding that retains its constancy over the years is that the more educated score lower on anti-Semitism scales, the less educated, higher. It's a stepladder. In 1964 some 15% of college graduates were found to be anti-Semitic, the percentage rising among "some college" respondents, continuing to rise among high-school graduates and cresting at 52% with those of a grade-school education only. In 1981 the stepladder, a shorter one now, rose from the same 15% level for college graduates to 28% for grade school graduates.

Levels of education are clearly related to income and to occupation, and the relationship holds fast when examined for anti-Semitism. The lower the income, the higher the anti-Semitism quotient, at least as measured by social scientists. The higher the income, the lower the quotient. Occupation follows suit. Professionals consistently score lower levels of anti-Semitism, blue collar workers, higher.

These statistical findings have given credence to and buttressed the long-in-place, commonsense emphases Jewish defense agencies have placed on education as a weapon against prejudice. It is a little known fact, but a large fact nonetheless, that the Anti-Defamation League, renowned for its watchdog role against anti-Semitism, expends a far greater proportion of its budget on educational programs, including the publication of teaching tools and guidelines and the development of human relations curricula, than on monitoring the Ku Klux Klan.

But questions remain. Granted that negative stereotypes

about Jews are a flashing stoplight and that relatively unhostile views a continue-with-caution signal, are the blue-collared, those of low education and low income, the currently dominant threat to Jewish interests? Substantial segments of the executive suites of corporate America remain inhospitable to Jews despite the substantial Jewish component in the graduating classes of the Wharton School and the Harvard Business School. That's not Archie Bunker barring the door. Interestingly too, the low-educational, low-income and occupational groups scoring highest on the scales of anti-Semitism are the very groups with which Jews have traditionally voted in concert. They are Democratic Party comrades-in-arms. If economic and political "liberalism" are indeed good for the Jews, might it be inferred from Jewish voting predilections that they have allianced with those least sympathetic to them and in social upheaval, the most combustible?

When respondents are sorted by age, anti-Semitic views are again stepladdered. Older people score higher in anti-Semitism than middle-aged people, and middle-aged people score higher than young people. But again, our qualifying clause: at least, as measured by social scientists. It was so in 1964 when the young (under thirty-four years old) scored 31% as anti-Semitic, the middle-aged (thirty-five to fifty-four years old) 40%, and the older, 59%. In 1981, again a shorter stepladder but again, too, one in place, the least anti-Semitic remain the young (eighteen to twenty-nine years old) with a 16% anti-Semitic rating. The highest scores are still for the oldest grouping (fifty-five years and over), 31%.

Both the overall decline in anti-Semitism and its distribution raise provocative questions.

Today's older people were yesteryear's young parents. Popular wisdom has it that we absorb our prejudices in our parents' homes. It would seem that the near halving on anti-Semitic prejudice among today's young, the bigots' brood of yesteryear, calls that wisdom into question.

As to the decline in prejudice among the older, also halved, this is not so much a case of their having experienced the glow of brotherly love in the intervening seventeen years as it is a case of their having gone to extremes to elude the pollsters. They died.

But why are the young today less prejudiced than their counterparts of almost a generation ago?

Quinley and Glock, in the Anti-Defamation League's study, attributed the improvement to education. Extrapolating from *The Tenacity of Prejudice,* they found that fewer than half of the older, more prejudiced respondents had more than a grade school education. Among the younger and least prejudiced, 91% had attended high school and one-third, college. Less education, more anti-Semitism. More education, less anti-Semitism, even unto the golden years.

In the Yankelovich American Jewish Committee study, the decline in anti-Semitism is attributed to today's increased tolerance for diversity—a perspective from the crest of the revolution in mores and values that occurred post–Steinberg and Selznick. Today's younger people, their rebellious "hanging loose" displayed in their uniforms of beards and jeans, their social sympathies ranging from furry seals in northern Canada to homosexuals wherever, are more tolerant than their more nationalistic and religiously more orthodox parents. In their roomier group sympathies, in their more lightly anchored religiosity, overt anti-Semitism is a less acceptable indulgence than it was in their parents' culture.

Of course, the difference in attitudes towards Jews among the old and the young may be explained by less exotic speculations. Part of the explanation may simply be a function of aging. Disillusion, the hardening of the arteries of diverse prejudices are attributes of age, not youth. Resultant scapegoating for which Jews have traditionally been practiced marks then follows as "naturally" as grumpiness. After all, the salad years of today's elderly were years in which openly spoken and openly practiced anti-Semitism was commonplace. Though a scorned value today, for many elderly it is a familiar childhood, mother-taught value, returning to which is an emotive homecoming. But whatever the mix of explanations for the attitudes of today's young, when they are probed a generation hence, and are themselves older, their now tolerance harbingers a still shorter stepladder.

Well, perhaps. On the issue of Israel, indisputably the over-riding concern of Jewry, the elderly who consider themselves to be liberals are more favorably disposed to Israel than are the elderly who consider themselves conservatives. However, information we will consider later in discussing Jews and politics reveals that younger self-described liberals are embarked on liberal paths divergent from their ideological forebears. When asked, for instance, if they would support United States military involvement in the event that "Israel were being defeated by the Arabs," younger liberals were much stronger in their opposition than older liberals and more strongly anti than young self-described conservatives.

The older liberals viewed Jews, especially in the wake of the Holocaust, as underdogs. They responded empathetically. Then, it was part and parcel of the liberal ideology. Younger liberals—and they are far more numerous than their political antecedents—view Jews for what we are, economically success-ful, an extension if not an integral part of the establishment, and they view Israel as a part of the dominant West. No underdogs, these; no social statement made in rooting for the Yankees. Conversely, young political conservatives, their parents' social biases outgrown, view Israel as a part of the West they would defend. Jews become, in a manner of speaking, the incidental beneficiaries of conservative ideology.

Relevant here, however, is a curiosity. Throughout the 1960s and 1970s social scientists probing the security of Jews paid far more attention to the danger from the Right than to the clearly visible and burgeoning danger from the Left. Was it because themselves liberals abhorring social injustice, they viewed violence as hooliganism—if engaged in by young racists and Klansmen, but if engaged in by college students protesting American foreign policy, simply thought that was "social protest"?

The relationship between political values that abhorred American military action abroad, indeed abhorred Amerika, and that abhorrence's implications for the democratic state of Israel, was consequently rarely examined. Moreover, as has been amply evident since the 1960s, the older who were classified as anti-Semites did not, beyond privately nursing their prejudices, act out the roles assigned them by the social scientists. Rather they were among those who in supporting increased expenditures for national defense were voting too, even if unwittingly, for the protective wherewithal with which to sustain Israel. And the young whose relative benign attitude toward Jews personally, an attitude credited by the Yankelovich study to their "increased tolerance for diversity," because of their political value system, are functionally indifferent to military threats that bode serious harm to Israel.

As recently as 1979, *Anti-Semitism in America* declared flat-out, "Anti-Semitism is most prevalent in the South, where 49% score as prejudiced and the Midwest where the figure is 44%." The least anti-Semitic regions cited were the Northeast and the West. Earlier Charles Herbert Stember found identical regional variations. *Anti-Semitism in America* was citing *Tenacity of Prejudice,* published in 1969, but a work in progress since 1964. By 1981 the South had experienced sea changes in levels of industrialization, in urbanization, in population growth and in political leverage. The Solid South was well on its way toward homogenization—downtowns indistinguishable from those north of Mason-Dixon, breathing air kindred to the pollution up North, watching the same TV fare damnyankees did, sleeping in cookie-cutter Holiday Inns, Howard Johnsons, Ramada Inns cloned from northern patterns. It had long since sheathed its determination to resist desegregation, and as Yankelovich revealed, had by now beveled the edges of its earlier reputation for anti-Semitism. In less than a single generation the South's dubious distinction as the most anti-Semitic of the nation's four regions was surrendered to the Northeast and to the Midwest. The South's 23% anti-Semitism index is lower now than the Northeast's 25% and the Midwest's 26%. The West, true to its pioneer traditions of judging people on their individual merits, has the lowest anti-Semitism index—17%.

In a 1979 observation Quinley and Glock, while asserting that "residents of the South and the Midwest consistently score as the most anti-Semitic; residents of the West and East as the least," observed too that these patterns pertain only to whites. We will look at Blacks' views of Jews later.

But it was left to Harvard University's William Schneider, in an unpublished paper prepared for the American Jewish Committee in 1978, to add a vital ingredient to this regional statistical soup. Again, it's the Israel factor, the factor so critically and so crucially related to the Jewish psyche. His data, he suggested, "show Southerners becoming more pro-Israel than Northerners . . ." Given the South is conservatism's citadel, Schneider's finding is a variation on our earlier theme reporting the respective views of conservatives and liberals toward American involvement in the Middle East in the hypothetical event of Israel's mortal peril.

Regional attitudes toward Jews are more complex than arbitrary cartographers' lines, riverway boundaries or mountain borders. Regions, after all, are composed of people and people manifest cultural styles, political views, social values, religious beliefs. People are also black and white and hues in between, and cumulatively these conditions shape a region's views. In this sense the regions of America are undergoing kaleidoscopic changes and as these comments on regional attitudes toward Jews suggest, it's the people-groupings and their views that need to be looked at more closely.

The data in *Christian Beliefs and Anti-Semitism* may have amused my mother, but it impressed Pope John XXIII. Advance tear sheets from the study were hastened by the Anti-Defamation League to Rome, where Vatican Council II, convened by the late pope, was in session. The study's findings documented the strongly negative effect of Christian teaching on attitudes toward Jews. In charts, graphs, numbers, percentages and commentary it revealed that overwhelmingly the one-third of Americans with anti-Semitic attitudes derived their prejudices from religious indoctrination. The jolting statistics became part of the deliberations of the College of Cardinals and were cited by Pope John's supporters during the debates leading to the Council's formal declaration repudiating Jewish guilt, past or present, for the death of Jesus. My private self thought, Thanks a lot. My public self welcomed the reprieve, late though it was.

Of course my response to my mother's question was essentially correct. But *essentially* is a qualifying word. What this study stipulated with the dispassion of scientific research—and without a trace of my mother's Yiddish accent—was that the literal acceptance of orthodox Christian beliefs, in which saved Christians have it made with God and all others are damned, leads, but not inevitably and not in all instances, to secular forms of anti-Semitism. This was buttressed with findings that Christian laity and ministers holding orthodox religious beliefs were disproportionately prejudiced against Jews. It is not that

anti-Semitism is purposefully taught—it rarely is—but by theologically singling Jews out as recalcitrants and culpables, they
become setups for secular persecution. In essence, bigotry
thereby becomes God's will.

The illustrative following chart is from the study.

PERCENTAGE OF CHRISTIAN LAYPERSONS SCORING HIGH
IN ANTI-SEMITIC BELIEF AT EACH LEVEL OF RELIGIOUS
BIGOTRY INDEX

Percentage scoring high and medium high on index of anti-Semitic belief	*Index of Religious Bigotry*						
	Low						High
	0	1	2	3	4	5	6
Protestants	10%	15%	28%	37%	46%	57%	78%
Catholics	6%	17%	19%	39%	40%	58%	83%

The variations retained their spread when factors of age,
education and socioeconomic background were taken into account. The more religious the respondent, the more likely the
greater his or her anti-Semitism.

Christian faiths looked at more closely revealed noteworthy
dissimilarities. While two-thirds of Protestant laity and half the
Catholics believed that acceptance of Jesus Christ as savior was
"absolutely necessary" for salvation and that consequently non-
Christians and backslidden Christians were damned, within
Protestantism there were wide variances in beliefs. Southern
Baptists' orthodoxy was 97% firm. On the low end of the scale,
only 38% of the members of the United Church of Christ
registered orthodoxy in their beliefs. It followed that Southern
Baptists scored high in the anti-Semitism index; members of the
United Church of Christ, low. Sixty-nine percent of Southern
Baptist clergy felt that Jews would remain unforgiven by God
until they accept Christ as their savior. Less than 4% of the
United Church of Christ, Methodist and Episcopalian clergy
felt that way. Laity responded in similar proportions, but at

moderately higher levels of orthodoxy than their ministers.

Seventeen years later, returning to the grounds searched by Glock and Rodney Stark in *Christian Beliefs,* Yankelovich found encouraging changes. For all that Christian fundamentalists have gained prominent visibility and have developed authority in their newly found political voice, Christian orthodoxy has declined since 1964. Christian fundamentalists are still more likely to register greater levels of prejudice than do nonfundamentalists, but the levels are lower than those of a generation ago. The 25% anti-Semitism score he attributes to fundamentalists is not, he feels, the result of their religious beliefs but of their lower levels of education. Indeed, in this most recent study, when such demographic factors as age, education and race are controlled, the association of religion and anti-Semitism disappears.

Whether Yankelovich's new data infers error in Glock and Stark's findings, or the polling vice is versa, or whether modest improvement in Christian orthodoxy's views of Jews is real we will leave to the next pollster or university social science department with a Proposal for mirror-transfixed Jews. What we find of interest and of some significance in these findings are the omissions once again of the functional distinction between simplistic anti-Semitic attitudes and actions which, while free of classical anti-Semitism, militate against Jews.

The modernist Christian denominations score low on indexes of anti-Semitism. The fundamentalists score relatively higher; they did then and they do now. But the National Council of Churches, eminent members of which include the United Church of Christ, the Methodists and assorted mainline nonfundamentalist bodies, time and again broadcasts resolutions which if heeded by our government would imperil the state of Israel. The fundamentalist denominations, responsive to their religious orthodoxy and not to the importunings of Jews, time and again broadcast positions supportive of Israel's security.

If the change in American attitudes towards Jews as a result of the passing of older, more anti-Semitic persons and their demographic places taken by younger, less prejudiced persons can be termed evolutionary, and if the increasingly Christian attitudes of Christians is benign gradualism, then the changes in the Black community qualify as revolutionary. In the sense that Black anti-Semitic prejudice is expanding within a context in which stereotypical prejudice is shrinking, it is counterrevolutionary.

No matter that as recently as 1979 Quinley and Glock in their *Anti-Semitism in America,* discussing the then fifteen-year-old data on Black anti-Semitism, rationalized it, and no matter Gary T. Marx in his subsequent University of California volume, *Protest and Prejudice,* came squeamishly close to justifying the Black prejudice his own data revealed, American bigotry's quintessential victim—the Black—was already showing a propensity for bigotry.

The following chart is from the Selznick and Steinberg, *The Tenacity of Prejudice.*

NEGATIVE ECONOMIC IMAGES OF JEWS BY RACE

Statement	Percentage Giving Anti-Semitic Response		Percentage Point Difference, Blacks Minus Whites
	Blacks	Whites	
Jews are more willing than others to use shady practices to get ahead.	58%	40%	+18
The trouble with Jewish businessmen is that they are so shrewd and tricky that other people don't have a fair chance in competition	46	34	+12
International banking is pretty much controlled by Jews	40	28	+12
Jews are (not) as honest as other businessmen	35	27	+8

	Percentage Giving Anti-Semitic Response		Percentage Point Difference, Blacks
Statement	Blacks	Whites	Minus Whites
Jews don't care what happens to anyone but their own kind	43	24	+19
Jews always like to be at the head of things	60	53	+7
Jews have a lot of irritating faults	44	40	+4
Jews stick together too much	48	53	−5
Jews are more loyal to Israel than to America	32	30	+2
Jews have too much power in the United States	9	11	−2
Jews have too much power in the business world	19	31	−12

In their commentary on these comparisons between Black and white acceptances of stereotypical put-downs of Jews, Quinley and Clark noted that Blacks scored higher in anti-Semitism only as it related to the economic image of Jews. Inasmuch as the ghetto merchant in the 1960s was often a Jew, presumably this form of anti-Semitism was natural. Moving right along, they then noted that on the last six questions in the chart, those without a business-practices component, the difference between Black and white responses was either negligible or revealed greater white anti-Semitism than they did Black.

Elsewhere they reassuringly found that Blacks were less anti-Semitic than whites as determined by the near unanimous Black opposition to discrimination in social clubs and their outnumbering whites two to one in their willingness to combat such discrimination. Finally they attributed the surprisingly high incidence (for 1964) of Black anti-Semitism to the education factor, asserting that "a relative lack of education thus appears to be a principal source of anti-Semitic prejudice for both black and white Americans."

They were supported by Marx, whose 1967 data told essentially the same story and led Marx to essentially the same conclusions—that Black anti-Semitism was either nonexistent, or the consequence of low educational levels, or a spin-off from antiwhite hostility, or "understandable" because of the consumer-merchant relationship of Black to Jew.

In 1978, the National Conference of Christians and Jews released a Harris study which included a new ingredient. In addition to comparing non-Jewish white responses and Black responses to anti-Semitic stereotypes, Harris interviewed Black leaders. Thirty-two percent of white gentile respondents affirmed that "when it comes to choosing between people and money, Jews will choose money." Blacks registered a 56% agreement; Black leaders, 81%. "Jews are more loyal to Israel than to America" elicited agreement from 28% white gentiles and from 37% Blacks. Black leaders however, agreed with a 50% score. On the standard catchall "Jews are irritating because they are too aggressive" the difference between white and Black views was insignificant, 27% and 29% respectively. Black leaders, however, scored 65%. Black leaders, one must assume, are more "educated" than their followers.

And so the statistical bad-news momentum increasing, we come to 1981 and the Yankelovich tracing of Selznick and Steinberg's footsteps. Same questions, the requisite sampling size, the controls in place.

Overall, this study found 21% of whites to be prejudiced, as compared with 37% of Blacks. Blacks scored 41% "neutral" and whites 30%, while the "unprejudiced" scores were 49% and 22% respectively for whites and Blacks.

The index toll of Black anti-Semitism, however, through the 1960s and 1970s is more clearly seen in a comparison of contemporary responses to the questions asked by Selznick and Steinberg.

The nonbusiness questions, to which comparable Black responses had comforted the University of California academics, now elicit Black anti-Jewish prejudice, consistent with rising over-all Black anti-Semitism. Where the social judgment "Jews stick together too much" in 1964 found agreement from 48% of blacks and 53% of white non-Jews for a 5% spread with Blacks scoring lower, today 63% of Blacks and 51% of whites agree with the statement—a 17% differential reversal. In 1964, the biracial civil-rights movement still on the march, only 9% of blacks felt that "Jews have too much power in the United States." Whites, 11%. Today, the civil-rights laws in place, the Black middle class expanding, 42% of Blacks attribute excessive power to Jews, while 23% of whites agree, a 21% differential reversal. That "Jews have too much power in the business world" was agreed with then by 19% of Blacks and 31% of whites; Black acceptance of the statement now has reached 51%; whites, 35%, a 28% differential reversal. In 1964, Blacks edged whites 32% to 30% in their belief that "Jews are more loyal to Israel than to America"; today the spread is 18%, 63% of Blacks agreeing and 45% of whites.

On the business-related questions, Blacks revealed uniformly higher anti-Semitic scores than they had for Selznick and Steinberg, while whites revealed somewhat lower scores, causing the differential margins of Black anti-Semitism to rise even higher.

A 1981 Yankelovich question elicited responses which Jewish organizations must ponder. He asked for a yes or no to the sentence; "Jews should stop complaining about what happened to them in Nazi Germany." An ominously critical, or so it seems to us, 40% of unscarred whites agreed. A sadly ironic, or so it seems to us, 34% of Blacks agreed. To be sure, Jews too from time to time experience the feeling "enough, already" but there's a difference between one's shying from repeated visits to the outer limits of sadness and another's insensitivity to one's grief.

It remained for Gallup in 1980 to pose to both whites and Blacks questions designed to probe their respective sympathies for Israel vis à vis its bellicose neighbors. Consistent with his findings that those who feel that Jews are more loyal to Israel than to the United States tend to be more sympathetic to the Arabs, he found that nonwhites were both more pro-Arab and less pro-Israel than the national average.

That anti-Semitism among Blacks has been on the rise is by now graphically demonstrable, and is an upwardly mobile curve predating the Andrew Young affair and its wake of Black recriminations against Jews. Most Jewish spokesmen and too many social scientists observing it described it circumspectly. After all, Negroes have long been the victims of discrimination, and consequently their prejudice was explained with rationalizations not nearly as readily offered to fundamentalist Christians or to the restricted country-club set. William Schneider, however, in a 1979 unpublished report to the American Jewish Committee's Milton Himmelfarb, saw what his contemporaries would or could not see. His testing revealed that "there is no difference between Black and white anti-Semitism among those fifty years of age and older, when education is controlled," but that the absolute increase in Black anti-Semitism was due to younger Blacks "who are significantly more anti-Semitic than younger whites, with education controlled." The older the white, the more likely he is anti-Semitic; the younger, the less likely to be anti-Semitic. With Blacks, however, anti-Semitism is inversely related to age, and contrary to earlier rationalizations, with education controlled, the strongest anti-Semitism is harbored by younger Blacks.

So, if the cause of Black prejudice is not attributable to a deficiency of education, and in fact the disease actually spreads in response to education, what is the cause?

Later on we will look at Black-Jewish relationships. At this point we want to say that the increased ideological sensitivity of young Blacks seems clearly related to both their hostility to Jews and to their Third World pro-Arab sympathies.

And a final statistic that bears on the gulf between younger and older Blacks in their attitudes towards Jews: Asked if they agreed that "Jews have supported rights for minority groups more than other white people," one-third of Blacks under thirty said yes, while older Black respondents affirmed the statement with a 42% score. That was in 1974. Since then ideological activism has increased, and memories of even past love affairs tend with time to fade.

The late Sebastian Owens and I started our respective careers in Denver as office assistants. He, with the Urban League. I, with the Anti-Defamation League. We became friends and one summer day, lunching together, I told him that my watermelon was just great. He said, No, thanks, I'd as soon not. I said he was missing something special. Laughing at what he began to tell me, and at himself as well, he explained that he never ate watermelon in public. The year must have been 1949 or 1950 and Sambo and Rastus and Negro-rolling-eyes stereotypes were still current. So believing that all eyes in the dining room would be drawn to him were he to animate the stereotype, he demurred.

Years later in Miami of the late 1950s, there was a synagogue bombing. It was during a period in which temple bombings pockmarked several Southern cities. One day someone drew to my attention an article on the bombings in a Jewish Communist publication and a quote in it attributed to me. I was reported as having advised the writer who alleged to have phoned me that we ought say nothing publicly about the outrages. He actually quoted me as counseling, "Sha, sha."

Weeks later, mowing my lawn on a Sunday afternoon, the father of a friend, an elderly Communist still campaigning against Tsarism, came by with another elderly gentleman. We exchanged greetings and sensing that they were really visiting, myself sun-drenched-tired, I invited them in for iced tea. As we were making ourselves comfortable my friend's father's conversation opener was that Mr. Federman, his companion, was a writer on Jewish issues and that he had long wanted the two of us to get to know each other. I smiled affably, and suddenly *Federman* rang a bell. I asked if he wrote for the Communist publication. Yes, he said, he did. I asked him if we ever met. No, we hadn't. More amused than cross-examining, I asked if we had ever spoken on the phone. Again, the answer, No. "Mr. Federman," I remonstrated, "how then could you have quoted me the way in which you did?"

His answer, hands outstretched, palms up, was a jewel. "Perlmutter, *if* I'd have called you, *what* would you have said?" It closed his case and we had our iced tea.

Owens was not altogether wrong, though wrong he was, and Federman was not altogether wrong, though wrong he was. Owens's image of the white-man's image was not imaginary, no matter that millions of whites would never have taken note of his watermelon. And the truth is that no matter "Sha, sha" was the antithesis of my response to the bombings, had Federman called and introduced himself as a writer for a Communist publication, I would not have spoken with him. His image of me, if not his reportage, had kernels of truth.

All of which is by way of introducing polling results of what Jews feel non-Jews think about them. Like Owens and Federman, they are wrong, but they're right too.

Yankelovich asked non-Jews whether they feel "Jews have more money than most people." Fifty-six percent said yes. Jews, asked for their perception of what non-Jews' responses to the same question would be, believed that 83% would say yes. Pressing his point, he asked non-Jews if they were bothered by the feeling that Jews have more money than most people. Thirteen percent admitted to being bothered. Jews, however, when asked if they felt non-Jews were bothered, registered a whopping 77% score.

"Jews are more ambitious than other people" was affirmed

by 45% of non-Jews. Seventy-nine percent of the Jews polled felt that the non-Jews would consider them more ambitious.

Thirty-two percent of non-Jews agreed to the statement "Jews have too much power in the business world." But more than twice the percentage, 76%, of the Jews felt that non-Jews would feel that way.

On "too much power in the United States," the Jewish estimate of what gentiles would feel again more than doubled the declared feelings of the non-Jewish sample, 53% as compared to 20%.

The hostile proposition that "Jews try to push in where they are not wanted" found agreement in only 16% of the non-Jewish sample. But more than three times as many, 55%, of the Jewish sample attributed to non-Jews the implied hostility.

What we find fascinating here is that despite our Jewish rejection of mischievous stereotypes, their mark is on us too. Indeed, we seem to mistake the length of its shadow for the real thing . . . assuming that the non-Jewish responses were candid and not, as may well be the case, answers given to "pass" the test.

And something else. Some group stereotypes are, alas, not groundless. Their mischief is in their application to an individual. The Japanese *are* extraordinary makers of transistor radios, cameras and the like, although there are untold Japanese who are all thumbs. The English *do* have a unique sense of humor, no matter the English clods one meets. This, by way of wondering whether "Jews have more money than most people" or "Jews are more ambitious than other people" is indeed something ominously more than a simple group fact.

Perhaps the Jewish responses suggest a touch of paranoia. If so, like they say, some paranoids do have enemies.

When Jews were seeking a surcease of humiliating and discriminatory advertisements—those No Dogs or Jews Allowed and Chr Only barbs—polls probing gentile attitudes toward Jews *qua* being Jewish had immediately relevancy. Bad news guided us to appropriate themes for our educational counteroffensives, and polls spotlighting the particular segments of the population harboring animus for us helped us to beam our messages accordingly. However, as Jews have hurdled or passed under exclusionary bars, and as the bars themselves have been discarded or at least lowered, the information derived from such polls has lost current pertinence. American attitudes toward Jews as marriage partners, neighbors, merchants are relative back-burner pots today when compared to American attitudes toward Israel—its defensive needs, its importance as a democratic oasis in an authoritarian desert, its bearing on American interests in the Middle East. Besides, Messrs. Gallup, Harris, Yankelovich and assorted social scientists have assured us that the elderly are more likely carriers of anti-Semitism than the young, and Metropolitan Life's actuarial graphs are assurance that time will heal this malaise too. So it comes down to what it is that concerns Jews most intimately. Given the critical role of the American presidency and the Congress in Israel's security, it is the American public's attitudes toward Israel that becomes most immediately relevant.

But alas, if tested polling questions designed to surface impressionistic pictures of the respondent's mind-frame reveal to us his attitudes about Jews, answers to questions related to Israel are not nearly as clearly focused.

While attitudes towards Israel are not free of feelings toward Jews, there are numbers of other considerations that affect responses. Expressed attitudes towards Israel are more likely to be conditioned by the timing of the question than is the case with views of Jews. Was the poll conducted following a PLO raid in which Israeli innocents were murdered? Following an Israeli preemptive strike in which Arab innocents were murdered? Is our country in the grip of an oil shortage? Have the

OPEC nations recently hiked their prices again? Have White House leaks hinted at Israeli intransigence? Has an Entebbe feat of derring-do fired the admiration of the American public? And what of the public relations image of the *dramatis personae?* One survey has revealed that the American public trusts Israel more than it does Menachem Begin, but trusted Anwar Sadat more than it trusts Egypt. But for all that these and other factors temper reactions to Israel and its Arab neighbors, both Yankelovich and Gallup have found that their samples' responses are not altogether independent of long-held feelings for Jews as Jews.

According to Yankelovich one in every three individuals who harbor negative attitudes toward Israel reveals himself in responding to questions on Jews as being anti-Semitic. This statistical relationship between anti-Semitism and negative views of Israel is surely ironic. Jewish organizations and spokesmen have eschewed reference to the equation. They have done so because it would constitute an unfair and inaccurate generalization, vulnerable to rebuttal, and would shade their credibility in other arguments. However, while Jewish organizations have shunned use of this pejorative association, highly regarded critics of Israeli policies have, turning it inside out, employed it to declare that no matter they will be accused of anti-Semitism they nonetheless feel compelled to reveal their current critical truth about Israel. This more-in-pain-than-in-anger resolve to fearlessly champion their freedom from intimidation, no matter that in doing so they become targets for unloaded guns aimed by nonexistent Jewish organizations, has been indulged by political leaders and journalists as diverse as Paul McCloskey and James Reston. The irony? The pollsters' findings proving that Jewish organizations have been overly shy of making an association which is, after all, if carefully drawn, demonstrable. And ironic too, because those who having voiced criticism of Israel while fantasizing countercharges of anti-Semitism, perhaps understand better than do Jews the vulnerability of their cheering sections.

The 33% of those negatively disposed toward Israel who are anti-Semites compare with 20% of those who are highly favorable to Israel but score as anti-Semites. The latter rather illusive finding may be suggestive of the timing of the poll—a particularly outrageous PLO or Libyan provocation might well outweigh a respondent's passive anti-Semitism. It may be, and we suspect frequently is, attributable to the respondent's anticommunism and his perception of the Israeli government as a Western advance point against Eastern communism. Anti-Semitism, at least as measured by surveys, would also be consonant with pro-Israel feelings for the proportion of the sample which identifies itself as Christian fundamentalists—high scorers on negative stereotypes of Jewish, but believers in the literal Word that the Jews are God's Chosen People and Israel their preordained final address.

A Gallup-polished facet of the same theme has revealed that those who are of the opinion that Jews' loyalty to Israel exceeds their loyalty to the United States tend also to be more sympathetic to Arabs. This group also believes that Jews have too much political influence.

And again, the stepladder. The American Jewish Committee's 1981 survey determined that among those qualifying as "prejudiced," the smallest number viewed Israel favorably and the largest number viewed Israel critically. Among those qualifying as "unprejudiced," the ladder saw the majority holding highly favorable views of Israel, and the smallest number bunched as critical of Israel. Across the board, those who hold generally favorable views of Israel are college graduates, Reagan supporters, conservatives, whites and males.

Interestingly, for all the apprehension Jews suffer about American public opinion and its influence on American Middle Eastern foreign policy, 44% of Americans in 1981 responded to the question, "If there was a war between the Arab nations and Israel, would you sympathize with: Israel, Arabs, Neither, Not sure," with the answer "Israel." Three percent selected Arabs. And for all that Menachem Begin has been faulted as wanting in "public relations" and Anwar Sadat extolled, American sympathies in response to this question have been on a plateau. In 1977, some 45% answered "Israel" to the identical question, and 2% opted for Arabs.

This continued positive level of popular sympathy for Israel, whether the offshoot of favorable attitudes toward Jews as compared to Arabs, whether the consequence of American anti-Communism or fundamentalist literalism, is in *realpolitik* terms tons weightier an assurance to Jews than their countrymen's increasing acceptance of them as neighbors, merchants, sons- and daughters-in-law.

De Tocqueville's *Democracy in America,* written 150 years ago, depicting Americans, our ethos and the society we were busily fashioning, retains its fascination for those seeking to understand our people and our land. Interestingly, it contains nary a chart nor a statistic. Of course de Tocqueville was an artist and social scientists are craftsmen, and so this aside admittedly lacks generosity. Polls do serve a useful purpose. We had a friend who owned a chain of supermarkets. Wednesdays, the *Miami Herald* would bulge with his advertisements, page after expensive page. I once asked him if his heavy spending for advertising paid off, and his answer allowed that half of it was a waste of money, the other half, useful. To my follow-up question, Why then don't you cut down on the ads?, he responded, "That's the problem. I don't know which half works and which doesn't."

We have referred to the utility in knowing the locus and the extent of negative views of Jews, but the curiosity of Jews for knowing how they are regarded by gentiles has sometimes served academic counterparts of the *Miami Herald* at least as

well as Jews themselves. Wanting so badly to *know,* we have
not always been wary buyers, and some of our silk-priced pur-
chases have been polyester—the periodic handing of cards to
respondents, for instance, on which are listed such groups as
labor unions, Blacks, the Catholic Church, business corporations, Jews and in recent years anti-abortion groups, conserva-
tionists, and the like. The interviewee is asked to indicate which
of the noted groups in his opinion has too much political power.
One Jewish organization has broadcast its comfort in the
finding that the perceived political power of business organizations, labor unions and assorted other secular groups exceeds
that of Jews. As if individual members of business groups and
Jews were apples and apples and had in common shared experiences of repeated dispersal and persecution. In a recent like
survey, satisfaction was derived from data suggesting that 30%
of Americans felt that environmentalists had too much power,
and that only 17% felt Jews had too much power. There have
been no subsequent reports that environmentalists have organized an Anti-Defamation League.

In some instances the social scientists have repeatedly posed
questions of dubious significance. High levels of acceptance of
Jews as being a "hard working people" have been interpreted,
correctly, as evidencing a positive image of Jews. But in the
same surveys affirmations by respondents that Jews are "more
ambitious than other people" is deemed a negative image. My
mother, let alone de Tocqueville with whom she had in common that they were both foreign born, would have caught this
silly, but hardy, inconsistency.

At times the questions seem programmed to elicit answers
bound to further disquiet their already apprehensive underwrit-
ers. A 1964 survey found that 13% of non-Jews with an opinion
on the subject believed that Jews have too much power in the
United States. A 1981 poll, noting that finding, forebodingly
revealed that currently 23% share that view. But the plain fact

is that since 1964 international harassment of Israel has es-
calated sharply, American interests in the Middle East have
increasingly preoccupied our presidents and our Congress, and
consequently the American Jewish community has been increasingly audible in the higher-pitched debates on this or that
foreign policy course. Is it to wonder then that with an increased awareness, accurately perceived, of Jewish participation in the debates, "Jewish power" would disconcert more
people than it had in the relatively low-key Middle East policy
debates of 1964? Besides, as we have seen, Americans remain
overwhelmingly sympathetic to Israel, due, to be sure, to the
parallel interests of the United States and Israel but in some
measure due too, perhaps, to the articulateness of Jewish participation in the political process. To argue is to be noticed; to
argue and win is to invite resentment. To not speak our mind
is to go unnoticed, not be resented, but, alas, to forfeit the
stakes. We can't have it both ways.

But if these illustrations of weaknesses in polling as a barometer of the levels of anti-Semitism are readily discernible, there
are less evident flaws, inherent in language itself, which have
long skewed polling results.

When a person professing Christian beliefs is asked whether
Jews are more likely than Christians to cheat in business, to use
shady practices, is he expressing anti-Semitism or is he rooting
for his home team? Or turnabout, is a Jew who abjures intermarriage so much anti-Christian as he is pro-Jewish continuity?
Roy Lutz writing in the *Review of Religious Research* found
that responses to anti-Semitism questions which did not contain
a reference to Christians—that is, "Do Jews have too much
power?"—were only weakly correlated with religious orthodoxy. These are sticky, tricky formulations and, in view of
the generally favorable attitude of orthodox Christians toward
Israel, have likely exaggerated the actual level of their anti-
Semitism.

Beyond the use of imprecise language, bad tools, the surveys are sometimes misleading as a consequence of the scientist's social biases. We have previously discussed Gary Marx's widely publicized *Protest and Prejudice,* and have commented on his rationalization of Black anti-Semitism as being reflexive to Blacks' proximity to Jews. Revealing more of his personal views than of the dynamics of prejudice, he summed up his findings with the observation: "While Negro anti-Semitism is deplorable, it certainly is more understandable than white anti-Semitism." In his preface, he confesses to his partisanship toward the civil-rights struggle and expresses the "hope" that his personal views have minimally affected his work. Also that " . . . someone with a different commitment might have written a different book." This is an unusual confession of partisanship, qualifying his own objectivity. The work, however, and its publicized findings have been long-lived, while the author's admission is as unintrusive as a footnote. One wonders, would a university or its faculty have countenanced a similar study by a scholar with an anti-civil rights laws bias?

Political particularism, a bias in the context of social scientific methodology, which after all aspires to objectivity, is also evident in the field of research into prejudice. In *Anti-Semitism in America,* published in 1979, a full chapter is devoted to "Politics and Prejudice." Given our long, often bitter experience with right-wing extremism, Quinley and Glock appropriately summarize and interpret the anti-Masonic, anti-Catholic, anti-Semitic propaganda and machinations of nativist right-wing movements. Not a word, however—in 1979!—about *left*-wing extremism. Their analysis is sound as far as it goes, but for not going far enough it is functionally truncated. It suggests the ingredients of the "politics of extremism." They are: "(1) the existence of large numbers of Americans who feel disaffected and frustrated by societal changes; (2) a willingness on the part of such Americans to ignore democratic norms and values and to violate the democratic rights of others; (3) a reservoir of minority group hate and prejudice which can be mobilized for extremist purposes; and (4) an acceptance of right-wing or 'preservationist' political ideology."

They also suggest that they have found "three very different groups of Americans who are most disposed to disaffection" and thus most attracted to extremist-style politics. These are "1. more privileged Americans, such as doctors or heads of family-owned corporations, who feel the weight of growing government controls; 2. less wealthy but predominantly middle-class Americans whose identity is closely bound up in traditional religious and secular values that are being supplanted by 'modern' values, which they consider to be immoral; 3. working-class whites who, after making some gains, feel their positions to be threatened, especially by the demands of poor minorities and by the attention given to those minorities by government and other agencies."

The story is told of the British defense of Singapore. Certain that the attack would come from the sea—the jungle to their rear seemed impenetrable—they fixed both their cannons and their attention accordingly. The attack, of course, came from behind, from the surprisingly penetrable jungle. And so with many of our social scientists. Accustomed to the rumblings of anti-Semitism and the grumblings of xenophobia from the far right, they are alert in one direction. The "disaffected and frustrated" and consequently potentially volatile are "doctors or heads of family-owned corporations," middle-class Americans," and "working-class whites." This discovery following a decade of inner-city riots, campus takeovers and international left-wing anti-Semitism and totalitarianism, none of which was examined in "Politics and Prejudice"! Violence launched from the right, it would seem, is extremism. From the left it is social protest. To Jews, scapegoated by both, the difference is without a distinction—a wisdom garnered more from our experience than from our academic surveyors.

In summary, statisticians, pollsters and social scientists have provided us with insights into the scope, level and locations of anti-Semitism. They have also roughly estimated the strength of the grip of particular stereotypes on the American consciousness. Moreover, for the intuitively aware they have provided the authority of their profession—all this so long as their small print is read carefully and the spaces between their lines weighed judiciously. This latter caution is well illustrated by the press releases flowing from the 1981 American Jewish Committee-Yankelovich after the Anti-Defamation League's Selznick and Steinberg study, which concluded that only 34% of the nation's non-Jews are anti-Semitic, a perceived improvement over 1964. Translated into numbers, the "good-news" 34% extrapolated, means that 70,000,000 men, women and children in our country are anti-Semites.

Beyond the layman's need to read surveys on anti-Semitism carefully there is a need for social scientists to craft their questions more probingly. The openness of American society through which haters of the Irish, of Catholics, of Masons, of Jews, of Orientals, of Blacks, of Mexicans, and of on and on has been more than matched by its resiliency in which the haters and their organizations have been absorbed, overwhelmed, ostracized from the mainstream. And so it has been the well-being of American democracy itself which has been the Jew's protective shell. Today, the Jew no longer the hapless victim but with the memory of having previously prevailed only to be persecuted again, we would do well to periodically take the temperature of our democratic institutions. Their good health is at least as relevant to our security as whether a gentile would buy a home if he knew his next-door neighbor was a Jew.

5

Allies and Adversaries, Then and Now

PHOTOGRAPHY COMMUNICATES AND paintings communicate, but for all of the sharp exactitude of literal portraiture the impressionists' truths are frequently more revealing. So it is that despite the statistical portraits of the pollsters, clearly evidencing the bettering attitudes towards Jews in the United States, Jews, responding to feeling tones rather than percentage points, are uneasy. No matter their organizational deliberations may be taking place in the posh baroque ambience of the Waldorf-Astoria or in the festooned ballroom of The Breakers Hotel plopped down in the tropical languor of Palm Beach, they worry. They worry about anti-Semitism. They know the polls, but still they worry. Not because they do not trust the polls but because their apprehensions march to a different drummer—their personal impressions. And so having discussed the graphs drawn by the social scientists, let us now view an impressionis-

103

tic portrait of the disturbances currently registering on the Jew's Richter scale, and his in-progress change of sociopolitical response.

Concurrently with the swelling good-news statistics, Jews have grown less surefooted. A decade ago who would have imagined that the Berrigan brothers, apostles of peace, would today be rationalizers of the terrorist PLO and that a brigade of Christian fundamentalists would be resolutely siding with Israel? Or that the United Nations, once the One World ideal, would turn lexicographer, brew antonyms—Zionism and racism—and in a reeking alchemy reconstitute them as synonyms? Or that Jewish defense agencies would still be filing friend-of-the-court briefs challenging racial discrimination, but that their legal adversaries would be led by the National Association for the Advancement of Colored People?

These questions, though posed rhetorically, imply our point: That the sector of American Jewry which counts itself as part of the Jewish community is being discomfortingly faced and challenged by political and social considerations unforeseen and alien to us only a blink in time ago. For it was only a short time ago that Jewish theoreticians and sword-carriers were in the vanguard of the political Left and of social reform. Our allies were "liberals"; our adversaries, "conservatives." Among us—outsiders, or at best possessing restricted passes to a restricted society, some (Communists, Socialists) sought to change the system, while others (liberals, reformers) sought to cause the system to function according to the democratic ideals it espoused. It followed that we were empathetic to other outsiders. Domestically they were political dissidents of the Left. The Left was part of us; those on the Right were viewed as an extremity of the very system that excluded us. And in foreign affairs our sympathy was for the Third World, our imagined overseas models of the minorities we supported at home.

Perhaps our political and social sympathies were fashioned

by the second clause of the Hillel tradition: If I am not for myself, who am I; if I am only for myself, what am I? Likely so. But whatever the reasons for our high profile in the Left, certainly anti-Semitism figured prominently. Long after we lost our Yiddish accents, long after we vacated the tenements of the lower East Side, established ourselves in the aeries of the upper East Side, even as we began to rue the distance we had put between our acculturating selves and our cultural heritage—a scalper's price of admission we had eagerly paid—*they* still would not fully accept us. So, as marginal Americans, we embraced and were embraced by the Left and by minorities, themselves outsiders.

But manifested anti-Semitism in the United States, as customarily we have experienced and measured it, is presently not the problem it was then. Consequently we are not the outsiders we were then. The interests of the Jewish community's political and social responses are undergoing, and will continue to undergo, marked, adaptive changes. In the 1940s and 1950s, when Jewish defense agencies were urging the passage of antidiscrimination laws for housing, education, employment and places of public accommodation we countered the arguments of our opposition by declaring we were not seeking to legislate against bigotry. We granted bigotry was a state of mind and consequently beyond the authority of the state. What we were seeking, we maintained, were laws to prohibit the transmutation of private bigotry into acts of public discrimination.

We succeeded. Today our residences are restricted only by our means. No religious or ethnic group boasts a higher percentage of college graduates. As for employment discrimination, despite its lingering persistence in executive suites, we have done very well indeed as a group. And in terms of acceptance in places of public accommodation, it is a not uncommon irony that resorts which then discriminated against us today are often dependent on our patronage.

But still we look, warily, over our shoulder. It's understand-able. For several years now, membership in the Ku Klux Klan has been increasing as have juicily reported incidents of anti-Semitic vandalisms. As with the Klan whose latter day mem-bership consists largely of young people, the vandalisms have largely been perpetrated by juveniles from fourteen to seventeen years of age.

At this point, we would, if we could, will this chapter to become a movie, and becoming a movie, freeze the foregoing paragraph as a frame, and in a voice-over, while the viewer contemplates the Klan's growth and the mushrooming (but unrelated) instances of anti-Semitic vandalism, the narrator comments:

Stand with me on the corner of Forty-second Street and First Avenue in New York City in front of the United Nations. Let us watch the diplomats on their way to work. Turbaned men, women in saris, tall Black men and short swarthy men, blond Europeans and yellow Orientals—all well groomed, educated, cosmopolitan. Diplomats.

Surely there isn't one among them who is a Klansman. Surely there isn't one who would, under night's cover, furtively sneak onto a Jew's lawn, daub a swastika on his door. But who threatens Jewish interests more ominously—the diplomats who regularly affirm that Zionism is racism, or the juveniles with paint cans?

Our contention is that in the near future, Jewish security will not be endangered by caricature anti-Semites. The Klansman, by socioeconomic definition, is a loser; by any comparison, American Jews have prevailed. As for the more educated, more polished anti-Semite, our achievements in the professions, in business and in the arts constitute our victory over and despite him.

We remain apprehensive because we sense that the cutting danger to us—potentially mortal to Israel, potentially maiming to the Diaspora—is in the sheath of certain governmental policies. These policies are in furtherance of perceived national interests and are essentially a-Semitic. Nonetheless they pose a Jewish problem.

When time and time again United Nations delegates repeat that Zionism is racism—sinking ever deeper, spreading ever wider the roots of our time's Big Lie—the instructed diplomats are attesting not to Jew hatred but rather to the oil thirst of their governments. Oil is not anti-Semitic. It has, however, altered the world's responses to Jewish concerns.

In 1980, delivering a rousing anti-Semitic peroration on the floor of the United Nations General Assembly, a Jordanian delegate fanned new sparks into the infamous "Protocols of the Elders of Zion." At its conclusion, silence. The delegate from France, birthplace of liberty, fraternity and equality, said nothing. The delegate from West Germany, a nation which has labored mightily to distance itself from its unspeakable past, sat silently. President Carter's delegate, himself no stranger to racism, deepened the silence with his silence. Not a murmur of protest . . . from anyone . . . save the Israeli ambassador. Jews heard him and while they have likely forgotten what he said, they heard the silence too, and the memory of it is longer lasting.

What is relevant here is not that a Jordanian let loose an anti-Semitic tirade—no surprise, that—but that no one even whispered "Shame." Because they are all anti-Semites? No. Because for reasons of national interest, such as maintenance of friendly relations with Arab OPEC nations and their wards, silence was the diplomatically preferred response. It was as if the expedient silence of the diplomats was a message to Jews saying, "You have been abused, and while our silence is our complicity, really, it's nothing personal."

Our thesis that today Jewish interests are beset by *realpolitik* devoid of familiar anti-Semitism finds resonance beyond the United Nations. The Common Market nations sell arms, packaged and beribboned with goodwill, to Israel's sworn enemies. Swelling Soviet and Arab choruses sing the virtue of the PLO. These policies—in the former instance, free of classical anti-Semitism; in the latter, flaunting it—are megatons more dangerous to Jewish interests than are neo-Nazis. Moreover, so often as to be predictable, these are policies of socialist governments and of nations whose freedom from colonialism Jews cheered only yesterday.

Domestically recent attempts to "reform" aspects of the American body politic have been carriers of fall-out corrosive of Jewish interests. The proponents of these purported reforms include many allies in Jewish battles against anti-Semitism. Indeed, the proponents include many Jews. For instance, many Jews were among those who challenged the electoral college as undemocratic.

Fortunately, the electoral college survived, until the next assault. Without it, presidential candidates would not need to factor into their campaigns the views of groups concentrated in swing states—and the political influence of the American Jewish community would dissolve. So would the ground on which Israel's cause is pleaded to presidential candidates—unless of course, one believes that justice is ever triumphant and that there really is a tooth fairy.

Of course, the electoral college is in fact democratic. It is democratic because in our system of balances, the House of Representatives is majoritarian. A presidency also reflective only of majority numbers is a political contradiction in terms, providing neither the check nor the balance of minority views, and consequently mocks pluralism and is wanting democracy. While attempts to scuttle the electoral college have been led by persons in no way anti-Semitic, if they are successful they will debase Jewish political currency—something anti-Semites have failed to accomplish.

The quota system has long stalked Jews. Anti-Semites sired it and universities, employers, home-owner associations and clubs whelped it. In the 1950s and 1960s, with the passage of state antidiscrimination laws and climaxed by the enactment of federal civil-rights laws, Jews, Blacks and others were freed of quota constrictions. But, alas, the system has returned. To be sure, it is incognito; its alias is "goals." Where once it scowled, now it smiles. For the old quota system barred the door, selectively; the new quota system opens the door, selectively. But irrespective of its intentions, a quota system remains a quota system—now arbitrarily bestowing opportunity, now withholding it, on whim reacting to race, religion or sex.

We will write more of the quota system, its hypocrisy and its cruelty later, but the relevance of raising the subject now is that it is another illustration of governmental actions which are free of intended anti-Semitism but nonetheless endanger Jews. For the justice for Jews and other minorities in the civil-rights laws was not that the laws mandated relief for Jews or other specified groups—they didn't—but that they prohibited racial or religious discrimination. With considerations of race and religion eliminated, the bigot's target was removed, or at least blurred.

Free of the quota system, Jews have done well. In universities, both as students and as faculty, in professional schools and as practitioners we number many times our 2.7% of the population. But, under camouflage of "affirmative action," legal precedents are settling and once again legitimatizing racial criteria for admissions and hiring, and racial percentages reflective of each community are being sanctioned.

And who is sponsoring and defending the new quota system? Not our familiar bigots; currently they are political lightweights. And if the quota's accessories include university administrations and personnel officers of corporate America, their complicity is mitigated by being hovered over by larger forces—the state, no less. For withheld government grants and contracts can be compelling arguments. No, the major proponents of the new quotas are past victims of the old quotas, shortsightedly turning racism's table. Their fellow travelers are persons whose motivations are to compensate for past wrongs. But for merit, for democratic government, and for unfashionable minorities—including Jews—it's all rather ironic. Those who had been victimized by racism now engaging in neo-racism.

Social and political arrangements are in flux in our country and our world. The Jewish community's position relative to governmental systems and to social and political groupings has changed. So have its interests. When assigned roles as outsiders formerly compelled Jews to oppose the establishment from its left flank and to make alliances with others similarly rejected, that served Jewish interests and the declared if not the practiced ideals of the nation. To suggest that we ought now tolerate what we only recently deplored simply because we have been accepted into the club would be cynical, and worse, dishonorable. But the fact is that we have largely won our battle not because we have done well but because the enabling principles for which we have fought have prevailed. It is our former allies and the beneficiaries of our moral and financial support who have abandoned our mutually shared ideals.

A Jewish Rip van Winkle who dozed off in the administration of Lyndon Johnson, waking this morning, would confront a disorienting day. The Shah of Iran is dead, the Savak secret police is no longer. But Iran's revolutionary reformers are no less despotic, and the Jewish component is that the risen-oppressed are anti-Semites. The Shah wasn't. Rip might recall the ousting of the Cuban dictator Batista and the Jewish component in that country, still a dictatorship, is that its new government would render Israel vulnerable to destruction. Batista didn't. And Nicaraugua and El Salvador, and a score of reform movements already victorious or in the process of "liberation" warfare are allied not with besieged Israel but with the colonialist Soviet Union or at the least with Jew-hating Yasir Arafat.

He would find peacemakers of Vietnam vintage, transmuters of swords into plowshares, championing the terrorist PLO, and the war-bemedalled generals and admirals protective of democratic Israel. What would he make of the respective roles vis-à-vis his Jewish interests of the civil-rights advocate, Reverend Andrew Young, and the evangelical Reverend Pat Robertson?

Plainly, the long-time conditioned response of the Jewish community to a panoply of social and political problems is undergoing and will continue to undergo significant change. That's as natural as the instinct of self-defense.

6

The Left and Jews

WE HAVE NOW stipulated what previously we have inferred. The preference Jews have manifested for the political Left over the Right requires reconsideration; characteristics of the socially conscious, modernist Christian denominations which traditionally comforted us and characteristics of the socially narrow-gauged Christian fundamentalists which traditionally discomforted us require our reevaluation; the mutuality of interests in our long-standing alliance with the Black civil-rights establishment is not as reciprocal as within easy memory it was.

In chapters seven and eight we will examine Christians and Jews and then Blacks and Jews. Consistent with the proverbial Elephant and the Jewish Question, in this chapter we will consider the Left and the Jews.

Where I lived in Brooklyn as a boy, the Democrats were a plurality and it was my impression that close behind them, at least in decibel count were the Communists and various Socialist factions. Republicans were as numerous as Whigs. When I say Democrats, I should explain. They were Democrats who, yes, they believed in socialism, but Roosevelt is good for Jews, good for the worker, and besides, a vote for the Socialists is a wasted vote. So socialism had our respect and the Democrats had our votes. For it was Roosevelt who seemed hawkish toward the Nazis, Roosevelt who led us out of the Great Depression, and it was Mrs. Roosevelt who spoke to our plaintiff's pursuit of civil rights. Besides, our district's office holders often being Jews, the Democratic party looked Jewish. Conversely, the Republican party looked gentile.

No longer a boy, Brooklyn a faded memory, during the Nixon-McGovern presidential campaign I met an old friend, Jewish, one whom I had known for more than a quarter of a century as a voting-booth Democrat and a living-room Socialist. We talked family, old times and some politics. On the latter, he offered, "I've been a lifelong Republican . . . the past six months." Of course he was half joking. But only half. Likely, Gallup never rang him, but his quip was the first ripple, to become wave-size in the Reagan-Carter election, in what may yet swell into a sea change in Jewish voting patterns.

The in-progress Jewish distancing of themselves from the perceived Left is not only a response to politics. Increasingly there is a social factor involved, less sentimental than Brooklyn Democrats having looked like us, but gaining in persuasiveness. In the Jewish ghettoes of our youth in Brooklyn, the Bronx and in the lower East Side we associated culture and learning with political "liberals"—beer, and suspected anti-Semitism in the counterparts of today's "hard hats." In the past decade these remembered associations, whether imaginings or accurately drawn, have lost their fit.

During the early 1950s, I used to travel the Mountain States, stopping in places like Casper and Laramie, Wyoming; Trinidad and LaJunta, Colorado; Las Vegas and Roswell, New Mexico. When I'd come into town the evening before my morning meetings I liked walking the city's downtown and nearby side streets around the bus or railroad station. Before leaving my hotel room, I'd hide my wallet under the mattress, remove my tie and "dress down," fearing, because the streets were not my streets and its leathery Anglo-Saxon and mixed-breed faces not the faces with which I grew up in New York, that business-suited I would seem wealthy, an inviting target for toughs. Nothing ever happened. Nothing ever nearly happened. But today in New York City, we have friends who will not take nighttime walks no matter the streets are their own, its faces childhood familiar. We have one friend on the West Side near Central Park who refuses to be intimidated, does take after-dinner walks, but leaves his wristwatch home, strategically walks the center of the sidewalk out of arm's reach of doorway or automobile-based accosters. New York City's parks, Central, Prospect, and dozens of smaller greenswards, are posted with signs cautioning strollers to Stay Out before sunrise and after sunset, graphic warnings just like the skull and crossbones of our medicine cabinet labels.

What has happened is that our big cities have become what my imagination feared the Southwest's skid rows were. LaJunta, however, turned out to be innocent, my fear of my own haunting, and East-Side, West-Side, all-around-the-town of the tuneful "Sidewalks of New York" are where the goblins are alive and well. Fear and filth, it seems, grow thick where music, art, theater, libraries and liberal constituencies thrive, and the streets are clean and safe where Babbitt lives. And this too is factored into my friend's political journey.

Beyond our favoring of the Left because it seems politically more sympathetic to our working-class and immigrant interests, and beyond feeling more comfortable with its political parties because its New York leaders even if Irish or Italian, let alone Jewish, seemed more of us than did native white Anglo-Saxon Protestants, Jews were drawn leftward because it was from there that the early calls for intervention in Hitler's Germany were heard; from the Republicans, many of them isolationists, we heard silence resonating as indifference.

In 1942, a freshman at Georgetown University's School of Foreign Service, I visited the Washington, D.C., Marine Corps recruiting station to enlist. The one question I wasn't prepared for was, "Why?"

"Why?" the sergeant wanted to know, and suddenly I was embarrassed. I had been trying to breathe slower, to will sedation for the excitement that for days had been welling larger and larger in me and on which I was now afloat. His surprise question drained my excitement and that was good because breathing regularly I felt mature, just as I had planned, but it embarrassed me and so again I felt my boyishness showing, compromising the maturity I was trying to project.

I was embarrassed because I didn't want to tell him why. It seemed too personal an answer, appropriate for late-night ice-cream-parlor bull sessions but inappropriate, even corny, somehow pompous, voiced to a Sigmund Romberg uniformed marine I had just met. Finally, my eyes shyer than my voice, I uttered my private truth.

"I want to fight fascism."

We had something in common, now. It was the one answer, ideological, for which the professional warrior wasn't prepared.

I have been thinking back to World War II. Likely, in part it's simply a matter of aging, reminiscing seems to be its by-product. But mostly, it was our war in Vietnam, its off-stage oxymoronic violent peace demonstrations, the popular European view Better Red Than Dead and the echoes of it in the American peace movement that draw me back to the Great War and to an accompanying nagging notion that nowadays war is getting a bad name and peace too favorable a press. What we are saying is that in the defamations by the Left of the promptings for our warring in Vietnam and latterly that in their sniping at American defense budgets, war *as such* is getting the bad name. So much so, for instance, that the late Margaret Mead described World War II as ". . . a war that culminated in the horrors of Hiroshima." To a point, true. An alternative more fitting truth, in the range of our then options, would be that the war in which I enlisted was a war that culminated with the closing down of the crematoria, in an end to ongoing genocide.

Plain and simply said, World War II was a good war and it wasn't the first such. More pertinently, given history's pages' endless accounts of man's propensity to subjugate, enslave and oppress, it must not be the last war, lest all the preceding good ones and their trophies of national and personal freedom are forfeit. Conversely, for all its currently good press, peace has been known to be bitter. In some places it still is and unless warred on, life is bitter too. Great numbers of enlistees, "interventionists" of the youth generation of the early 1940s, intellectually nursed by the old Left, understood that peace can be war's progeny, tyranny, the miscarriage of peace, and they understood it with an idealism more reality-based, and a love of life less self-referent than is evident in the young liberals referred to earlier, whose testimony to pollsters reveals them as less disposed than conservatives to American military preparedness, let alone to supporting United States military involvement in the event that "Israel were being defeated by the Arabs." And this neo-isolationism contributes to the appearance of Jews as politically exiting left, entering right.

Strongly held political views, whether generated by personal fear or by altruistic social convictions, whether sustained by illusions or by delusions, have been propellants for Jews, coalescing us, driving us inward from the wide margins of America but driving us outward too by freeing us from our own marginality. And there's no mistaking it, in our time and in this place, it's been the politics of the Left that has opened and freshened the way. There on the Left is where this land's windows have been raised. We associated anti-Semitism with the political Right, from the Spanish Inquisition, to the tsars' pogroms, to the tribunal that tried Dreyfus, right up to Adolf Hitler. By and large, the isolationists of our youth, those insensitive to spilled Jewish blood were of the Right too. But we were emancipated from the walled, sometimes figuratively, sometimes literally, ghettoes by revolutions from the left in the eighteenth and nineteenth centuries; and in the United States we donned our civil rights, tailored by the political parties of liberalism. Our parents' affinity—overwhelmingly, they were poor working class—was for the redolent-with-promise rhetoric of the Left. When political loyalties are so long in place, the gears —no matter that what discomforts us on the left today is hauntingly familiar; it frightened us as youths when we discerned it in the right—just do not change easily.

What is bemusing about Jewish tolerance of or expectations for or even participation, often as leaders, in Socialist and militant left movements is the shortness of those Jews' memories. They remember Haman more vividly than Marx. But historically, the far Left's fruits were as bitter to Jews as those harvested by the far Right. Nor did it begin with Stalin whose consuming anti-Semitism was more logically an offshoot of radicalism's roots than it was an aberration.

In Germany at the turn of the eighteenth century Johann Gottlieb Fichte, the noted philosopher and early Socialist, deplored Jews as "a powerful, hostile state perpetually at war with other states," and wrote, "The Jews must not be granted civil rights, unless one night one could cut off all their heads and replace them by others in which there would not be a single Jewish idea." Ironically, at least in retrospect, he saw "no other means of protecting ourselves against them than by conquering their Promised Land for them and sending them all there."

In neighboring France his contemporary, the father of French socialism, Charles Fourier, was warning the masses that "in dealing with Jews one is bound to expect lies and nothing but lies." Rather unsocially, the progenitor of Gallic socialism described Jews as the "worst exploiters (who) do not shrink from high treason" and as "the spies of all nations and if need be informers and hangmen."

Pierre Joseph Proudhon, a chief protagonist in the French Utopian Socialist movement of the latter part of the nineteenth century, reviled Jews as worthless, they being, in his Socialist vision neither farmers nor industrialists. Proudhon's influence on the way in which Socialists regarded Jews prompted historian Edmund Silberne to observe that during the Dreyfus Affair many socialists accepted anti-Semitism as a "preparatory school for socialism."

Proudhon's contemporary, Ferdinand Lassalle, himself a Jew and the acknowledged initiator of modern socialism in Germany, denigrated Jews as "the sons of a great but vanished past," publicly boasted that there was not a single Jew close to him, and in his Socialist paper published the writings of vitriolic anti-Semites. This, however, did not dissuade Friedrich Engels, who second only to Karl Marx is credited as being the intellectual source of modern socialism, from decrying Lassalle as "the silly yid" and "the greasy Jew of Breslau." Marx's own anti-Semitism (and Jewish ancestry) is well known, but apparently not widely enough, even among Jews. It was Marx himself who wrote, "What is the worldly basis of Judaism, if not practical need, egoism? What is the worldly cult of the Jew? Huckstering. What is his worldly god? Money."

Nor were these simply the offstage fulminations of socialism's founding fathers, voiced out of earshot of the madding crowd, confined to unread, esoteric journals. Anti-Semitism served as a brightly colored lure for the downtrodden masses, themselves prepared, often eagerly, to scapegoat Jews. Lucy Dawidowicz in *The Golden Tradition* unearthed an 1881 edition of the Russian Socialist paper "Narodnaya Volya," written for popular consumption, justifying Russian pogroms.

> Good people, honest Ukrainian people! Life has become hard in the Ukraine, and it keeps getting harder. The damned police beat you, the landowners devour you, the kikes, the dirty Judases, rob you. People in the Ukraine suffer most of all from the kikes. Who has seized the land, the woodlands, the taverns? The kikes. Whom does the peasant beg with tears in his eyes to let him near his own land? The kikes. Wherever you look, whatever you touch, everywhere the kikes. The kike curses the peasant, cheats him, drinks his blood. The kikes make life unbearable.

Some Socialists were offended by the diatribe and made their displeasure known. The response of the party, however, was to declare that the statement represented its official position: "We have no right to respond hostilely or even indifferently to a truly popular movement." The "popular movement" was the Socialist euphemism for "pogroms."

Abraham Cahan, later to become the celebrated editor of the Yiddish-language American newspaper the *Forward,* in 1891 served as a delegate from the United Hebrew Trades of New York to the Socialist International Congress convening in Brussels. Alarmed by rabid popular anti-Semitism and the complicity of Socialists in the spreading and stirring of it, he petitioned the International to repudiate anti-Semitism and to affirm "that you are the enemies of all exploiters be they Jew or Christian and that you have as much sympathy for Jewish workers as for Christian workers."

They refused. Finally, the would-be reformers of capitalist decadence passed a compromise resolution condemning "anti-Semitic and philo-Semitic excitations"!

But our exclamation point completes neither the story, nor the point of its telling. Cahan, the wise Socialist counselor to New York's teeming, disoriented, immigrant Jewish proletariat, a respected journalist and a regarded intellectual, was so embarrassed for his comrades that upon his return, reporting on the congress in the *New York Yiddish Zeitung* he omitted any reference to the rebuff. It took thirty-five years for Cahan, writing his memoirs, to finally accommodate for anti-Semitism and zeal for social reform as possibly occupying the same place at the same time, and albeit belatedly, at last reported on the full truth of the Brussels' Socialist International.

In the United States one of populism's most articulate excoriators of the railroads, the banks, the corporations, all of the forces which presumably were embittering the life of the masses, was Georgia's U.S. Senator Tom Watson. During the Carter-Ford presidential campaign, President Carter's mother, Lillian, in a television interview, boasted of having reared her children in the teachings of this socially conscious champion of the people. Tom Watson, of course, it was, whose anti-Semitic invective is credited with the arrest, trial, conviction on suborned testimony and subsequent lynching of the ill-fated Jew, Leo Frank, whose innocence has been irrefutably established by a recent confession.

The story, perhaps apocryphal, is told of the great American Socialist leader Eugene V. Debs whose initials for decades have been the identifying letters of the New York foreign language —largely Yiddish—radio station, WEVD. Upon his death, lying in state, by his bier were two immense wreaths. One, presumably on the left side, *in memoriam* to the great leader, was the offering of the Communist party, U.S.A. On the opposite end, *in memoriam* to the great leader, was the offering of the Ku Klux Klan, U.S.A.

But it was Isaac Babel in his story "Gedali," who neatly and tellingly captured the sad irony of Jewish confidence in the Left as an antidote to the Right. The Russian revolution is afire and Gedali, a Jew, is talking with a revolutionary, a non-Jew.

"Revolution? 'Yes' we say to it, but shall we say 'no' to Sabbath?" . . . " 'Yes,' I cry out to the revolution, 'yes,' I cry out to it, but it hides from Gedali and answers only with bullets . . .'

" 'You don't know what you like, Gedali. I am going to shoot at you and then you will know, and I cannot help but shoot, for I am the revolution . . .'

" 'But the Pole shot at me, my kind sir, because he is the counter-revolution. You shoot at me because you are the revolution . . . Who, then, will tell Gedali which is revolution and which is counter-revolution?' . . ."

Babel, the Jew, created Gedali as his witnessing surrogate. Generations later Alan Dershowitz, the Harvard law professor, played himself. Visiting Spain in 1980, in Madrid on the Sabbath eve, he decided to attend synagogue services. At the entry portals guards frisked and searched him, asked him to produce his passport and to explain his presence. In response to his puzzled question he was advised that there had recently been two assassination attempts on leaders of the Jewish community. "By the Right or the Left?" Dershowitz asked. The revealing unrevealing answer: "We don't know."

What other group marked for violence does not even know whether the attempts come from the Right or the Left?

When we lived in Colorado in the early 1950s, so did a right-wing fundamentalist preacher who stocked his trade with anticommunism and anti-Catholicism. He was also *pro patria.* His audiences, mainly religious fundamentalists, thirty, on a good night maybe forty in attendance, came to hear his fear-lessly revealed TRUTH about COMMUNISM in OUR NA-TION'S CAPITOL, and about PAPIST TREACHERY. He instructed them on the RED MENACE and alerted them to the WHORE OF BABYLON and buttressed his points with here-tofore OFFICIALLY REPRESSED EVIDENCE. Among his sermons was one in which he described rapes of Spanish nuns by Communist troops during the Spanish Civil War. He was so explicit you could almost see the huge Red phalluses sundering the poor nuns. You were supposed to. His congregants seemed to love it. Imagine, passing righteous judgment on the Commu-nist anti-Christ and simultaneously—vicariousness for their prophylaxis—hate-screwing his Whore. God was good.

In my memory's eye I saw them again on a TV news sequence showing hundreds of students massed in front of a hotel in which candidate Ronald Reagan was at a presidential campaign meeting. Their right arms extended in the Nazi salute, the students were mockingly chanting, SIEG HEIL!, SIEG HEIL!, SIEG HEIL! Animated hyperbole, rhythmically, insistently, declaring Reagan equals Hitler, Reagan equals Hitler, Reagan equals Hitler, and all the while they were indulging their free-dom of speech and assembly, they were frustrating Reagan's. The association in my mind with the Colorado pietists? The students too seemed to be pleasuring in their hatred, in damning Reagan for their own fantasies. Back there in the tabernacle, those wet-dreaming, nun-defiling Christians had become the Communist hordes, and on my TV screen the Left had become what it always warned us the Right will be.

They were also *pro patria,* or if it makes any difference, *pro publico.* The more things change, the more they remain the same.

As the span bridging Babel in revolutionary Russia and Der-showitz in newly democratic Spain is contracted in the eye of the Jewish beholder, the not altogether surprised Jewish eye which has seen-it-all and cynically understands the seeming immutability of anti-Semitism, so is there a span reaching from 1891, Brussels, the Socialist International, Abraham Cahan, to 1974, London, the Socialist International and Golda Meir. The Jewish experience contracts this span too, makes the distantly separated places, the generations-separated protagonists seem as one.

"Enraged"—her word—over the refusal of "my Socialist comrades" in Europe to permit American Phantoms and Sky-hawks en route to Israel from the United States to land for refueling as part of the American airlift operation to help the Israelis against the Arabs' surprise Yom Kippur attack of 1973, she phoned Willy Brandt, requesting a meeting of Europe's Socialist parties. "I have no demands to make of anyone, but I want to talk to my friends. For my own good I need to know what possible meaning socialism can have when not a single Socialist country in all of Europe was prepared to come to the aid of the only democratic nation in the Middle East. Is it possible that democracy and fraternity do not apply in our case? Anyhow, I want to hear for myself, with my own ears, what it was that kept the heads of these Socialist governments from helping us."

Brandt convened the heads of the continent's Socialist parties, those in government and those in parliamentary opposition. Since Israel's prime minister had requested the meeting, Mrs. Meir opened the session, explaining the unanticipated attack, confessing her government's misreading of its intelligence reports, and how, following days of touch and go, Israel fended off the invaders. Then, with the candor old friends indulge with each other, she addressed them as if one-on-one. "I just want to understand, in the light of this, what socialism is really about today. Here you are, all of you. Not one inch of your territory was put at our disposal for refueling the planes that saved us from destruction. Now, suppose Richard Nixon had said, 'I am sorry, but since we have nowhere to refuel in Europe, we just can't do anything for you, after all.' What would all of you have done then? You know us and who we are. We are all old comrades, long-standing friends. What did you think? On what grounds did you make your decision not to let those planes refuel? Believe me, I am the last person to belittle the fact that we are only one tiny Jewish state and that there are over twenty Arab states with vast territories, endless oil and billions of dollars. But what I want to know from you today is whether these things are decisive factors in Socialist thinking too?"

When she was through, the chairman asked if anyone wanted the floor to speak.

Nobody did.

The functional indifference of the 1974 Socialist International's 1891 antecedents to the Jewish condition had been attributed to their overriding concern that they retain close links with the masses, no matter the latter's endangerment of Jewish populations. First things first. When she returned to her seat, deafening silence her platform successor, she heard the new, updated overriding Socialist concern. ". . . someone behind me—I didn't want to turn my head and look at him because I didn't want to embarrass him—said, very clearly, 'Of course, they can't talk. Their throats are choked with oil.' " First things first.

Indifference to one's friends is a kind of foreplay to the embrace of their enemies. By 1979, Socialist chieftains Willy Brandt and Bruno Kreisky, the latter playing, as we have seen, a long familiar if not honored role as a Jewish "freedman," welcomed Yasir Arafat at a well-publicized, elaborate banquet in Vienna. This time the Socialists whose ideals warmed our Brooklyn tenement houses and who figuratively looked and sounded so much like our uncles and aunts were not silent.

They held a joint press conference with Arafat and in effect recognized the PLO as "the sole legitimate Palestinian representative." Somewhat on the order of the Illinois Better Business Bureau solemnly appointing as the sole legitimate representative of the Chicago Correction Board, Al Capone.

When the American hostages were seized by the Khomeini Iranians, the Socialist International's response, fully three weeks germinating, was "the struggle for the independence of a people and the realization of social justice should not be hampered by actions which cast doubt upon the dignity of Iran." At about the same time they issued a publication without a trace of the tied-tongue of their response to Iran's gangsterism. In it the then prime minister of Jamaica, Michael Manley, vigorously defended Fidel Castro and extolled the Bolshevik Revolution as having been the "catalyst and rock" which irrevocably shifted "the balance of the forces in the world" against "imperialism."

Such reluctance to defend, even rhetorically, the largest democracy in the world, coupled with such corresponding enthusiasm for that democracy's totalitarian opposition, placed in realistic context the extent to which Jews, a relative handful in the world's population, can rely on presumably humanistic socialism.

Apologists for the Left—like those for the Right—have frequently rationalized anti-Semitism or indifference to Jewish interests as being merely a transitory phase. In the ripeness of time such social peccadilloes, and those of harassment of dissenters and the adoption for themselves of their deposed predecessor's undemocratic practices, would, like scabs, fall off, and benign socialism would blossom. The scabs were capitalism's, or imperialism's, and socialism's very ethics would safeguard its citizenry from bigotry and political repression. This has been the rationale for Western Socialist championing of, and the

Left's sympathy for, Third World governments, a variation on the paternalistic theme, "Give them time, they'll grow up."

In this context, the annual reports of Freedom House, whose board of trustees include notable human-rights advocates, civil-liberties advocates, Social Democrats and distinguished academics, are especially edifying. The following chart is adapted from its 1981 report on the status of world freedom. In the column Political Rights, the rating 1 reflects a state with a fully competitive electoral process and that those elected do in fact clearly rule. A 2 means that political rights are not as fully realized as in 1 and so on to 7 where political despots feel little constraint in exercising dictatorial rule. In the column Civil Liberties, the rating 1 is for states the publications of which enjoy freedom of expression and are free of governmental propaganda; the courts, protective of individual rights; persons not imprisoned for their opinions; private rights and preferences in education, occupation, religion, residence, etc., respected. The scale proceeds to 7, along the progression reflecting declining conditions of civil liberties. *F* means freedom; *NF* means not free; *PF* means partly free.

Patently the people of the West whose governments have been reviled by the Left as decadent and repressive, and of capitalist or mixed economies, are likely to be freest; the Communist, Arab and Third World nations are far more apt to eat their own. The gods of liberationism, who if they haven't quite failed, move with a decided limp.

The failure of leftist governments and systems, even when viewed through the haze of our sympathy for their peoples' earlier plight, is only disappointing. Absent an Idi Amin, an exposed as distinguished from a closet brute, the shortcomings of the objects of our compassion when manifested by their governments disappoint rather than personally pain us. Not so when the heroes of the Left, intellectuals, or from the ramparts,

TABLE OF INDEPENDENT NATIONS:
COMPARATIVE MEASURES OF FREEDOM

	Political Rights	Civil Liberties	Status of Freedom
Afghanistan	7	7	NF
Albania	7	7	NF
Algeria	6	6	NF
Angola	7	7	NF
Argentina	6	5	NF
Australia	1	1	F
Austria	1	1	F
Bahamas	1	2	F
Bahrain	5	4	PF
Bangladesh	3	3	PF
Barbados	1	1	F
Belgium	1	1	F
Benin	7	6	NF
Bhutan	5	5	PF
Bolivia	7	5	NF
Botswana	2	3	F
Brazil	4	3	PF
Bulgaria	7	7	NF
Burma	7	6	NF
Burundi	7	6	NF
Cameroon	6	6	NF
Canada	1	1	F
Cape Verde Islands	6	6	NF
Central African Rep.	7	6	NF
Chad	6	6	NF
Chile	6	5	PF
China (Mainland)	6	6	NF
China (Taiwan)	5	6	PF
Colombia	2	3	F
Comoro Islands	4	5	PF
Congo	7	7	NF
Costa Rica	1	1	F
Cuba	6	6	NF
Cyprus	3	3	PF
Czechoslovakia	7	6	NF

	Political Rights	Civil Liberties	Status of Freedom
Denmark	1	1	F
Djibouti	3	4	PF
Dominica	2	2	F
Dominican Republic	2	3	F
Ecuador	2	2	F
Egypt	5	5	PF
El Salvador	6	4	PF
Equatorial Guinea	7	6	NF
Ethiopia	7	7	NF
Fiji	2	2	F
Finland	2	2	F
France	1	2	F
Gabon	6	6	NF
Gambia	2	2	F
Germandy (E)	7	6	NF
Germany (W)	1	2	F
Ghana	2	3	F
Greece	2	2	F
Grenada	5	5	PF
Guatemala	5	6	PF
Guinea	7	7	NF
Guinea-Bissau	6	6	NF
Guyana	4	4	PF
Haiti	6	6	NF
Honduras	4	3	PF
Hungary	6	5	NF
Iceland	1	1	F
India	2	3	F
Indonesia	5	5	PF
Iran	5	5	PF
Iraq	6	7	NF
Ireland	1	1	F
Israel	2	2	F
Italy	1	2	F
Ivory Coast	6	5	PF
Jamaica	2	3	F
Japan	1	1	F
Jordan	6	6	NF

	Political Rights	Civil Liberties	Status of Freedom
Kampuchea	7	7	NF
Kenya	5	4	PF
Kiribati	2	2	F
Korea (N)	7	7	NF
Korea (S)	5	6	PF
Kuwait	6	4	PF
Laos	7	7	NF
Lebanon	4	4	PF
Lesotho	5	5	PF
Liberia	6	6	NF
Libya	6	6	NF
Luxembourg	1	1	F
Madagascar	6	6	NF
Malawi	6	7	NF
Malaysia	3	4	PF
Maldives	5	5	PF
Mali	7	6	NF
Malta	2	3	F
Mauritania	7	6	NF
Mauritius	2	4	PF
Mexico	3	4	PF
Mongolia	7	7	NF
Morocco	4	4	PF
Mozambique	7	7	NF
Nauru	2	2	F
Nepal	3	4	PF
Netherlands	1	1	F
New Zealand	1	1	F
Nicaragua	5	5	PF
Niger	7	6	NF
Nigeria	2	3	F
Norway	1	1	F
Oman	6	6	NF
Pakistan	7	5	NF
Panama	4	4	PF
Papua New Guinea	2	2	F
Paraguay	5	5	PF
Peru	2	3	F

	Political Rights	Civil Liberties	Status of Freedom
Philippines	5	5	PF
Poland	6	4	PF
Portugal	2	2	F
Qatar	5	5	PF
Rumania	7	6	NF
Rwanda	7	6	NF
St. Lucia	2	3	F
St. Vincent	2	2	F
São Tomé and Principe	6	6	NF
Saudi Arabia	6	6	NF
Senegal	4	4	PF
Seychelles	6	6	NF
Sierra Leone	5	5	PF
Singapore	5	5	PF
Solomon Islands	2	2	F
Somalia	7	7	NF
South Africa	5	6	PF
Spain	2	3	F
Sri Lanka	2	3	F
Sudan	5	5	PF
Surinam	7	5	NF
Swaziland	5	5	PF
Sweden	1	1	F
Switzerland	1	1	F
Syria	5	6	NF
Tanzania	6	6	NF
Thailand	3	4	PF
Togo	7	6	NF
Tonga	5	3	PF
Transkei	5	6	PF
Trinidad and Tobago	2	2	F
Tunisia	6	5	PF
Turkey	5	5	PF
Tuvalu	2	2	F
Uganda	5	5	PF
USSR	6	7	NF
United Arab Emirates	5	5	PF
United Kingdom	1	1	F

	Political Rights	Civil Liberties	Status of Freedom
United States	1	1	F
Upper Volta	6	5	PF
Uruguay	5	5	PF
Vanuatu	2	3	F
Venezuela	1	2	F
Vietnam	7	7	NF
Western Samoa	4	3	PF
Yemen (N)	6	5	NF
Yemen (S)	6	7	NF
Yugoslavia	6	5	NF
Zaire	6	6	NF
Zambia	5	6	PF
Zimbabwe	3	4	PF

Published by Freedom House
January–February, 1981
Dr. Raymond D. Gastil

fail us. For having engaged our personalized political affection, their dalliances or worse pain us.

In this century few if any intellectuals have as persuasively argued the desirability of the coming of the triumphant Left as Jean-Paul Sartre. In his surgical exploration of classical anti-Semitism, his work was seminal. His sympathies for Jews made him pro-Israel; his political philosophy made him supportive of revolution in the Arab world. He was confident that came the revolution, leftist Arab regimes would accept Israel's existence. Saul Bellow, our Nobelist, neatly flicked off this simplicity. "The Marxist-Leninist leaders of the Arab world were and remain even more hostile to Israel than the feudal princes of the oil kingdoms."

Sartre posited, "You cannot invite both Israelis and Arabs to an international conference. You can't because the Arabs won't have it." Asked why give in to the Arab boycott, the old philo-Semite responded, "Because the left seems to have more sympathy for certain liberation movements—think of Algeria for us—than for a government or a country which up to these last years was not threatened the way it is now. The real problem for us was, 'What is going on in Algeria?' . . . Actually it is shameful not to invite them—let us not be hypocritical—that means not inviting the Arabs." One doesn't know if Sartre's subscriptions included Freedom House's annual reports, and his explanation for the miserable political and civil-liberties lot of the revolution-liberated Algerian people. But Bellow's observation is more pointed. "In other words, there are millions of Arabs; they are politically big. Neither the State Department nor the Politburo nor Jean-Paul Sartre can afford to disregard them."

Sartre's head, were Left intellectuals to pin up superhero posters in their dens, would enjoy a corresponding place of honor to Che Guevara's in the dens of Left activitists. If Sartre can be said to have been the Guevara of the cerebral Left, Guevera was the Sartre of the emotive Left.

The heroic Che Guevara: "We must above all keep our hatred alive and fan it into paroxysm, hate as a factor of struggle, intransigent hate of the enemy, hate that can push a human being beyond his natural limits and make him a cold, violent, selective, and effective killing-machine." This Hitlerian hurricane of intentions *cum* social disposition provides depth of focus for our earlier reported views of Zionism enunciated by his comrade, Fidel Castro.

Jane Fonda is by no means a Guevara or, to be sure, a Sartre. Politically, however, she has long symbolized a persistent and gritty independence of establishment views. She, too, blown poster-size, has adorned the college dormitory walls of the young in search of Left solutions to Right injustices. In the Soviet Union for filming a movie in 1975, she was questioned by American reporters about her views of Soviet civil liberties. She reacted by describing the press's curiosity as "ironical" because "it's understood throughout the world that the major

police states in the world are created by the United States." Her
view of Senator Henry Jackson's effort on behalf of Soviet
Jewry likely escaped the study of her Jewish admirers. "I don't
think that whatever goes on inside the Soviet Union should be
used to destroy détente, as I think Jackson is doing." First
things first.

She stipulated that she was "extremely critical of the deprivation of civil liberties in any country," and added, "If Jackson
is so concerned about civil liberties, where is his voice speaking
out against Lon Nol or General Thieu?" Here, too, one doesn't
know if this heroine of the Left reads either Freedom House
reports or the *Los Angeles Times,* and their accounts of latter-
day human rights in Cambodia and Vietnam. But times both
change and they don't change. Came 1981 and Jane Fonda, her
husband the once prominent leader of the radical Students for
a Democratic Society but now seeking political office in California, adorned the dais of a rally protesting the Soviet Union's
treatment of Jews! That's the change in the times. However,
that the Jewish sponsors of the rally would invite Ms. Fonda,
whose activism contributed to the ascendancy of the very governments in Cambodia and Vietnam, whose people have since
suffered genocide and the pitiable birth of the boat people,
suggests that times do not altogether change. Even some Jews
still more readily forgive a complicitor of the far Left than one
whose mischief was in concert with the far Right.

Surely there were lessons in the geometric progression of
human misery under the Cambodian and Vietnamese governments who assumed power immediately upon American withdrawal from Southeast Asia. But they seem not to have been
learned by this decade's Leftists, here and abroad, as they demonstrate against and scold the United States for its involvement
in Nicaragua and El Salvador. For Jews who, if they are not
anything else, are not slow learners, the lessons should be clear.

On the occasion of the first anniversary of the Sandinista victory in Nicaragua, Yasir Arafat's greeting was: "The way to Jerusalem leads through Managua." Arafat's presence in Managua for the Sandinista's celebration was not that of a Johnny-come-lately. The anti-Somoza revolutionaries, as long ago as 1970, had received military training from the PLO and Patrick Arguello Ryan, a Middle-East-trained Sandinistan, was a participant—killed—in a PLO abortive attack on an El Al airplane. In El Salvador the leader of that unhappy nation's guerilla forces is Shafik Handel. He is also the leader of El Salvador's Communist party, and a frequent visitor to Libya.

The Left's sympathy and support for those victimized by Rightist governments is not the issue. In fact, their compassion is shared, or worthy of sharing, by all who treasure political freedom and a fed stomach. The problem, however, is that too often, historically as well as contemporaneously, the Left's sympathizers have not thoughtfully weighed the alternatives, carefully evaluated those who in battle with the faulted status quo would replace it with a new, often crueler authority. In today's world ascendant revolutionary governments all too often have aligned themselves against the United States, along-side the Soviet Union, or with the Arab powers. In the United Nations they have contributed to the increasing of the voting margins of victory for Israel's enemies.

In the 1980 elections Senator Frank Church, chairman of the U.S. Senate's Foreign Relations Committee, suffered defeat. Israel and American Jews lost a good friend. Time and again, when Israel's very security hung in the balance of this or that American foreign policy determination, the Idaho senator with hardly a Jewish consistituency brought his considerable influence to bear in behalf of the peanut-sized democracy. Similarly, in behalf of Soviet Jewry. And yet Church, the credentialed liberal, symbolizes within his very political gestalt problems for Jewish interests, which while not as readily recognizable as those of the hard core Left for being relatively more centrist, contain seeds of future mischief for Jews.

In the contemplative freedom from pressing political decision-making that is the defeated candidate's consolation prize, Church bared a quintessentially liberal—and mischievous—foreign-policy view. Writing in the *New York Times Magazine,* he charged the Reagan administration with holding a "view of the Soviet Union (which) fails to distinguish between the Russian leaders' more fanciful aspirations and their actual capabilities. The attempt to translate this flawed analysis into foreign policy puts the United States at odds with a diverse collection of stubbornly independent nations, including our principal European allies, that are far less mesmerized by the Kremlin than our present White House team.

"In El Salvador, for example, the conflict between armed guerillas and Government forces is portrayed by the Reaganites as a 'textbook case' of Soviet-inspired insurgency, but Mexico, Venezuela and Western Europe disagree, viewing the conflict as rooted in the intolerable condition of life in that beleaguered land."

Continuing, he rhetorically inquired, "How can the perceptions of so many other countries, including our closest allies, be reconciled with his (President Reagan's) own preconception?" Noting that England is retiring about a third of its largest ships while the United States Navy is being expanded on a crash basis, he rued, "Ironically, within the Western alliance, the United States alone has embarked upon a massive rearmament program."

Political musical chairs, and the chair designated "isolationist," occupied in the late 1930s by a Senator Nye, in 1981 seized and occupied by a liberal. Because rational people yearn for peace through accommodation? To be sure. But that was Chamberlain's hell-paved intention too.

The Jewish component? In the years prior to World War II, the functionally isolationist Right blinked at Germany's rabid anti-Semitism. Today, peace-treasuring liberals, many proven friends of Israel and of Jews, blink at the Soviet Union's standing as unabashedly the dominant purveyor of anti-Semitism in the world, and as in the instance of Hitler's Germany, the most powerful and truculent enemy of democracy—the political system that is always Jewry's safest harbor. Moreover, that "so many other countries, including our closest allies" remain cool to our rearming program is also not without precedent. England's military unpreparedness in 1940 bordered on suicidal.

The peculiarly Jewish perception of "our closest allies"? Mrs. Meir's overheard "their throats are choked with oil" is part of our picture frame, but an insight that, after all, holds true for fuel-parched European nations regardless of their governments' political persuasion. Beyond oil it is the very ideology of the liberals in which peace, even if it is pockmarked by injustice, is preferable to the prospect of confrontation that today imperils Jews. The foreign policies vis-à-vis Israel of the liberal, Social Democratic parties in such diverse nations as Sweden, Denmark, England, Austria and Germany have been far more placatory of the Soviet Union and far less tolerant of Israel's concerns than have their conservative oppositions. Not, we hasten to add, because the conservatives love Jews more, but because the impersonal consequences of their ideology secures Israel and Jews—communism's scapegoats—more safely than the liberal ideological value that in opting to shy from military preparedness lest it offend the enemy exposes Jewish security. Accommodation between partners with a community of interests contributes to peace; unilateral accommodation to bullies is appeasement, endangering all manner of species, first among whom—once again—are Jews.

Perhaps the real propellant moving the Jew toward the conservative ground is his traditional liberalism. Perhaps in wanting to conserve liberalism's harvest of individual rather than group rights and the rejection of appeasement of anti-Semitic governments Jews are in fact still liberals and it's the Left that is sliding further left, causing the illusion of Jews as conservatives. Perhaps, too, the political change in residence now evident is attributable in part to feeling unwanted, to the sense of having been used and discarded. In an essay, really a confessional, the liberal journalist Jack Newfield writing in the *Village Voice,* a bellwether of Leftist political and social views, had this to say:

> The *Village Voice* has been my home for 17 years. And it has become painful to me that my own house is not as concerned about anti-Semitism as I wish it were. The *Voice,* to its everlasting credit, has played a significant role in defending the rights of other groups that are discriminated against—blacks, women, gays, union dissidents, artists. The *Voice* has been a vigilant watchdog on abortion, civil liberties, and militarism. But the rights of Jews have been a secondary concern. Jewish nationalism has been treated differently than every other nationalism.
>
> The thing that troubles me about a part of the American left doesn't have an official sociological name. It's more than anti-Zionism, and different from traditional anti-Semitism. Its impact is often in omissions—the injustice not mentioned, the article not written, the petition not signed. It is often communicated in code words. But it is essentially a series of dual standards. It is a dual standard for the human rights of Jews in certain countries. It is a dual standard that questions Israel's right to exist by denying to Zionism the same moral legitimacy that is granted to every other expression of nationalism in the world. And it is an amnesia of conscience about the creation of Israel, and about the Holocaust, symbolized by Noam Chomsky writing an introduction to an insane, anti-Semitic book that alleges the Holocaust is a Zionist hoax. And by Jesse Jackson saying he is sick and tired of hearing about the Holocaust.

Power, whether wielded by the good or the bad, requires a counterforce. After all, it is exercised by persons, and whether they have worn white hats or black hats, their unchallenged exercise of power has ever been corrupting. So it is that when conservative views have held sway, liberalism played an important counterbalancing role. Conversely, conservatism has been a critical balance to liberalism's reigns. Today in the United States the conservative political philosophy enjoys ascendancy. If liberalism is to fill the role preordained for *outs* by democracy, it needs to recognize democracy's requirement of power adequate to its defense; it needs to recall its earlier dedication to equality of opportunity rather than continue to drumbeat its latter-day theme of equality of results. It must recognize that important though they are, issues such as equitable tax policies, health insurance, abortion, prayers in the schools, noise levels, gay rights are secondary to the very viability of the United States in its deadly earnest game for keeps in which life and freedom are the stakes.

Are these the precise views of those, both Jewish and non-Jewish who have moved, or seem to have moved to the starboard in their politics? Hardly. But increasingly they are heard views, and the graphs of change suggest that they may be inchoate in larger numbers of one-time liberals who increasingly turn up in polls as "no opinions," "don't knows," or are closet conservatives who emerge on election day.

Of course for Jews it's always more complicated. As Nathan Glazer's already mentioned survey of campus radicals a decade ago revealed, young Jews rebelling against parental allowances among other injustices were disproportionately evident in the counterculture revolution. An intergenerational conflict has surfaced in Latin America, where Jews have been an integral part of the modernization of a number of republics and where a generation ago they were poor, but are now middle class, light years removed from the proletariat of which they were only yesteryear members. The radical Left, as seemingly it has always been, is not without its Jewish component of young reformers. In Iran, the Iran of Khomeini, the politically radical strain as distinguished from the religious zealots boasts the presence of intellectuals, young Jews included. It would seem that young Jewish Leftists may be the second most self-destructive species known to man, the first being the lemming.

We have been discussing the Left, or more accurately perhaps, the Left's left. Also the danger-in-waiting for democracy and for Jews in liberal policies packaged as peace but containing defeat. Does this constitute an endorsement for the Right? Far from it. If Golda Meir's Socialist friends slaked their thirst with oil, rather than their ideology with assistance to beleaguered fellow Socialists, capitalism, whose oil thirst is prodigious and whose ideology is profit, is certainly a no more reliable friend. Witness the formidable pressure—successful—on the administration to reinstitute grain sales to the Soviet Union, emanating from the very heartland of American anti-Communism, our Midwest. Indeed, Lenin's dictum that capitalism would sell communism the rope with which to hang capitalists is being slavishly implemented by patrons of the American Right, the big-business interests. No, we have not discussed the Right, not because it is not of concern to Jews but rather because that danger is so well known by Jews. The Left, however, for all its contemptuous and bitter treatment of Jews, continues, because of the coquettishness of its rhetoric, to appeal to some Jews. And so this discussion, saying in essence, in politics as in snake oil, *caveat emptor.*

One can make too much of the differences between the far Right and the far Left. During the late 1930s one Kenneth Goff, a member of the national committee of the Young Communist League informed on his erstwhile comrades at hearings of the U.S. House Committee on Un-American Activities. Shortly thereafter he assumed the national chairmanship of the neo-Fascist Gerald L. K. Smith's Christian Youth for America. Given that there were only months between his residence in the leftmost end of American politics and his new address in the spectrum's furthest right reaches, it would seem that considering the political distance covered, his speed and stamina were awesome. Not really. From the Communists Goff had learned that Stalinism could be candied over with appeals for support of justice in the Scottsboro case; from Nazism that Hitler could be sugared with appeals for America First. He had but to change the names of the bogeymen and his panaceas and the distance between the polar extremes of our politics turned out not to be linear but contiguous points on a circle. For Jews, aware that we are not the only group reviled and condemned around the world, we are also aware that we are the only group against whom discrimination has been officially sanctioned by both the far Right and the far Left.

The word *far* is of critical importance here. No more than conservatives may logically be viewed as far Rightists can liberals be considered as far Leftists. We are discussing changes relevant to Jews taking place in the ample distance between the two extremes. Not long ago, that Jews by and large were to be found in the Left where needed social change was fermenting, was a supportable generalization. Today it is statistically demonstrable that Jews are increasingly evident in the Right where long fought for and only recently achieved social values are being conserved. When, precisely, did the change happen?

The Jewish story is told of the old woman who was given a small, lovable calf. So caring for it was she that nightly she would raise it in her arms and carry it up a long flight of stairs to her bedroom. After some time, the woman was carrying a cow.

When did the calf become a cow?

7

Christians and Jews

HISTORICALLY, WHEN THE planes of Christendom and Jews have met, the resultant friction has not been equally wearing on them. And for all that "things have been getting better," the facts that the one's animus against the other is currently abating, and the other's reactive foreboding abating too, suggest which has been the aggressor, which the aggressed upon. Israel's first President, Chaim Weizmann, once observed, "We are a cinder in their eye." Sigmund Freud, more occupationally referent, put it this way: "The Jews had a father religion and the Christians a son religion, and the subconscious wish is to kill the father from time to time."

For Christians, the meeting of the planes dates as far back as Scriptures and is as recent as this morning's mass. As Harry Golden has put it, "The Jew bears an identity with every step of the Christian's way; with his birth, his marriage, his Church and his death. The Jew is identified with the Man on the Cross, *his* birth, *his* death, *his* Second Coming, and with the life everlasting." For the Jew, the meetings of the planes have left so indelible, so throbbing a memory that even the very sight of blond hair, any time, anywhere and even in our homogenized society, still registers Christian.

We have written about my growing up in Brooklyn, about my neighborhood having been virtually all Jewish and so my boyhood assumption that the world was Jewish too. As I grew older, eight, nine, and began walking long walks to other neighborhoods, I discovered the Irish and the Italians. The south side of the Williamsburg section of Brooklyn was Jewish, the north side, Italian. It was with the Italians that we had our fights. Wintertimes, when it snowed, we'd pile high arsenals of snowballs, some filled with coal ashes, some with horse dung, and our gangs would engage each other across the no-man's-land of Metropolitan Avenue, which in intervals of truce was our demilitarized zone. But we never really considered the Italians as full-blooded Christians, or as enemies. Perhaps because it was the Pole who figured in our parents' accounts of old world anti-Semitism, perhaps, too, because the Italians were neither blond nor thin-lipped; but whatever, the Italians, albeit antagonists, were a kind of distant kin.

I'm not quite sure just when, but it was in my young manhood that I became aware of Protestants as contemporary Christians, as distinguished from history book Germanic sects wakening to the rousings of Martin Luther. Somehow I sensed them to be more civilized, less anti-Jewish than Catholics. Theretofore I had considered Christians (that was the term we used, not *gentiles*) as pretty much all the same, and if differing among themselves, inconsequentially, like the physiological differences between a Thai and a Cambodian. Soon, I "liked Protestants better than Catholics." Protestants were suggestive of England and in my public school that meant "cultured."

They were also Emerson and Thoreau, Brahmins, graced in Letters with a social conscience; they were Jefferson and both Roosevelts, providing an imagined patrician sanction for my vague stirrings of democratic socialism. Our Polish janitors didn't. Viewed thusly, I classified Protestants alongside the Italians of my earlier youth as not being fully Christian, like the Catholics were, the "real" Christians whose fathers haunted our parents' memories.

Even today the word *Catholic* registers in me images of Irishmen and of Eastern and Southern European nationality groups, the ism coming on later, with second thought. And for all that I know better, the word *Protestant* conjures icons of socially haloed patricians, a kind of group photograph of the board of directors of the Bell Telephone Company or of Consolidated Edison, to be followed, but also on second thought, by the garden-variety Protestant sects.

Today, however, I suspect my boyhood Protestant icons and find myself disposed more kindly to my ethnic images of Catholics.

I've thought about both changes in me and in the case of Catholics it has a lot to do with the ethnicity of the Catholic, the Irishness, or Italianness of him that is his resonancy, and which is proving more durable than his crucified, bleeding-Christ statuary, my boyhood's nervously heard ticking bomb in all Christians. Also, John XXIII figures in the change, and no matter that Lincoln turned out to be not really Jewish, sometimes I revert to childhood imaginings, suspecting that John was, at least through a distant maternal ancestor.

As for those Protestant icons, it figured that I would have a change of heart. How long can one, and a Jewish one at that, remain innocent about Consolidated Edison?

Of course these recollections are through a half-century-old glass, surely as much romanticized as real. Twenty years later, more than thirty years ago, my interaction with gentiles had upgraded from dung-filled snowballs to civil rights. My responsibilities as a young Anti-Defamation League staffer in the mountain states included the development of interfaith dialogues and the furthering of support for fair-employment-practices state laws. (Jews in Colorado, New Mexico, Wyoming and Utah were mostly middle class, doing well, thank you; the underprivileged—an ugly word, then not yet in vogue—were Americans of Mexican descent and the smattering of Rocky Mountain "Negroes.") Church bodies and clerics were prized allies. After all, interfaith dialogue with gentiles in secular organizations in practice simply constituted dialogue with liberals, and useful though it was to relate to such organizations as the American Civil Liberties Union, the Japanese American Citizens League, the Urban League and several labor unions, it was also political impotence. With their small memberships and their having a readily evident self-interest in civil rights, they were not nearly equal to the legislative influence wielded by the more representative, more regarded church bodies. In those years the "modernist" or liberal Protestant denominations were relatively responsive. The fundamentalists were more absorbed in Scripture than in Constitution. Catholic priests, as a matter of church policy, did not in those days participate in interfaith dialogues. Ecumenical camaraderie was restricted to the movies, to Bing Crosby and Pat O'Brien films.

And so once again, and not only because the boy is father to the man, I found myself preferring the mainline Protestants, and now having discovered the diversity of Protestantism (they *didn't* all look alike!), I reexperienced my foreboding about the "real" Christians, the religious fundamentalists.

And it wasn't only because they were unresponsive to the problems of religious and racial discrimination. Rather my view of their enmity was the direct consequence of the flamboyant self-advertisements of bigots and Elmer Gantrys who professed

Protestant fundamentalism. On the national scene the anti-Semitic and racist rantings of such fundamentalists as Gerald L. K. Smith, Gerald B. Winrod and William Dudley Pelley reverberated throughout the land, and for Jews were echoes of the piercing shrillness of Nazism. In the mountain states a popular Stetson-hatted cowboy evangelist, Harvey Springer, the Reverend William L. Blessing, whose sermons drew some twenty of his faithful but whose printing press amplified his hate ten thousand times, the aforementioned Kenneth Goff, now become a fundamentalist preacher, all provided local harmony to the nationally broadcast melodies of the Smiths and Pelleys and Winrods.

One did not visit the tents and churches of the fundamentalists whose preachers preached Gospel, period. But one heard and read the outpourings of the haters, the exhibitionists and con artists who in their exploitation of fundamentalism pandered anti-Semitism. One's impression then of the corpus of fundamentalism was garnered from its warts. "I met a state department man in the train on my way here to Greeley (Colorado). Got to talking with him about Uncle Joe Stay-lin and things. Know what he told me? 'You goddamn Christians keep your nose out of world affairs.!' " Kenneth Goff's voice was metallic, insistent. In minutes it hammered into silence even the restless children brought along to hear the well-advertised "big city preacher saved from communism by Jesus." As he warmed to his task, children as well as parents sat awed and frightened in hard wooden chairs that ceased their creaking as he recalled "a particularly revolting picture hanging on the wall of the Jew-controlled Communist party. It showed Christ's intestines hanging from his stomach while workers gnaw at his entrails, drinking from his veins . . . "

"Showers of Blessing," William Blessing's gaudy publication, subtlety the least of its attributes, regularly described Jews as "the black, greasy-skinned false Jews," the real biblical Jews being Christians, and supplemented the *Denver News*'s wire services by reporting to his subscribers on current events. "Bernard Baruch outlines 11 point program for world recovery— *one point more than God gave to Israel on Mt. Sinai* (Ex. 20). What strange power does this Jew hold over America and the world?"

From the hindsight provided by the distance Jews have come from their hapless victimization by the Third Reich, the words seem ludicrous. Jabberwocky talk. But not so then. The defamations heard in the Munich beer halls still audible, it is no wonder that in our apprehensions we were more emotionally reactive to these hatemongers than the mass of fundamentalists were cerebrally responsive. That we are here and the Smiths, by and large, are gone is partial testimony to that reassuring truth. But because our ears were nervous and because there was no fundamentalist pope or hierarchy to officially discipline or defrock a Smith or a Blessing, and because demographically, culturally and educationally we did not and do not know each other, fundamentalists remain for Jews a source of suspicious concern.

Catholics in those years were not a dominant factor in either the civil-rights issues in the mountain states or in my pursuit of Christian markets for our do-good efforts. The first stirrings of change in my responses to Catholicism, responses seeded by the stories of our parents' treatment by Poles, nursed by boyhood readings in European history, fertilized by taunts of being Christ-killers, occurred at Georgetown University. There I began to distinguish between Catholics and Catholicism. That a faculty member could, pointing to a map of the Far East, declare that Shanghai was no more typically a Chinese city than Jew York was typically American was angering, but did no more than confirm my judicial notice of Catholicism's anti-Semitism. But that colleagues who were Catholic were "regular guys," that in studying together, drinking ice-cream sodas together in hours-long bull sessions our religious differences could recede into inconsequentiality, was small *r* revelation, at times sweet and warm. I could thusly retain my hostility to Catholicism, the frequent persecutor and sometime butcher of my ancestors, and simultaneously feel free of myself harboring religious prejudice. The big change, however, in my reactions to the ism of Catholics—and the major influence, I am confident, in the change of attitude of most Jews—came in the 1960s. Pope John XXIII. This amply girthed man (that he was stout, not ascetic, subtly matters); this Italian (that mattered too); this man who spoke of opening wide the church's windows (the church's, not of individual hearts, which while a pretty thought would, practically, mean little); he, alone, diluted the centuries-old bitterness of remembering Jews. That the final vote of the Second Vatican Council repudiated Jewish guilt, past or present, in the death of Jesus and deplored "hatred, persecutions, displays of anti-Semitism directed against Jews at any time and by anyone" was welcome. That it was passed, not without political lobbying to be sure, but by a vote of 2,221 to 88 was assurance that the windows were indeed open. But basically it was the person of John that refocused my conditioned wary reaction to Catholicism.

It was significant to me both as an interested party and as the boy I once was who held the views I then held that the Protestant World Council of Churches, the uptown Protestants who are shunned by the fundamentalists, passed their resolution absolving Jews in the death of Christ even before the Church hierarchy formally approved Pope John's proposal.

In 1979, my automatic childhood suspicions of Christians now long dissipated, my adulthood's reservations, always, I'd assumed, considered, now relaxed, and if not myself an intent hunter of or exuberant player in ecumenism, surely a cheering fan, our field observations of Christians were advanced by a tête à tête with Pope John Paul II. Actually, there were several têtes;

ourselves, Maxwell Greenberg, the then chairman of the Anti-Defamation League, three colleagues and a like number of Americans of Polish descent. Months earlier we had communicated to the pope our concern that the Polish government was planning to commemorate the one hundredth anniversary of the birth of Janusz Korczak. Korczak, a doctor and a writer, had also operated orphanage homes. One of the homes was for Jewish children. Korczak's prescription for the healing of the hurts of orphanage was love. His stock of this primitive cure was boundless. During the Nazi occupation of Poland, Korczak, a Jew, was ordered by the Nazis to bring his Jewish children to the railroad station. The train, as was well known, ran to the dreaded concentration camp in Treblinka, the last stop.

Because of his wide-ranging friendships and the universal regard in which he was held, Korczak had opportunities to hide, to go underground, to at least postpone if not altogether escape his and the children's sentence. He chose, however, to accompany his wards to the railroad depot, onto the train, to Treblinka's camp, and finally, still with his children, into the ovens.

Now, the Communist Polish government was honoring its heroic son, Korczak, the Pole. No reference to his having been Jewish; no reference to the fact that had he not been Jewish his fate would not have been sealed. And so the Anti-Defamation League and the Polish American Congress sought the assistance of Pope John Paul II in an effort to focus public attention on Janusz Korczak, the Jewish martyr and the Polish patriot.

We were in Jerusalem when the Vatican's invitation to visit with the pope reached us. It seemed a symbolically appropriate place to be, to hear the telephone operator's "Jerusalem? This is Rome." Our parents, if not fully comprehending and certainly not fully approving of their children entering the very maw of the Polish *goyim* they'd fled, would nonetheless have smiled a complex, private thought.

That John Paul II was warmly agreeable to the proposal that our group made to him for commemorating both Korczak's Jewishness and his Polish patriotism is not quite the point here. Rather is it that his naturalness of manner, our admiring awareness that he was an athlete as well as a scholar, his moving remarks weeks earlier during a visit to Auschwitz all made for easily liking him, accelerated the continuing evaporation of our still lingering charyness of the Church. How not but reciprocate warmth to a man, the pope yet, who personally greets you at his door. Upon taking leave, I expressed appreciation for his remarks at Auschwitz, saying they were moving and well noted by Jews. His response, the authenticity of its modesty unquestionable, was that it was too early to thank him, he had not yet served long enough to be judged so kindly.

Reminiscences. Recollections of Christians. The earliest, parent-witnessed, parent-experienced accounts of flesh and blood bogeymen. In time the personal encounters, the gained experience out of which one sorts, discriminates between stereotypes of Christians and Christians. And latterly, the polls. Polls without the burden of memory, their statistics coolly counterweighted against our hot memories, authoritatively reporting the continuing lessening of Christian anti-Semitism. And in the foreground of this collage, Christians remembered, Christians known and Christians studied, Pope John Paul II standing in his library's doorway, smiling "Come in, come in"; and juxtaposed with him, a composite photograph of a socially attuned minister, urbane, benign, his smiling greeting, the news that anti-Semitic stereotypes among the member denominations of the liberal National Council of Churches continues to be an exemplar for Protestants.

Alas, something there is that is the matter with our collage. It is true that we have been absolved of guilt in the murder of Jesus and by no less authorities than the Second Vatican Council and the Protestant World Council of Churches. But it is a reprieve which were it not for the heinous cruelty of our served sentence, would be absurd. Grown men, twentieth-century man, heirs of the framers of the Constitution, of the draftsmen of the Magna Carta, of the French Revolution, of the Renaissance, of the splendor that was Rome's and the glory that was Greece, soberly gathering in earnest deliberation to weigh evidence against *me,* from the south side of Williamsburg in Brooklyn, whose only unaccounted-for night was a clandestine trip to a Newark burlesque in 1940, in the dock for a crime two thousand years old! Pity, that it is neither Jewishly prudent nor gracious, sinfully delicious though the notion may be, to convene a World Council of Jews to consider the proposition that Christians "past or present" be absolved of guilt for their recidivist crimes—in jurisdictions the world over—of murder, looting and indifference.

But private, perhaps mean, admittedly cynical fantasies aside, in our real world, Christendom's absolution of Jews was a functional blessing and our collage of post–World War II symbols of bettering Christian attitudes toward Jews do represent welcome and substantial changes for the better.

Or do they? Is it hopelessly paranoid, while clearly recognizing that Jews are no longer theologically despised, that the resentment of us is abating, to nonetheless reserve judgment for fear that this time we are vulnerable to being loved to pieces?

The love. In France, in recent years pockmarked by anti-Semitic incidents, many violent and inclusive of murdering bombs, the French bishops' conference in what after all is "Catholic" France, spoke eloquently, clearly. "It is too easy for us to become indignant at (such) horrible attacks on our Jewish brethren. Too often, alas, the blame is also due to our prejudices and our ignorance about the Jewish people and their history."

In the United States, the bishops from whose ranks Pope John XXIII received important support during the Second

Vatican Council, likewise spoke caringly.

"The Catholic community cannot be indifferent when a wave of anti-Semitic violence strikes at the Jewish people . . . It is a time to stand beside them in their anguish and to reaffirm, in the words of the Second Vatican Council, our absolute opposition to all 'hatred, persecutions or displays of anti-Semitism directed against Jews at any time and by anyone.'

"In condemning the bombing of the synagogue in Paris, Pope John Paul II said he shared the indignation of Catholics and others in France in response to this outrage . . ."

Beyond this succor tendered timely, tendered warmly, in contradistinction to the distant Pope Pius XII, Pope John Paul II is the first pontiff to have publicly acknowledged Israel's origin in the Holocaust and its right to security.

And yet.

No matter the Vatican has excoriated terrorism in Italy, in Germany, in France, in Latin America, and the pope himself has been gunned down by its savagery, and despite the documented direct linkage between these acts of wanton terror and PLO training camps for international terrorists, the Vatican has provided the PLO with aid and comfort.

Farouk Kaddoumi is the PLO's second-in-command to Yasir Arafat, chieftain of the terrorist organization's foreign-relations desk. Cardinal Agostino Cassaroli is Pope John Paul II's secretary of state. In 1981, on the ides of March, the two met in Vatican City. One, the representative of an organization boastful of its murders of Jewish women and children, intransigently committed to the destruction of the state of Israel. The other, the foreign policy spokesman of—in matters Jewish—a reborn Catholic Church. According to a Vatican communique, " . . . the principal subjects of the discussion were how to reach just and stable peace in the Middle East, the Palestinian problem, the question of Jerusalem, and the Palestinian presence in Lebanon." But according to Kaddoumi at a press conference held on the grounds of the Vatican," . . . the position of the Vatican is one of solidarity with the Palestinian people and their struggle for liberation." Given the well-known PLO definition of "liberation" and the Vatican's compassion for the death by bombing of random Jews in France and elsewhere, one waited for a demurrer from the Vatican to the Kaddoumi version of the meeting. It was not forthcoming.

Instead one week later another meeting took place, placing the earlier one in perspective. The pope himself granted an audience to Habib Chatti, secretary-general of the Islamic Conference Organization, the very group before which earlier in the year a Saudi call for *jihad,* a holy war against Israel, had been issued. Chatti's account of the meeting was that "we had identical views on some issues, parallel views on others, but no opposing views on any issue. Neither the Vatican nor the Islamic Conference accepts the Judaization or annexation of Jerusalem." Chatti boasted: "I came away from the meeting convinced that the pope shares our sentiments." There was no papal or Vatican disclaimer.

As to the "Judaization" of Jerusalem, earlier the Vatican Permanent Observer Mission to the United Nations had distributed a document to United Nations delegates on the Holy See's position on Jerusalem. It called for international guarantees for the holy places and the city, but made no mention of Israel's administration of the holy places which unlike Jordan's earlier administration provides access to Christians, Moslems and Jews. Nor, strangely for a church steeped in history, did it contain reference to the absolute lack of access by Jews to their holy places when Jerusalem's old city was under Jordanian-Arab rule.

One does not, or at least we do not, question the earnestness of the Vatican's expressions of fraternity with Jews and the church's remorse for "our prejudices and ignorance." Evidence supportive of the sincerity of these expressions is persuasive.

But evenhanded compassion for Jews and those who joy in the
killing of Jews raises questions, if not hackles. Questions an-
ticipated in the private thoughts we ascribed to our parents,
who if they had heard we were on our way to the pope would
have smiled, enigmatically, for us; knowingly for their longer
remembering selves.

In 1974 Monsignor Hilarion Capucci, archbishop of the Mel-
kite branch of the Greek Orthodox Church which owes allegiance to Rome was arrested, tried and convicted by the Israelis. The charge was gun running. His sentence was twelve years
imprisonment. The benefactors of the priest's rifles, pistols,
explosives, grenades and detonators? The PLO. He had been
caught red-handed. In 1977 the late Pope Paul VI sent a plea
for clemency to Israel's then president, Ephraim Katzir. The
Holy See's pledge that Capucci's release would "not be detri-
mental to the State of Israel" and that the cleric would leave
the Middle East permanently and remove himself from further
involvement in Arab-Israel disputes was favorably acted on.
Capucci was set free.

Since his release Capucci has repeatedly and flagrantly vi-
olated Pope Paul VI's solemn pledge. In frequent press inter-
views, in speeches on two continents and in his writings he has
championed the PLO's claims to the whole of Palestine. Further, it was Capucci who brought Kaddoumi and Cardinal
Cassaroli together. And it is Capucci who has been serving as
a roving ambassador for the PLO. Despite the Vatican's pledge,
despite Capucci's violation of that pledge, despite Jewish protestations made to the Vatican, he has not been disavowed and
continues to propagandize in behalf of Yasir Arafat's terrorists.

Why the Vatican has chosen to remain silent and in its silence
to dishonor its agreement under which the gun runner was
released is a matter for speculation. For America's distinguished Catholic scholar, the Reverend Edward Flannery, noting Catholic calls for involving the PLO in Middle East negotia-

tions, it is anguishing. "I cannot understand why religious bodies should risk giving encouragement to self-proclaimed destroyers of Israel by sitting down with them or urging others to do so." Writing in another context, one in which he was deploring a Maryknoll Father's official publication's idealization of Fidel Castro, William Buckley, Jr., wrote, "What is needed . . . is a significant enhancement of the curriculum at Maryknoll. Because although these men and women are to be praised for their corporal acts of mercy, they must be reminded that the sovereign law is to love the Lord, and one cannot do this, and also love either Fidel Castro or the hideous policies evoked by the mention of his name."

For Maryknoll we would substitute Vatican, a change which would not offend logic; for Fidel Castro we would substitute Yasir Arafat, a distinction with little difference; there being but one God, the Lord remains in place. In this formulation, Jews cannot but praise the Vatican's words of fraternity and of remorse for sins past. However, consorting with our enemies today, providing the PLO with image-enhancing propaganda forums, failing to support Jerusalem as an undivided Jewish city, indeed, having yet formally to recognize the state of Israel —for Jews all this is more compelling a caution than words of fraternity are an assurance. It's the rabbinic story, relevant here too: "How can you say you love me if you don't know what it is that brings me pain?"

In this instance, however, not so much pain, as death.

The relationship between Jewish social-action organizations and liberal Protestant bodies has been long standing and fruitful.·Not so our interaction with evangelical and fundamentalist Protestants. Still, the closer we have teamed with the former, the farther have they moved from us on the issue central to our beings, Israel's security. The further the distance on social issues that has separated us from the latter, the nearer have they approached us on that same core issue. Not long ago, suffering the stings of religious persecution, it mattered comfortingly to us that the modernist Protestant sects registered relatively high levels of religious tolerance and disturbingly, that fundamentalists scored high in intolerance. But today religious tolerance of Jews is belated balm for the memory of pains past, and, as we will see, is little better than a placebo for what currently anguishes Jews. And the fundamentalist's relative religious intolerance can and does coexist with religious and political attitudes supportive of Israel's well-being. In short, liberal Protestantism's tolerance is not so helpful to us as its political hostility to Israel is damaging to us. Fundamentalist intolerance is currently not so baneful as its friendship for Israel is helpful. For remembering Jews, it all needs sorting out. Our friends of yore now insensitive; the fundamentalists whose amens warmed hostile preachers and chilled overhearing Jews, now our limited partners. As Adam is reputed to have said when beholding Eve, "We live in an age of transition."

Earlier, in our consideration of attitudinal polls, we discussed the relationship between Christian orthodoxy and anti-Semitic attitudes. The more fundamentalist the respondent's views, the more likely was he to harbor anti-Semitism; the less fundamentalist, the lower his anti-Semitic quotient. So it is that 69% of Southern Baptist clergy (nonmembers of the National Council of Churches) agreed that Jews remain unforgiven by God until they accept Christ as their savior, in contrast to 3% of the clergy of the United Church of Christ, Methodists and Episcopalian clergy (mainstays of the National Council of Churches) holding that view. The views of laity follow a similar pattern.

Why then do we feel more comfortable today with the Reverend Bailey Smith, leader of the Southern Baptist Convention, who has seriously declared, "With all due respect to those dear people, my friends, God Almighty does not hear the prayer of

a Jew," than we do with the socially conscious National Council of Churches? After all, the Southern Baptists have yet to
disclaim the charge of deicide against me, while member organizations of the National Council of Churches acquitted me even
while the Vatican Council II's jury was still out.

The answer lies not in their measures of anti-Semitism, but
in their political postures. Christian-professing religious attitudes, in this time, in this country, are for all practical purposes,
no more than personally held religious conceits, barely impact-
ing the way in which Jews live. Their political action, as it
relates to the security of the state of Israel, impacts us far more
meaningfully than whether a Christian neighbor believes that
his is the exclusive hot line to "on high."

More specifically:

As long ago as 1967, in the days that led into the Six-Day
War, when at the behest of Nasser the United Nations with-
drew its cushioning forces from the Sinai, and when the Egyp-
tian army ominously marched into the vacuum in step with
clamorous Arab threats of destruction against Israel, the National Council of Churches with whom Jews had been dialogu-
ing, ecumenizing, and Brotherhood Weeking, was silent. Immediately however that Israel's Davidlike victory was achieved,
the National Council of Churches recovered its voice and declared that it "cannot condone by silence territorial expansion
by armed force." No comment, however, on the Arab precipita-
tion of the war.

In 1972, the National Council of Churches selected as its
principal speaker at its Triennial General Assembly a vitupera-
tive anti-Semite, Imamu Baraka, formerly known as LeRoy
Jones. Jones was then on the screaming high notes of his Jew
hatred. Jewish organizations protested his scheduled appearance to their colleagues at the council—to no avail. It was a
time when Black militancy was gaining ascendancy as fashionable, and Jewish apprehension becoming a bore.

In 1973 during the Yom Kippur War, while the Soviet Union was infusing massive arms into the Arab war machine and Israel was in desperate need of war matériel, the National Council of Churches called for "an immediate mutual cessation of arms shipments . . . either directly or indirectly to the belligerents." In view of the remoteness of the possibility that the Soviet Union would heed their call, and in view of the utter dependency of Israel on American arms, the liberal churchmen were in effect politicking America for the defeat of the aggressed-upon Jewish state. The call had emanated from the National Council's governing board. As reported by Rael Jean Isaac, "Gerald Strober, then on the staff of the American Jewish Committee, who was present at the meeting as an invited observer, recalls that David Stowe, an official of the United Church of Christ, said to him 'Israel might have to die for the cause of peace.' "

When in 1975 the United Nations voted its infamous resolution equating Zionism with racism, the National Council of Churches, at the ready with resolutions in behalf of varied and sundry radicals and militants, passed. But several months later, in the wake of widespread criticism of the United Nations' twisted equation, the National Council again found its voice and resolved its supportive approbation for the U.N., without any qualifying but or however.

The National Council of Churches' position calling upon the American government to establish contacts with the PLO dates back to 1974. The United Methodists, however, are on record since 1976 as favoring a PLO state. This, without ameliorating context that would require the PLO to recognize Israel. Methodist clergy, as we have seen in polls, are amongst the least anti-Semitic denominations in America.

In 1978, the council displayed its selective compassion again. The PLO had landed terrorists on an Israeli beach and in an orgy of wanton murder massacred thirty-seven Israeli civilians. Israel retaliated with death-dealing military strikes. The coun-

cil's governing board responded by calling upon the United
States to cease furnishing antipersonnel bombs to Israel. The
resolution, understandably commiserative of the deaths of Arab
men, women and children as a result of Israel's action, made
no reference to the PLO raid and to its innocent victims. A
drafting oversight? Hardly. The board had considered and specifically rejected an amendment to the resolution which would
have deplored the deaths of those "wantonly killed or maimed"
in the PLO terrorist action which had precipitated Israel's
retaliation.

In 1980, a Methodist layman, David Jessup, reported to the
United Methodist Church's General Conference that:

> Most Methodist churchgoers would react with disbelief, even
> anger, to be told that a significant portion of their weekly offer-
> ings were being siphoned off to groups supporting the Palestine
> Liberation Organization, the governments of Cuba and Vietnam,
> the pro-Soviet totalitarian movements of Latin America, Asia
> and Africa, and several violence-prone fringe groups on this
> country.

The church did not dispute Jessup's supportive evidence—
his documentation was gathered from the Methodists' own records—nor did it contest his political characterization of the
donees. Instead, Jessup was name-called as engaging in "right-
wing extremism," no matter his curriculum vitae's description
of him as a staffer for the AFL-CIO, his service in the Peace
Corps, in the civil-rights movement and with the farm workers
in California. Somewhat disingenuously, but revealingly
nonetheless, Bishop Roy Nichols, president of the Methodists'
Board of Global Ministries, declared, "When the church commits itself to identification with the poor and oppressed we may
sometimes become involved with people whose blend of Marxist interpretation and Christian theology may be different from
our own."

Later in 1980 the National Council of Churches adopted a policy statement on the Middle East which called on Israel to include the PLO in its Middle East peace negotiations. Ghoulishly, the advice came on the heels of a Palestinian terrorist squad's murder of six Jewish worshippers in a Sabbath ambush. The terrorists' commander, captured, confessed to having been trained in the Soviet Union. Presumably his "blend of Marxist interpretation and Christian theology" mitigated the heinousness of his crime.

As reported by Rael Jean Isaac, during the Governing Board of the National Council of Churches' discussion of the resolution cleansing the PLO, there was heated discussion as to whether the resolution should include approval of the continued existence of Israel. "The 250-man board voted in favor of retaining Israel as a Jewish state by nine votes. Henry Siegman, executive director of the American Jewish Congress who was present at the discussion, reported that this vote was to him the most disturbing aspect of the 1980 policy statement."

Predictably, following Israel's 1981 lightning strike against Iraq's nuclear reactor, the president of the National Council of Churches, the Reverend William Howard, condemned the raid. However, so did many editorials, organizations and individuals, including friends of Israel. But the National Council's political bias, if not its Christian charity, was uniquely predictable. Howard's communication to President Reagan went on to assert that American "moral credibility" hinged on our unilateral embargo on arms to the Middle East. Once again the peace-professing National Council was calling upon America, where it is with some influence, to cease shipment of arms to embattled Israel while the Soviet Union and Western Europe, where it is without influence, continue to arm Israel's enemies. The United Presbyterian Church, the United Methodist Church and the Church of the Brethren, none of them fundamentalists or high scorers on anti-Semitism scales, issued similar communications.

Given the overwhelming sympathy of Americans for Israel
as compared to the PLO and indeed as compared to the Arabs
in a hypothetical war, it is clear that the National Council of
Churches' bureaucracy does not reflect the views of the 41
million Christians who are members of its thirty-two Protestant
and Eastern Orthodox denominations. Let alone on the subject
of the Middle East, it is equally clear that the vast majority of
American Christians, including the membership of the United
Methodist Church, United Presbyterian Church in the United
States of America, United Church of Christ, Christian Church,
Episcopal Church, Presbyterian Church in the United States,
Lutheran Church in America, all of whom contribute millions
of dollars annually to the council, do not share the bureaucracy's views on a broad spectrum of related international issues. For instance, in 1976 in a resolution par for the course of
the World Council of Churches in which the National Council
is a dominant factor, South Africa, Brazil, Argentina and Chile,
as well as the United States were excoriated. The lineup of
villains did not, however, include the Soviet Union. Indeed,
passed at a meeting in Nairobi, the resolution took no note of
Idi Amin's neighboring Uganda! Eugene Carson Blake, the
longtime leader of the National Council, described its and the
World Council's financial aid to terrorist organizations as "the
greatest evangelistic influence there is in our times to win belief
in Jesus Christ." In view of mainstream American attitudes
toward communism and terrorism, it is a safe assumption that
Professor Martin Marty, the University of Chicago's distinguished theologian, more closely approximates the views, if not
the articulated revulsion, of American Protestantism:

> The advocates of revolutionary socialism, whether they ground
> their advocacy in Christian millenialism, in mixed Christian and
> Marxian "liberation theology," or in simple secular philosophies
> of history cannot point—or at least have not pointed to my

satisfaction—to post-revolutionary resolutions that allow true intellectual and religious freedom.

They complain about "repressive tolerance" in our own current society without letting us point to the "repressive intolerance" of Socialist regimes everywhere. They may say that I am demonstrating the provincialism of a Westerner with a full stomach when I cherish religious freedom without noting that other economic systems bring fuller stomachs. They have not shown that such systems are all that provident. And they slide past the murder of perhaps 7 million under Maoism or of too many millions to count under the Stalinist system (which none of them any longer favors or even likes to hear brought up), and past the persecution that most postrevolutionary socialisms enact.

To be told that such systems tolerate "religious freedom" because some of them allow churches to remain open so long as church people do not criticize the regime, is to leave us no further along than we would be under right-wing regimes in, say, Korea or Chile.

But alas, neither Marty's nor the voices of other Protestant critics hold sway in the council's bureaucracy. And on the subject of Israel, Jews must ponder the real significance to them of liberal Protestantism's low scores in scales of anti-Semitism. What solace to us, what significance for us, in a National Council policy statement in 1980 which deplored "the resurgence of anti-Semitism," cheek by jowl with their finding that in the Middle East "the consensus of opinion supported the settlement of the Palestine issue along lines suggested by the Palestine Liberation Organization." No reference, of course, to either its implication that the PLO's solution means the destruction of Israel, or that Palestinian Arab demurrers to the PLO have resulted, as in Gaza, in executed death sentences.

Why this constant, persistent, mounting pressure by the National Council's ruling hierarchy against Israel?

Dr. Franklin Littell, the prominent Protestant theologian and Holocaust scholar, attributes it to insensitivity. "Six mil-

lion Jews were murdered in the heart of Christendom by baptized Christians, none of them rebuked, let alone excommuni-
cated . . . They strut callously on, issuing their pontifical phrases
that deal frivolously with matters affecting the life and death of
real Jews, without any sense of how vulgar and pretentious they
sound to persons (Jews and Christians) who have passed
through the fires or walked through the ashes of Auschwitz."

In *From Pariah People to Pariah Nation,* Richard D. Hecht
probes beyond insensitivity, considers the transformation in
Christian attitudes from anti-Semitism against Jews to anti-
Semitism the object of which is the Jews' surrogate: Israel.
Tracing the charge of "intransigence" against Jews as far back
as Tacitus's argument that the Romans had no alternative to
the capture and destruction of Jerusalem because the Jews were
unbending and obstinate, Hecht finds the metaphor of "intransigence" a major element in Christian persecution of Jews in the
Middle Ages. He cites David Berger: "Every major Christian
doctrine could be supported by several verses in the Hebrew
Bible, and some of these appeared utterly irrefutable. Indeed,
a few verses seemed so impressive that the persuasive force of
any one of them should in itself have caused the Jews to aban-
don faith. Only preternatural blindness or conscious refusal to
accept the truth could account for Jewish resistance, and both
of these explanations played an important role in the medieval
conception of the Jew." Today, Hecht maintains, the idea that
Jews are intransigent, unbending and even blind to the theological claims of Christianity has been transferred to the state of
Israel. Israel has become, so to speak, the voodoo doll into
which latent anti-Semites, camouflaged in the fashions of ecumenism, manifesting not anti-Jewish hostility but rather expressing purely political views, can stick pins, intending the
curse, as in days of old, for Jews. "Consequently . . . Israel is
continuously portrayed as being intransigent to the 'legitimate'
demands of the Palestinians or to its Arab neighbors, but scant

attention is given to the fact (of) Arab intransigence to the
legitimate rights of the Jewish people to its homeland . . ."

Littell is perceptive; Hecht may be right; but Hecht's argument is speculative, not easily proven and consequently is a
set-up for rejoinders that Jews differed with, too reflexively
charge "anti-Semitism." But there is another answer to the
"why" of our question that is on its face persuasive. This answer
is in the very arguments stipulated by council leaders in defense
of council actions. It lays exposed between the lines of Methodist Bishop Roy N. Nichols' earlier-cited rationale for Methodist underwriting of terrorists, "When the church commits
itself to identification with the poor and oppressed, we may
sometimes become involved with people whose blend of Marxist interpretation and Christian theology may be different from
our own." It is hidden in, but protrudes from the United
Church of Christ's David Stowe's one-liner, "Israel might have
to die for the cause of peace." It is an ominous presence in the
candid observation by the council's Robert Turnipseed, addressing a Jewish organization and declaring, "The Palestinians
have been seen as an oppressed people. Israel has been seen as
part of the oppressing forces."

And so there it is. In part, insensitivity to Jews, whose Auschwitz evoked easy and therefore cheap sympathy but whose
Jerusalem dearly taxes Christian intransigence; in part, perhaps
subtly, psychologically, transferred anti-Semitism from this or
that Jew to the impersonal corpus of Judaism, the Jew's state;
but in substantial part too a trendy charity for revolutionaries
so long as they are of the Left, coupled with an animus-riddled
guilt for themselves being part of the West, the "oppressor
forces." Israel, being of the West, being "white," beset by "un-
derdeveloped" masses whose very terrorism is perceived as
evidence of their victimization, becomes in this selective perception of good and evil expendable alongside the United States,
capitalism, imperialism and all the bogeymen long aborning in

Communist propaganda and today strapping heavies in the foreign policies of the World and the National Council of Churches.

This mind-frame was nowhere and by no one as exquisitely portrayed, unwittingly to be sure, as at the Fifth Assembly of the World Council of Churches by Dr. Robert McAfee Brown, professor of World Christianity at New York's Union Theological Seminary. Addressing his confreres in Africa, he allowed that as a white, a male, a bourgeois and an American, he himself embodied "racism, sexism, classicism and imperialism." He lashed America for its sins and the evil it continues to seed, and mea culpa'd, "You may feel that I have not made Jesus political enough, and that I am too conditioned by bourgeois categories to understand the full thrust of liberation." Then, finally, in a supreme act of public penitence, he announced that he would no longer be guilty of "linguistic imperialism." He continued his address in Spanish.

There is a Sholem Aleichem story of a mendicant who weekly solicited the town's rich man as he left his plant on payday. Invariably—well, almost invariably—he'd receive several coins from his generous patron. On the occasion which makes the story, the rich man passed him by, offering nothing more than regrets. The beggar asks why? The rich man tells him, "I had a bad week." To which the mendicant answers, "You had a bad week, so I have to suffer?"

And so with Jews and their erstwhile friends in the National Council. The council's clergy are on a high of guilt, paying political penitence for being white, being affluent, being American, but a high which like the beggar's patron, they'll eventually get over. So, meanwhile we have to suffer?

We have suggested that the appearance of consistency in liberal Protestantism's early-on denial of Jewish responsibility for deicide and its latter-day declared abhorrence of anti-Semitism, is deceptive. In fact, no matter its good intentions toward Jews, the National Council of Churches' road to Middle East peace, for Israel leads to hell. At first impression there is the appearance of consistency, too, in the narrow sectarianism of the fundamentalist Reverend William Blessing's 1950's anti-Semitic fulminations and the Reverend Bailey Smith's 1980's confidence that God does not hear the prayers of a Jew. But here, too, appearances, functionally, are not what they seem to be.

Blessing, Gerald L. K. Smith, Winrod, Goff, et al., enjoyed or at the very least profited in their anti-Semitism. They professed it, practiced it, commercialized it in a time in which Jews were the butt of religious discrimination. That they did not represent mainstream America, that they themselves were attitudinally marginal Americans, parasitically feeding on prejudice, was small comfort to us because, understandably, we were not surefooted. How could we be otherwise, when in our memories and on Fox Movietone News the ovens of Auschwitz figuratively were still smoking?

When in 1981 the Anti-Defamation League communicated to the president of the Women's Division of the Board of Global Ministries of the United Methodist Church its concern with the group's funding of PLO propaganda organizations and requested a meeting to discuss its concern, two letters went unanswered. A third letter elicited a response from its president, Ruth A. Daugherty, in part saying ". . . my schedule is heavy for the remainder of the summer. I cannot presently arrange to meet with you." "Presently" has not yet expired.

When the Reverend Bailey Smith, president of the world's largest Protestant denomination, the Southern Baptist Convention, representing 14 million Baptists, opined about the tinniness of God's ear to Jews, once again we were "concerned," a condition experienced by Jews with the near frequency of the common cold. At the time, I was quoted as observing:

Dr. Smith did not say how he came upon this information. A phone call from God? A mail-o-gram from Torquemada? A chance encounter with a burning bush?

Skeptics might dismiss the Baptist leader's prattle as fallout from the long, hot summer's siege, a fantasy fevered by ayatollahs and cultists. But Dr. Smith is a "spokesman" of sorts, and his Southern Baptist Convention a major religious force in America. Consequently, ludicrous though his comments are, the implication of his revelation is real, and it is clear. Jews, he means to tell us, are incomplete. Christians, or at the least, Baptists, or, at the very least, Southern Baptists are whole. Because Jews are incomplete God does not hear them. Get with it Jews—he is saying—if you want God to hear you, convert.

Several weeks later, Smith, his cheek turned, wrote me: "I have a great desire for better understanding with you and your people. I deeply regret any hurt that may have come by remarks credited to me." Unlike the Women's Division of the Methodists' Board of Global Ministries, to whom we had written evenly if not deferentially, the Southern Baptist leader wanted to meet and to talk.

Months later, following several encounters between the leadership of the Southern Baptist Convention and the Anti-Defamation League, Smith wrote to President Reagan:

> I want to respectfully request that you continue to give the ultimate amount of aid and assistance to our very dear and important friends in Israel. I believe that they are worthy of our most conscientious efforts in their behalf. I am certain that I speak for many of my fellow Baptists when I say that we support anything that supports Israel.
>
> I admit that I have grave doubts about selling the AWACS to the Arabs. I feel for certain that it would jeopardize the security of Israel and we must do nothing to put them in any jeopardy at all . . ."

In November of 1980, then President-elect Ronald Reagan received a mailgram saying in part:

> ... We are concerned about morality and reaffirmation of princi-
> ples of faith not only on the domestic scene but also in terms of
> our international affairs. From our religious, moral and strategic
> perspective, Israel supremely represents our values and hopes for
> security and peace in the Middle East.
> ... We therefore urge you to implement this national security
> and moral perspective through your appointments in the foreign
> affairs and defense fields. Unfortunately many of those vying for
> such positions hold views which are incompatible with your
> policy perspective on Israel . . .

The signators were the Reverend Jerry Falwell, president of the
Moral Majority, Edward E. McAteer, president of the Religious Roundtable and Paul Weyrich, president of the Committee for the Survival of a Free Congress.

The fundamentalist Jerry Falwell, again: "God has blessed
America because America has blessed the Jew—His chosen
people." And again, "I want to stand with the Jews. If that's
where God blesses, I want to walk close by." And in criticizing
President Reagan's controversial AWACS package before the
City Club of Chicago: "If we are so concerned about protecting
our oil interests in the Middle East, we should have the installa-
tions to defend them. We should control the defense of this area
instead of handing over the military might to nations that could
turn it against Israel."

Support of the state of Israel by fundamentalists like Bailey
Smith, Falwell, the Reverend Pat Robertson and the various
television ministries whose "parishioners" are estimated in box-
car numbers is consonant with surveys of rank-and-file fundamentalists. In his studies of American attitudes towards Jews
and toward Israel, William Schneider has found two strains

running in opposite directions. On questions probing anti-Semitic attitudes, conservative white Protestants trail Blacks and Hispanics in their anti-Semitism, but outpace white Catholics and the least anti-Semitic, the liberal white Protestants. However on questions relating to Israel, while Blacks, consistent with their position on the anti-Semitism track, lead in antipathy, again followed by Hispanics, the smallest anti-Israel scores are those of conservative white Protestants. Parenthetically, but relevantly nonetheless, Schneider observes that among white Christians and Blacks, the irreligious are the least sympathetic to Israel and the least supportive of U.S. military aid to Israel. He conjectures that Christians who reject religion tend to reject Israel, and that sympathy for Israel among Americans is rooted in religious beliefs. As one Southern fundamentalist who had never met a Jew explained her sympathy for Israel: "I have prayed to the God of Israel all my life."

There is a difference between the fundamentalists of the Gerald Winrod time and stripe and today's fundamentalists. It is marked; it is deep, in reciprocal charity, it richly deserves Jewish awareness. Earl Raab has expressed it this way:

> Let's just make a comparison on a common-sense level: Can you conceive of Winrod inviting Jews to join his organization? Can you conceive of Winrod being willing to accept an award from a Jewish organization? Can you conceive of Winrod contributing heavily to a Jewish welfare federation, or politically supporting the state of Israel? Can you conceive of Winrod saying publicly, as Falwell has, "I want to stand with the Jews?"

Per our high-school physics class, things in motion tend to stay in motion, unless acted on by an outside force. Similarly there is an inertia in our attitudes, whether they have been spawned in bias or born in experience. So it is that Jews, generally speaking, remain more comfortable with liberal Protestants than with evangelicals and fundamentalists, despite the outside force of changes in our times and our agendas. The "Jewish agenda" is a varied one. The fundamentalists' support for prayers in the public schools, the Moral Majority's activism in behalf of conservative political candidates, fundamentalist opposition to ERA and to abortion, indeed, the very accents of their social conservatism grate on the liberal political creed. Because of these issues, let alone our having long been "neighbors" of the liberal Protestants by virtue of our demographic distribution, we feel ideologically closer with them than with fundamentalists. Indeed, I sometimes wonder if some of our biases would be more comforted, less bruised if only those Israel-supporting fire-and-brimstone preachers would slip and let loose some old-fashioned anti-Semitism. That would be reassuring of our preconceptions. More, it would relieve us of the confusion we experience in hearing expressions of love in accents that are unfamiliar and within easy memory had been threatening. After all, confirmation of our prejudices requires less of us than a change of mind.

At this point, several questions beg asking.

1. Is the security of Israel the sole criterion by which we judge who is our friend of opportunity, who our adversary? Are we not in effect advocating single-issue politics?
2. What about the polls which consistently reveal a co-relationship between anti-Semitism and literalist interpretations of the New Testament? Are we not for the expedience of gaining political support for Israel embracing and thereby strengthening a segment of society which is intrinsically prone to anti-Semitism?
3. Anti-Semitism aside, are we, like Major Barbara, prepared to take the Devil's help to do the work of the Lord?

These are logical and important questions. Moreover, they are challenges which examined carefully are posed by friendlies.

As a response to the first question, we are, admittedly, in

effect suggesting a bottom-line single-issue political evaluation
of the friendship of fundamentalists who are committed to the
security of Israel. We suggest that all issues are not equally
weighted in importance to Jews and that agreement on one
issue may outweigh in importance differences on a variety of
issues. Further, that agreement on that overriding issue does
not obviate one's options to continue debating the issues of
difference.

The issue of abortion is important. Fundamentalists largely
oppose abortion. We favor the legislation and court rulings
which have made abortions available where not long ago they
were legally denied.

We favor ERA. Fundamentalists largely are opposed to it.

We question the effectiveness as a moral spur of prayers in
the public schools and oppose trespassing by church upon state.
Most fundamentalists favor prayers in the schools.

While we doubt that the framers of the First Amendment
had in mind the protection of filmed fellatio, we deem the
excesses of pornographers to be less threatening to freedom of
speech than those who in their understandable revulsion
against those excesses would qualify and weaken the First
Amendment. Fundamentalists view this issue differently.

However, when these issues on which we differ, singly or
together, are weighed against our agreement on the prerequisites for the physical security of Israel, they simply do not
balance the scale.

Jews can live with restricted abortions. Indeed, societies have
through the centuries.

ERA is an important issue, but Jews can live without ERA.
Since its inception, this nation has, and the women's liberation
movement has made and is making dramatic progress without
it.

Prayers in the public schools would constitute problematic
scaling of the wall separating church and state. It would not,

however, mean the death of the Bill of Rights or seriously impact Jewish life.

Banned pornography is not by the remotest of reasoning as telling a setback to Jews as would be the alienation of allies who oppose the political imposition of a PLO-dominated state on Israel's borders.

Said otherwise, Jews, like farmers, union members, members of chambers of commerce, Democrats, Republicans and all groups, are hosts to convictions on multiplicities of issues. They will continue to express those views even when differing with allies who are like-minded on the subject of Israel. But all of the issues on which we hold views are simply not of equal importance. The security of the state of Israel is far more crucial an issue, in terms of that nation's life and death and in terms of the lives and deaths of its population, than the issues on which many fundamentalists and many Jews differ. And so, netted out, the bottom-line answer is, Yes, the conservative fundamentalists today are friends in deed, because unlike the National Council of Churches' liberal Protestants, they have been friends in need.

The second question has been posed frequently, concernedly, by persons dubious and prudently so of expediency as a guide to combating anti-Semitism. They maintain that the relationship between fundamentalist religious beliefs and anti-Semitic stereotypical views being well established, Jewish approbation for fundamentalist positions on Israel may, over a distance of time, become a boomerang. They feel it is a faulted strategy because it renders respectable people who are basically unfriendly. Further, that their very sympathy for Israel is the antithesis of friendship for Jews. This, because fundamentalists' support for Israel is rooted in their interpretation of Scripture which views Israel as having to be a fully secured Jewish state before Jesus Christ can return. When he does, Jews, the reasoning has it, will convert to Christianity. Essentially then, fundamentalist friendship is nothing more than a patiently played conversion ploy.

Fundamentalists do indeed interpret Scripture as predicting the Messiah risen when Jews are returned to Israel and in time promising the acceptance by Jews of Jesus Christ. It is neither our intention to be flippant nor disrespectful when we say, When that day comes, we'll see. Meanwhile, however, we need all the friends we have to support Israel against the political machinations of petrodollars, against the bias of the United Nations, against the connivance of the Soviet Union with Arab rejectionist states, against Arabists in the U.S. State Department, and against those who in pursuit of the abstraction of peace would sacrifice the security of the reality that is Israel. Interestingly, in the United States Jewish opposition to consorting with fundamentalists supportive of Israel comes more forcefully from secular Jews and from religiously liberal Jews than from orthodox Jews. The orthodox Jew, more zealously the guardian of his religious traditions than his coreligionists, is nonetheless seemingly less nervous about his down-the-road vulnerability to conversion. As for the concerned secular Jews, perhaps their discomfort with Jerry Falwell is not so much their fear of being converted as it is their aversion to his political profile. But conservatism is an affordable indulgence for Jews in America. For Jews in Israel, fundamentalists are comrades-in-arms on a vital front: the United States. For ourselves, however, no matter Pat Robertson's, Bailey Smith's, Jerry Falwell's friendship for Israel is rooted in the New Testament, we've an open mind. If the Messiah comes, on that very day we'll consider our options. Meanwhile, let's praise the Lord and pass the ammunition.

We have seen in our commentary on Christian beliefs and anti-Semitism the mischief for Jews in literalist interpretations of the Christ story. But literalism is two-sided. As it relates to Israel that same literalism registers higher support for Israel by

fundamentalists than by more liberal Christians. When Bailey
Smith made his notorious observation about God not hearing
the prayers of Jews, the media dramatized the commonplace.
In *Christian Beliefs and Anti-Semitism,* Glock and Stark found
that fully two-thirds of Protestant America and half of the
nation's Catholics agreed that a belief in Jesus Christ as the
savior was "absolutely necessary" for salvation. Also that a
majority of Christians hold beliefs that would condemn non-
Christians to damnation (including those Christians who do not
accept Jesus as the Son of God). Bailey Smith simply said aloud,
but dramatically and within earshot and eyeshot of the media
what an awful lot of people quietly believe. Besides, if Christians did not believe in salvation through Jesus Christ, it could
be argued, and not without persuasiveness, Why be a Christian.
Surely, or at least arguably, the Christian tenet that salvation
comes through Jesus Christ need not be any more prima facie
an evidence of anti-Semitism than Jewish rejection of Jesus
Christ is prima facie an evidence of anti-Christian prejudice.
Indeed, when our first meeting with Smith concluded and we
faced waiting reporters and cameras, I was asked right off
whether we had changed his mind. My response was, "No. It's
precisely his religious beliefs that make him a Baptist and mine
that make me a Jew." The importance of our meeting and our
dialogue, we suggested, was in our mutual desire to bring the
two faith communities closer in understanding of each other
and of our respective concerns.

To be sure, religious conceit has historically had baneful
effects on Jews, and the Anti-Defamation League's and the
American Jewish Committee's continuing dialogue with fundamentalists is explicit recognition of the requirement of Jewry
not to be forgetful of the lessons of history. But not all religious
conceits need be seen as a clear and present aggressive enmity.
Nor do Christians have an exclusive franchise on religious conceits. A chief rabbi of Jerusalem, himself of course Orthodox,

has observed that God does not hear the *shofar* ("ram's horn") when at Yom Kippur services it is blown in a Conservative synagogue.

We are aware that to this point our argument for *ad hoc* political alliance with fundamentalists is more suggestive of practical politics than of political purity. For do not the second tier of questions and our responses to them really grant the poll-revealed anti-Semitism of fundamentalists? The questions, yes. Our responses, not really. To the extent that we have implicitly granted anti-Semitic attitudes as lacing fundamentalist religious beliefs it has been for the purpose of weighing anti-Semitic attitudes as traditionally defined against the relevance to Jews of religious and political attitudes toward the security of the Jewish state. The former weigh less. However, that argument now made, our proposed definition of contemporary anti-Semitism presses for remarking. Previously we have suggested that the social, political and economic stations enjoyed by American Jews today has rendered the anti-Semite's rejection of us as a residential neighbor, or his resentment of us as being overly ambitious, with lessened importance than such attitudes bore when Jews were vulnerably segregated and impotently discriminated against. Still, no matter we have "made it," we remain apprehensive, on guard against "anti-Semitism." What then is the definition of this latter-day anti-Semitism which despite our achievements continues to haunt us? And why do we seem to absolve so many prominent fundamentalists of being its carriers while questioning the friendship of the dominant leadership in the National Council of Churches?

A formal declaration by the Union of Jews and Christians at the German Evangelical Churchday, issued to the West German government in the summer of 1981, defines what it terms the "New Anti-Semitism." Affirming in a preamble their notice of increasing "evidence of a regression into hostility towards Jews," the group declared that "behind the criticism of the

Israeli government, which is of course open to criticism as
much as the politics of any government, the old anti-Semitism
is visible." Thusly introducing their premise, they proceed to
define the new anti-Semitism:

> 1. It is anti-Semitism when Israeli politics is judged without
> regard for the special position of the state of Israel: a small state
> in a state of war for thirty years, surrounded by enemies who
> deny it recognition and peace—a state whose people would not
> survive a military defeat.
> 2. It is anti-Semitism when erroneous actions by the Israeli gov-
> ernment are judged one-sidedly, without regard for the actions
> of Israel's enemies, and are pointed out and judged more sharply
> than similar actions by other governments.
> 3. It is anti-Semitism when the "special relationships" between
> the Bundesrepublik and the state of Israel, which have been
> recognized up to now by our government and which are a conse-
> quence of the persecution of Jews perpetrated by Germans and
> in the name of the German people, are denied and the responsi-
> bility of German politics for the existence and security of Israel
> is denied or forgotten.

The definition is a good one. Besides, German evangelicals and
German Jews, no casual authorities on the subject of anti-
Semitism ought to know.

The final question, raising the issue of propriety in accepting
the Devil's help to do the work of the Lord, purposefully sets
aside the consideration of anti-Semitism. To this point our
discussion of fundamentalists has been largely referent to Jewish *qua* Jewish interests. But Jews are not an island. And even
if fundamentalists were philo-Semitic, a disposition not in evidence, if they pander hatred of others or conspire to undermine
democracy, certainly the embracing or whitewashing of them
would be an act wanting in ethical behavior, let alone being a
failed tactic with which to serve Jewish interests. All this, by
way of introducing the observation that in recent times in

America rarely has a religious persuasion been as broadly smeared as have fundamentalists. As excoriations of Zionism have served to camouflage raw anti-Semitism, so have swollen hyperboles descriptive of the Moral Majority and the Religious Roundtable beclouded the image of fundamentalists. Ironically fundamentalists, believing in Satan, have themselves been pictured as satanic, an irony compounded by persons scornful of bogeymen. So it is that the president of Yale University, his adjectives darkly peppering his forebodings, can declare, "A self-proclaimed 'Moral Majority' and its satellite or client groups, cunning in the use of a native blend of old intimidation and new technology, threaten the values" of the nation. "And they have licensed a new meanness of spirit in our land, a resurgent bigotry that manifests itself in racist and discriminatory postures, in threats of political retaliation, in injunctions to censorship, in acts of violence." And the president of Georgetown University, whose Jesuit founders even in these United States were vilified by the stereotypes of anti-Catholic bigots, can compare the Moral Majority with the Ku Klux Klan. "Whether hatred comes wrapped in white sheets or the scripture, it is still a denial of man and his works. America is in a rancorous mood these days . . . These moods have found different names: nativism, know-nothingism, America First, the Ku Klux Klan, McCarthyism. Now we have the new righteousness and its prophet, the Moral Majority." Neither president suggested that his conclusions were reviewed by professors of evidence in their distinguished law schools.

But are the conservative fundamentalists political devils? And are their legions, if legions they are, really managed by the Moral Majority? Or have they, like Jews and Catholics, been branded monolithic when in actuality they are a politically diverse breed?

George Gallup, testing evangelical fundamentalist opinions on politically revealing issues, found that there was no statistically meaningful difference between them and nonevangelicals. More specifically, on the issue of defense spending, no difference. On whether the government should spend more or less on welfare, no difference. On such issues divisive of liberals and conservatives as gun registration, building of more nuclear-power plants, capital punishment or the need for governmental social programs, no difference. Indeed, a *Los Angeles Times* national survey revealed that there was no significant difference between evangelicals and nonevangelicals even on the Vietnam War, both groups believing it to have been ill advised by three-to-one margins.

As indicated earlier, there are differences between fundamentalists and Jews, and between fundamentalists and liberal Protestants, let alone among Jews and let alone too among fundamentalists. Gallup has found that evangelicals are evenly split on the question of abortion, while nonevangelicals oppose the banning of abortions two to one. Evangelicals heavily favor prayers in the schools. The rest of us do not. These differences, however, are hardly suggestive that heaven is our intended destination, hell their natural habitat.

Likely, these facts are welcomed by neither the Moral Majority nor its more severe critics. For the former, it suggests their charismatic leadership is with pale followship; for the latter, that their verbal volleys are being fired at civilians. Facts still further confound both the Moral Majority and its would-be exorcists. The University of Texas in a survey conducted in the Dallas-Fort Worth area, a presumed center of Moral Majority ideological sway, found that in 1981, in the wake of its purported victorious campaign in the 1980 elections, a scant 14% of the 771 sampled expressed support for Falwell's organization. To what should have been the dismay of the Moral Majority and the embarrassment of those who see in it the singleness of purpose of the Ku Klux Klan, fully one-third of those supporting the Moral Majority disagreed with the statement:

"Abortion is a sin against God's law." Thirty-four percent of
Moral Majority supporters answered affirmatively when asked
to agree or to differ with the statement: "I believe in the ERA
to guarantee women's rights." The study found that 28% of the
respondents in this Bible Belt area were nonsupporters of the
Moral Majority and that 49% had either not heard of, or were
indifferent to the Moral Majority. Drs. Anson Shupe, Jr., and
William Stacey, the study's directors, concluded, to their admitted surprise, "that the 'Religious Right' may be largely a
media creation . . . the product of systematically conjured imag-
ery and public relations 'hype.' " They might have added that
there is one fruitful field of cooperation between the leaders of
the religious right and their more newsworthy critics. Both,
with the enthusiastic assistance of the media, successfully contribute to the exaggeration of the religious right's political influence.

But regardless of the puffery in the criticism of the religious
right, are they, as distinguished from fundamentalists at large,
a devil, albeit a pint-sized one?

The Moral Majority has been charged with contributing to
a resurgent bigotry. There simply is no substantiating evidence
to support this serious charge. Bigots eschew the support and
membership of Jews, Catholics, Blacks or whomever, singly or
in combinations. The Moral Majority solicits their membership.

The religious right marks political candidates for defeat
based on their voting records or platforms on selected issues.
This time-tested, if not time-honored, expression of group interest has been and is used by liberals, by farmers, by union
members, by Blacks, Jews, Catholic organizations and moreover is the basis on which candidates themselves regularly appeal to voters. When the National Council of Churches issues
statements on nuclear energy or urges the United States to
recognize the PLO, that's "prophetic witness," but the religious

right's opposition to abortion or its support of Israel is "single-issue politics."

The Moral Majority has encouraged boycotts of sponsors of television fare it considers pornographic. In our view, mistakenly so and in the long run, mischievous. But fascistic? Within easy memory, Black and white civil-rights advocates have boycotted segregated lunch counters and racially discriminatory companies, while war protestors have boycotted chemical companies, and environmentalists have boycotted despoilers of our air and water, and for a spell of years, untold numbers of Americans protesting working conditions on California farms made do without lettuce.

The religious right has been accused of censorship activities. Some thirty years ago, a neophyte in the Anti-Defamation League, I dutifully advised a radio-station executive in New Mexico that one Upton Close, whose recorded commentaries the station carried, published anti-Semitica which he mailed to corresponding listeners. The executive considered my evidence and to my naive surprise, then and there instructed an aide to stop carrying the Close recordings. Several weeks later, Roger Baldwin, the founder and for generations leader of the American Civil Liberties Union, visited our home and I confessed my abashment with having been party to the abridgement of Close's freedom of speech, no matter his sideline was anti-Semitism. Baldwin, the very personification of civil liberties, smiled, "Why are *you* embarrassed? You exercised *your* freedom of speech. The station manager is the culprit." The Moral Majority has publicly declared its belief in the right of the Women's Liberation movement to boycott states which have not ratified ERA. Certainly their own right to wield the boycott weapon—in a democracy whose Justice, blindfolded, must not peek lest she be swayed by the identity of the litigants before her, and who is programmed to be responsive to precedent—is precious to us all. The protestor, whether of the religious right or the Communist Left gives substance to freedom of speech. It is undermined not in its exercise but in its abandonment, and responsibility for the latter is with the media and our government.

The Reverends Falwell, Bakker, Robertson, Robison and the long right flank of Christian political activists have been accused of mixing religion with politics, blurring God's and Caesar's jurisdictions. But so did the Reverend Martin Luther King. So do the Fathers Berrigan. So does the Reverend Andrew Young, the Reverend William Sloane Coffin, the reverend leaders of the National Council of Churches, sundry rabbis, and all of them with accompaniment from volume-amplifying press releases. The danger to democracy is not in the participation of clergy in political debate but in the establishment by the state of religious doctrine as a public policy engraved in law. The commonweal is not so much served by clerical abstention from participation in political discourse as by vigorous participation by citizenry from which develop constraints upon the state from transmuting the views of any creed into law.

In this context, it is noteworthy that the decibel count of fundamentalist political expression, recently so audible, is not without precedent. Evangelicals were prominent in the abolitionist movement, in prison reform, in lobbying for child-labor laws, and as long ago as the mid-nineteenth century. And at the turn of this century William Jennings Bryan, had he been polled on social issues by a Gallup, would have registered as a reactionary—his Scopes-trial performance—and simultaneously as a radical—in time, to be vindicated by the New Deal's social-welfare revolution.

In conclusion, we need not agree with fundamentalists in their millennial theology, to accept their proferred friendship on shared worldly concerns. And although we differ with many of them on particular secular and sectarian issues, we can no more rationally ascribe deviltry to them than Godliness to ourselves. Given the actuality of their political and social diversity and the pejoration in the stereotype of them as monolithic, they and fairness merit fresh evaluation by Jews even as Jews have pled for bias-free consideration of their own diversity, and have insisted on the secular merit of their own religiously shaped values.

Oscar Cohen has observed that today the fundamentalists are on our side, but if Jews work hard at it, they won't be.

Who needs that? And to what end?

8

Blacks and Jews

For American Jews, Christian watching is something on the order of a farmer's weather watching. One cares; given past performances, one had better care; but it's nothing personal. Or, perhaps more accurately, it's like apprehensively watching an erratically behaving stranger. The feeling, be it of suspicion, even if buffered with hope, or of cool, even if laced with preparedness, is relatively free of personal feelings. No past alliance to stir ambivalence, no trenches shared, certainly no great expectations. Not so for Jews vis-à-vis Blacks. Precisely because Jews, both as Hillel's legatees and as liberals, have invested themselves in the civil-rights movement, shared as it were, the once so lonely, often besieged trenches, the statistics in chapter four on Black anti-Semitism evoke more layered Jewish reactions than does white anti-Semitism. The unraveling of old friendships, just because the parties know or think they know each other so well, is further frayed by the very intimacy that once bound it.

Public discussion of Blacks (and for that matter of Jews too), requires tiptoeing care and grace. The field is mined with white prejudice and with Black pride, with white insensitivity and with Black soreness, with white words unartfully crafted and with Black hearing selectively tuned, and they are all detonators. Sometimes, however, our self-imposed restrictions on easy discussion of Blacks get silly. Two illustrations:

In the early 1950s, we saw *Billy Budd* with a Communist couple we knew. It was a Wayne State University production featuring a Negro student in a lead role. But such a Negro! He was so deeply, darkly complected that he suggested charcoal. This, plus the fact that he was playing a period-piece British naval officer, prompted Ruth's intermission conversation opener: "Isn't that something, casting a Negro in that role."

The ensuing silence sounded and felt like plop. Then, tartly, but in a voice not yet prepared to break off diplomatic relations, the she-"progressive" answered: "Really, I didn't notice his race."

We had been sitting front row center.

In those days, when racial enlightenment shone portside, it was de rigueur to not notice the differences in race. Ruth, alas, had let go a boo-boo more socially compromising than underarm odor. Today, social fashions having fickled our race values, her 20-20 vision of the youth's Blackness has become "race-sensitive," while our acquaintances of yore, for having been color blind, are *ex post facto* "functional racists."

For their times, however, both liberal styles, yesteryear's mini-seeing of Negroness, and today's maxi-seeing of Blackness, make some sense. When color was a civil liability, let alone socially leprous, color-blind whites served Negroes to hurdle discrimination, and to a chance at self-realization. Color blindness was an humane attitude, largely held and proselytized by the white Left. When during Lyndon Johnson's administration racism's pall began lifting, color blindness was relegated to the status of horse-and-buggy race relations. It was now necessary to see the Blackness of the Negro so that we could more responsively minister to those of his Black-class and Black-culture wounds that were beyond the medications of color-blind civil-rights laws. The white Left accommodated itself, albeit in this phase of the accelerating race evolution Negroes led the way. I'm sure that our *Billy Budd* dates made the transition but equally sure that being politically programmed, they are still punching out rote answers to questions the critical nuances of which they hear deafly. They were not our companions in the following story, but they might as well have been. It occurred twenty years later in the early seventies; racism now on the defensive.

In truth, in retrospect, the gore of the story seems plasticized by the setting, a schlock–French Provincial Miami Beach hotel. We were visiting with old friends and dinner over, caught up now on each others' intervening years, we were talking of race. Our friends told the story of their friends, a white couple who had sought out and moved into a mixed school district. They wanted their grade-school daughter to experience racial integration. One day after class the girl was accosted and captured by three Black girls. They roped her to a tree, pummeled her, scratched her, tore her hair and spat on her. Screaming abuse all the while, one finally threatened they were going to roast her, cut her open and eat her insides. At this point adults happened along, routed the Black children and freed the white child. She ran home and sobbingly recounted her experience to her mother, climaxing with her classmates' threats to eat her insides. Her mother, besides herself, moaned, "The cannibals!" And the child, her sobbing trailing off, her voice firming, responded, "Mother! That's prejudice!"

Marvelous punch line, but it's not the point of the story. It's the manner in which our friends told the story that is. In low tones, not hushed tones unconsciously pitched to befit the recounting of dread, but controlled low tones, dialed, consciously to keep from being heard at the next table.

Why? Would the story have been as furtively told in the same giddily named Café Pompeii if it were of white youths mutilating a Black child? I think not. That story and the passionate telling that is its due would have developed freely, its possibility of being overheard a standing invitation to those in earshot to join in the indignation without which the story's significance is unrealized. But the villains of the story were Blacks, moreover, Black children, and the tellers of the tale are well educated, well off, politically liberal, whites, and while we would presumably understand them, the Pompeians at the next table might not, might instead think them—as the white child did her mother—prejudiced. And so as more fittingly becomes the telling of a bigoted lie, our friends whispered a true story.

Of course, the story is racially flammable and it might be argued that in telling it in the manner they did they sought to control, to avoid spreading, its licks. True, in part. But something else is involved too. Surefooted when we explore white aberrations, we have grown cautious, but self-consciously and apologetically, when publicly discussing Black aberrations. As well-intentioned Southerners once feared being sent to Coventry as "nigger lovers," Americans have become apprehensive lest they be shunned as "racists."

While our friends at the university in Detroit and in the café in Miami Beach are Jews, today, in this racial context, their race sensititivy is no longer the prima facie evidence it was then that they are Jews. The Jewish franchise on white racial compassion has been broken. White Anglo-Saxons, as editors, clergymen, academics, government bureaucrats, politicians, dawdlers in the nascent civil-rights movement, are today as illogically rationalizing of race wrongs as recently they were insensitive to race rights.

To return, however, to Jews and Blacks and their long-in-place, now tenuous special relationship. And long in place it is. At the turn of the twentieth century Zionism's founder, Theodor Herzl, authored a novel, *Old-New Land,* in which he fantasized the future Jewish homeland, today's Israel. Remarkably and given contemporary Third World political attitudes towards Israel, ironically Herzl's concentrated zeal for a Jewish state was not mutually exclusive of others whose homes were not their own. The 1902 Zionist work included this passage:

> . . . There is still one other question arising out of the disaster of the nations which remains unsolved to this day, and whose profound tragedy only a Jew can comprehend. This is the African question. Just call to mind all those terrible episodes of the slave trade, of human beings who, merely because they were black, were stolen like cattle, taken prisoner, captured and sold. Their children grew up in strange lands, the objects of contempt and hostility because their complexions were different. I am not ashamed to say, though I may expose myself to ridicule in saying so, that once I have witnessed the redemption of the Jews, my people, I wish also to assist in the redemption of the Africans.

The American Jewish component in the civil-rights movement, its doting role in the nourishment of the infant NAACP and Urban League, its lawyers, strategists and activists in behalf of racial justice stand as compelling testimony to the Jewish universality of Herzl's dream of redemption for Blacks. And despite the polls we have discussed which reveal rising levels of Black anti-Semitism, despite the genuflections to the PLO and thinly veiled appeals to anti-Semitism by such prominent and popular Black figures as Jesse Jackson, in the Congress of the United States Black and Jewish members of the House of Representatives have reciprocated votes of group interest collegiality. As the Jewish legislators, by and large, are dependable votes affirming the Black agenda on domestic issues and on African concerns, so have the members of the Black caucus, overall, been responsive to Jewish concerns for Israel's security. Indeed, for all that the evidence of Black sympathy for the Arab cause is mounting and tolerance for Jews ebbing, in 1981's rancorous AWACS debate, sixteen of the seventeen Blacks in congress voted against the arms sale to the Saudis. Analysis of the ideological and/or psychological and/or opportunistic nature of this still pulsating Black-Jewish political alliance may be instructive, but in the face of the widely acknowledged cooling of relations between their constituencies, no more so than the very fact of the alliance's continued life—at least in the Congress.

Still, there is a catch. For Jews, and for Blacks too, there seems always to be one. Recently, as an expression of its appreciation for a Black congressman's supportive votes in behalf of Israel's security, an American Jewish organization offered the legislator a testimonial dinner at which it would publicly manifest its gratitude. The congressman declined. "If you really want to do me a favor, forget it. In my district," he smiled apologetically, "a Zionist award, one, won't help me, and two, can only hurt me."

To be sure, the Black-Jewish halcyon days of song-festing against Southern centurions, of arms locked marching to Selma, of raptly amening stentorian assurances that we shall overcome were somewhat less than unremittingly comradely.

In 1962, well before the fire-eating acts of Rap Brown, Eldridge Cleaver and Stokely Carmichael, well before the Black-Jewish confrontation over community control in Ocean Hill-Brownsville, well before the muzzles of Arab propaganda took dead aim at Black communities, well before reverse discrimination wedged Black and Jewish communities, James Baldwin, in *Notes of a Native Son,* observed:

Jews in Harlem are small tradesmen, rent collectors, real estate agents, and pawnbrokers; they operate in accordance with the American business tradition of exploiting Negroes, and they are therefore identified with oppression and are hated for it. I remember meeting no Negro in the years of my growing up, in my family or out of it, who would really ever trust a Jew, and few who did not, indeed, exhibit for them the blackest contempt.

Elsewhere Baldwin has observed that every society needs someone to hate, requires its very own scapegoat. In Alabama, he said, it was the Negro. In Harlem, the Jews. Dick Gregory, also the product of Black urban poverty, in his book *Nigger,* also written in the 1960s, also recounted a Black bill of particulars against the Jewish ghetto merchant. Recalling sales of no longer fresh bread, spoiled fruit and rancid butter, he nonetheless added a revealing dimension to Baldwin's remembered view of Jews:

When it came down to the nitty-gritty (however) you could always go to Mister Ben. Before a Jewish holiday he'd take all that food that was going to spoil while the store was shut and bring it over to our house. Before Christmas he'd send over some meat even though he knew it was going on the tablet and he might never see his money. When the push came to the shove and every hungry belly in the house was beginning to eat on itself, Momma could go to Mister Ben and always get enough for dinner.

Quinley and Glock who perceived Black anti-Semitism as stemming from the economic relationship between the two ghetto-bound minorities, saw in it too the source of Black ambivalence toward Jews. Resentment with indebtedness. "Black Americans," they wrote in 1979, "would be a great deal more anti-Semitic if it were not for the positive side of their relationship with Jews." Perhaps. Perhaps that's why remembering older Blacks tend to be less anti-Semitic than younger Blacks. But in recent years entrepreneurial Jewish moms and pops have vacated the Black ghettoes; young Blacks have consequently neither the grateful nor the resentful memory of Goldberg their parents retain; and yet they are more anti-Semitic than their Jewish-crossed elders. Moreover, the thinning of the Jewish presence in the ghetto seems to have fattened anti-Semitism without nourishing the meanness of poverty.

But simply to assert the foregoing, the Jew as year-round exploiters and as holiday gift-bearers, and to allude to the popular wisdom that the Jewish mercantile presence in the ghetto accounts for, rationalizes ghetto anti-Semitism, grants too much. The stereotype of the Jewish ghetto merchant, no matter that Jews remained in blackening ghettoes long after white gentiles had fled, no matter their wares were available on trust long before banks were required by law to be equal-opportunity lenders, has been one which if it didn't inspire anti-Semitism, tended to condone it. And the stereotype is not a solely Black-fashioned one. Well-intentioned whiteys have nurtured it. In 1968 President Lyndon Johnson's highly publicized Kerner Commission studied racism and urban disorders and reported that the "typical" ghetto merchant was a Jew. Also, that ghetto merchants charged exorbitant prices. This, in the newsy text of the report. In the supportive statistical tables, however, "typical" turned out to constitute 39% of inner-city merchants. A commission less intent upon sociologically explaining and thereby absolving the shattering of storefront windows and the stealing of liquor and television sets, less itself given to the acceptance of acceptable stereotypes might have observed in their commentary that 61% of ghetto merchants were gentiles! Indeed, 25% of the merchants, according to the back-page charts, turned out to be Black.

During the strife-torn years of the late 1960s when "telling it like it is" about honkies and Jews seemed a more popular pastime in the inner cities than stickball, a Cincinnati newspaper ran an editorial explaining why a small merchant had to charge higher prices in the ghetto. The editorial pointed out that the small merchant couldn't buy in the quantities that larger merchants did and consequently couldn't pass on the discounts his larger competitors could manage. It explained about higher levels of pilferage in the ghetto than uptown and the resulting higher insurance rates—if insurance was available—as a factor in ghetto prices. What made the editorial significant, if not popular, was that it appeared in a Black newspaper trying to explain why a Black ghetto merchant had to charge higher prices.

The Kerner Commission's report purporting to explain and in doing so rationalize Black fury undoubtedly was written with a compassion not readily evident in the reports of the Bureau of Labor Statistics and the Department of Labor. The latter, also prepared in the late 1960s, studied comparative prices in the ghettoes. Studying six cities, these studies found that the small ghetto merchants' prices were, in fact, not different from the small merchants' prices outside the ghetto. Also, that supermarket prices in and out of the ghetto were on a par with each other. Temple University and St. Joseph College studies of the same period uncovered similar findings in Philadelphia, as did studies in St. Louis and Newark.

During those years of riving Black-Jewish relations in New York, tight and troubled home for the nation's largest Black and Jewish communities, the epithet *Goldberg* was the spat synonym for *slumlord*. It was a time in which maharajah-rich foundations, preeminently the Ford Foundation, financed Black-activist programs designed to wrest control of community institutions from whitey, as if color was a determining pedagogical talent in the teaching of mathematics or spelling. On a more constructive tack, the Rockefeller Brothers Foundation undertook a project designed to prove that landlords in slum areas could indeed earn a financially viable return on their property while providing acceptable services. At a cost of several hundreds of thousands of dollars, the foundation financed a three-year experiment in New York's depressed lower East Side. Its results, fit enough to print in the *New York Times,* revealed that even a Rockefeller could not break even by following the dictates of conscience and housing regulations in ghetto rental property. The Rockefellers, no Jews they, abandoned the experiment. The lesson, however, is that Goldberg's evacuation of ghetto rental properties, the sale or abandonment of candy stores, tailor shops, grocery stores and small appliance stores by Jewish moms and pops has relieved neither ghetto poverty nor Black anti-Semitism.

In 1979, just prior to Andrew Young's resignation as our ambassador to the United Nations and its wake of winds of acrimony, their gusts flurrying the air with recriminations and anti-Semitism, *Politics Today* published what in retrospect proved to be a barometer:

> Most surveys show blacks less sympathetic to Israel than whites, and more likely than whites to accept anti-Semitic stereotypes. To some extent, the difference is attributable to education. With education controlled, however, an interesting relationship appears: using an anti-Semitism scale based on negative stereotypes . . . one finds no difference in anti-Semitism between whites and blacks fifty years of age and older. But there is a substantial difference between whites and blacks under the age of fifty, with younger blacks considerably more anti-Semitic and anti-Israel than younger whites.

In its next issue, the Andrew Young storm now about to form but its fury unimagined by most Jews, *Politics Today* observed:

> Anti-Semitism seems to be highest among younger, better educated, less religious and more politically conscious blacks.

With this insight, a new flavoring was added to the brew of Black anti-Semitism. Marx, Gary that is, had rationalized it as being brought on by mom and pop merchants. Baldwin, much earlier, provided Jews with a blame-mitigating accomplice, "the American business tradition of exploiting Negroes." Others have attributed Black anti-Semitism to Blacks being, after all, Christians. Still others, to capitalism's forcing its subjects to compete scroungingly for its meanly rationed favors. Others still, accounting for Black anti-Semitism, have recalled Boswell's account of Johnson arriving at a party and noting a friend turning away from him. Said Johnson to his companion, "What's he got against me? I haven't done anything for him."

But here was something new. "Politically conscious" Blacks led not only whites, but their own elders, as carriers of anti-Semitism and hostility for Israel. Popular wisdom would not have it so. Popular wisdom attributes prejudice to the disappointments of age; these anti-Semites are young. Popular wisdom ascribes prejudice to the uneducated; these anti-Semites are educated. Better educated, consequently with greater opportunities for making it, their anti-Semitism belies the theories of both Marxes. In the past, studies have linked anti-Semitism to religious orthodoxy; these young are less religious than their less anti-Semitic seniors.

During the hullabaloo of the Andrew Young resignation, in a walk from a cooling-it meeting with the Urban League's Vernon Jordan, NAACP's Benjamin Hooks, the American Jewish Committee's Bertram Gold, Bayard Rustin gave theoretical perspective to the term, "politically conscious." "There was a time," he told me, "when the class struggle was intranational. The *haves* against the *have-nots*. What we're witnessing now is a new class struggle, an international one. Have-nations in conflict with have-not nations. The have-nations are perceived as supporting Israel, the Third World have-not nations are perceived as supporting the Arabs. Jews are haves; Blacks are have-nots. The alliances consequently fall in place."

In a word, for many young politically conscious Blacks, the Third World has become their Israel; Jews, their Arabs.

The anti-Semitism journaled by Black artists, the anti-Semitism located, counted and weighted by pollsters, long simmering, boiled over with Andrew Young's sudden resignation. Young had lied—his own term was "shaded the truth"—to Secretary of State Cyrus Vance about his forbidden liaison with the United Nations agent of the PLO. No matter that he could claim, had he chosen, inferred approbation for his clandestine tryst by citing President Carter's comparison of the PLO to the "civil-rights movement here in the United States," he didn't. Having lied to his government, hence to the American people, and caught *in flagrante,* his relationship with the State Department became untenable, his resignation, if not actually sought by the president, nonetheless had to be accepted. Let alone an embarrassed, lied-to secretary of state, face would not have it otherwise. Immediately Jesse Jackson, his voice megaphoned by the media, declared that the Ku Klux Klan didn't file the Bakke case, the Ku Klux Klan does not deal with South Africa, the Ku Klux Klan did not pressure for Andy's resignation. Demagoguery's verdict: The Jews are guilty. On all counts.

Actually, of the dozens of national Jewish organizations, only one's leader had called for Young's removal. But no matter, the word was out: The Jews got Andy. Black anti-Semitism broke free of its mean streets, moved into meeting halls and on to TV land; long corseted in pollsters' charts, its figure suddenly bulged.

Within days of the resignation, Benjamin Hooks called a meeting in Harlem of Black leadership. A cross section of national Black leadership, some 200 attendees, churchmen, representatives of Black women's organizations, political leaders, academics, educated, politically and socially conscious, middle-class, arrived Blacks filled the hall. Percy Sutton, a former Manhattan borough president and unsuccessful candidate for mayor of New York City brought greetings and set the mood: "After all I did for the Jews, in the clutch, they left me. The Jews are part of the establishment and don't intend losing their power." Dr. Kenneth B. Clark, the well-known psychologist, reacted to resolutions which the *New York Times*'s Roger Wilkins felt would "certainly . . . change the historic relationship between Blacks and Jews" with the pointed opinion: "It was our Declaration of Independence." An account of the proceedings given me the following morning by a worried, long-time civil-rights leader included:

> I have never seen such intense anti-Jewish feeling, coupled with fantastic anti-Semitism. People I generally respect deeply, jumping to their feet cheering whenever anti-Semitic remarks were made. If I had to describe the mood, it was wrapped up in one young man who walked along side of me as I was leaving. "The goddamn Jews don't want us. Why the hell do we need them? Screw them. We've got the Arabs."

Stating, as we have, that the head of only one national Jewish organization had called for Young's firing is a truth, but only as far as it goes. The waves of words now ebbed, is it time to voice a quiet, inhibited truth? The ADL had declared then that Young's race was an irrelevance; that had he been a white man, for having misrepresented the truth to the secretary of state, the course of events would have been no different. But isn't there in that statement a skirted proposition that merits public discourse? Andrew Young's race *was* relevant. Had he been white and expressed his view that Cuba was a stabilizing force in Africa, which he had; or voiced his views concerning the sainthood of the Ayatollah Khomeini, which he had; or that communism wasn't his enemy, which he had; isn't it reasonable to assume that his resignation would have long since been asked for? It is an irony for the delectation of footnote writers of history that irrelevant as Young's race was to his resignation, it was a substantial relevancy to his tenure. Jews did not call for Young's resignation in part because he was Black and their consequent disinclination to stoke the embers of Black anti-Semitism, and, for myself at least, because the pressure mounting for his resignation was doing well, thank you, without the need for Jews to position themselves as scapegoat. While we may have been more prudent than the lone caller for his resignation, we were less courageous. And given that the absence of Jewish insistence for his resignation simply stimulated Sutton and Clark and Jackson and Lowery, *et al.,* to invent Jews, we relearned an old lesson about anti-Semitism.

There was even difference within the Jewish establishment as to how to react to the anti-Semitism spilling, flowing and bubbling in the wake of Young's resignation. Some preferred to not respond to it. They sought to avoid the extension of confrontation. What, they argued, are the Jewish weapons in such a confrontation? Words? Press releases? The rhetoric of "more in pain than in anger"? But Black weaponry, they feared, included contributions of Arab dollars, even violence against Jewish properties in the ghetto. ADL, an equal indignation employer, labeled black anti-Semitism for what it was: anti-Semitism, regardless of the race, creed or national ancestry of its purveyor. In doing so, we heeded our intuitive selves as well as such Black leaders as Bayard Rustin and Vernon Jordan, who counseled that Jewish silence would simply encourage the anti-Semites in their midst to greater vituperativeness. The blood of the lamb excites the tiger. Besides, our manifested anger, they advised, would provide resonance for their own appeals to argue the Young case on its merits, rather than by our silence desert them and leave the battleground to the bigots. Some Jews counseled dialogues with Blacks and goodly numbers of Black-Jewish dialogues were held in cities across the country. By and large, the further culturally removed from the New York scene, the more healing they were. At one such meeting in New York with the Reverend Joseph Lowery and the District of Columbia's Representative Walter Fauntroy, the Jewish braves at the peace powwow were reprimanded because Jewish bankers were allegedly "oppressing our people," and challenged, "Why should we speak out against anti-Semitism? You never have on the KKK!" ADL, widely acknowledged by the media, by government agencies, and inferentially by the Klan itself as the Klan's primary bête noire, was at the meeting and did not want for a loss of words. On the heels of these contributions to "dialogue," the SCLC's reverend president prayed for peace, urged Jewish support of his peace efforts and Jewish assistance in soliciting support from their "Black friends"!

It was John Roche, an Irishman as green as a shamrock, whose comment on the reactions of some Jews was among the more memorable of the millions of words written and broadcast at the time:

> Instead of telling Young to shove it and riding out the hot air gale, Jewish leaders rushed to organize rap sessions with blacks. Jews seem to have an unmatched sense of guilt for sins uncommitted, a fact that has motivated their singular humanitarianism and simultaneously made them the softest target in town for a sadistic pirate like Young. Alas, the Jewish rush to "reconciliation" with blacks provided a kind of legitimacy to the squalid accusation.

The "Declaration of Independence" was not unremittingly abusive. There were those who independently declared contrary views and, for running into the prevailing winds of Black hostility, courageous views.

Bayard Rustin chose the *New York Times* as his dais:

For seriously considering links with a group like the PLO, the Black community is moving beyond the realm of mundane politics as usual. We are moving into an area where we face three enormous risks. First, we risk causing serious divisions within our own ranks; second, we risk the forfeiture of our own moral prestige, which is based on a long and noble tradition of non-violence; and third, we risk becoming unwitting accomplices of an organization committed to the bloody destruction of Israel— indeed the Jewish people.

Vernon Jordan, in his Group W Broadcasting Network commentary, cautioned:

The role of the PLO has been injected into the continuing dialogue between Blacks and Jews. I think it's a mistake to flirt with an organization that has no claims on Black sympathies. It is wrong to claim that the PLO is fighting for freedom or that it resembles the Black civil rights movement . . .

And Julius Lester, veteran black activist, writing in the *Village Voice:*

I don't recall angry pronouncements from black leadership when 18 Jews were killed at Qiryat Shemona by Palestinian terrorists. I don't remember black hands held out in sympathy when 20 Jewish children were murdered at Ma'alot, where Palestinians held a school of children hostage. When 31 Jews were killed in a Palestinian attack on a bus, black leadership did not gather before the televisions cameras and microphones to say, "No! No! No! Not another Jew can be murdered on this earth."

But their voices were barely audible in the din of angry charges emanating from the more flamboyant, more media-adapted spokesmen. And when Benjamin Hooks, who had participated in a Black-Jewish meeting designed to stem angry rhetoric, later felt compelled to explain himself, he opted for defensiveness as being least offensive:

I never made a statement critical of the efforts made by Jesse Jackson, Joe Lowery, or Walter Fauntroy. I got a bad rap on that.

The media slurped the bitter brew. Understandably, too. When, if not really lovers, nonetheless demonstrably cohabiting allies carry on in public, that's news. When they are cultural exotics—Blacks and Jews—the news is newsy. But the scandal of the rift wasn't its only noteworthy media aspect.

Roger Wilkins, then a *New York Times* staffer and an attendee at the Harlem rally of Black leaders, led off his *Times* coverage of the meeting with a quote he attributed to Bayard Rustin. "What we accomplished in there was a miracle." Rustin having told me that the meeting was rife with anti-Semitism, I called him, curious about the quotation. The civil-rights' dean, a usually gentle man, was outraged. The night of the meeting he had said to Wilkins that it was the most racist meeting of Blacks that he had ever attended, and that the expressed anti-Semitism was frightening. Wilkins then asked, Didn't you find *anything* good that happened tonight? To which Rustin sarcastically countered, "I suppose it was a miracle that given the attendance, they didn't endorse the PLO." Two months later, an unchastened and apparently unrepentant Wilkins, writing in the New York *Amsterdam News,* a Black community paper, looked back at the meeting and recalled it as the beginning of a "process of effort, of idealism and of intellect."

During that period I phoned one of television's elder statesmen to seek his counsel concerning the then seemingly endless stream of broadcast Black vitriol against Israel. His advice was that we not respond, that we let it run its course and that soon the media would tire of it. While I did not immediately agree, I respected the source of the advice; it was prudent and I planned to weigh it carefully. As we were uttering our closing,

about-to-hang-up niceties, his prudence for Jews turned to de-
light for theater. "Oh yes," he suddenly remembered, "watch
for us Sunday. We've got Jesse Jackson on 'Meet the Press.' "

We suspect that the very subject of Black-Jewish relations
has more widely occupied Jews than Blacks. Perhaps because
of that temperature-taking tic of Jews and because Blacks are
still outside must of necessity concentrate their attention on
nearer problems. The facts of life for poor Blacks simply do not
qualify Jews as a front-burner preoccupation. For some educated Blacks, Jews are in the way and hence the rancor attend-
ing the quota issue. But arriving Blacks remain a minority
within a minority. With the abatement of press coverage of
frictions, with the dawned realization that Martin Luther
King's popularly celebrated disciples are the Jesse Jacksons and
Andrew Youngs, and not the Vernon Jordans and Bayard Rus-
tins, Blacks in turn are receding as a preoccupation of most
Jews. And beyond these symbolic allusions, the two groups are
simply not as relevant to each other as they were during the
civil-rights era when Jews as a group were among the few
activist allies Blacks could count on. The fallout from the Andrew Young affair did not shape these facts, but did tear their
veil. The unraveling relationship, however, was indeed further
loosened by Young. Because of the surfacing of the heretofore
repressed anti-Semitism, yes, but also because so few, so very
few Black leaders disavowed the uninhibited racism. That some
Blacks murmured that for them to speak up would cause them
a loss of credibility in the Black community was understandable
as a tactic, but a melancholy and distancing confession nonetheless.

Will time heal the wounds, reverse the pollsters downward
edging graph lines on Black-Jewish relations? Perhaps. But
there are issues down the road which, though they may not be
clearly labeled "Jewish" or "Black" seem likely to impact and

to further try Black-Jewish attitudes toward each other. Given that younger, more educated Blacks tend to favor Third World nations of color, the evolvement of the relationship between these nations and the Arab nations, in the context of Arab-Israeli relations, will certainly affect American Jews' views of Blacks and Blacks' views of Jews.

Beyond political issues, however, new patterns of relationships between the two minorities are already aborning. The old patterns were based on our respective identities as Jews and as Blacks. As Jews, we were for civil rights. The Jew in us propelled us to speak out, to march, to vote in order to break down racial barriers to first-class citizenship. Like Herzl, way off in Austria and in another century, we had been there, so to speak, and so as Jews we knew that discrimination was painful and that it was wrong. It was wrong for us. It was wrong for Blacks. Similarly, Blacks related to us on these issues precisely because they were Blacks. Had they not been Black, they would not have been discriminated against. It was that simple, that fragile, our relationship—one forged in discrimination, the direct consequence of our being remembering Jews and of their being forgotten Blacks.

But racial discrimination in housing, in employment, in education, in places of public accommodation, in government service, in voting is now illegal. Indeed, the quota system today penalizes whites. Nonetheless, as is plainly evident, Blacks have not yet entered the mainstream in numbers sufficient to dilute the Blackness of ghettoes, the Blackness of poverty, the Blackness of both the victims and the perpetrators of street crimes.

So it is that the new pattern of Black-Jewish relations we foresee is one that will be issue-related, rather than one that is essentially race- and religion-centered. Blackness no longer being as dominant a causal factor in sentenced poverty as it once was, Jews will continue to support measures that are aimed at ameliorating the circumstances of the poor—because they are poor, rather than because they are Black. In short, reflexive sympathy to color will no longer come as automatically as once it did. Jews will continue to support social and political programs that are both compassionate and racially equitable. As a group, we always have, and if hints of change are wafting in the political breezes, they do not augur abandonment of racial justice but rather our awakening to the difference between political medications that are labeled racially responsive and racially neutral programs that may hopefully succeed in helping those who are in need, many but not all of whom are racial minorities.

For instance, we have seen no evidence that current high unemployment levels among Blacks is attributable to employment discriminations based on race. It is attributable to an amalgam of factors, such as our government's economic policies, the catch-up time required to offset the effects of past discrimination, the sociology of family life in Black ghettoes, the very statistical formulas used which do not separate out the disproportionate numbers of young in Black families and consequently convey even bleaker news, etc. If, as concerned citizens, we are to be helpful, ought we not, as seems to be happening anyway, lower the banners we carried for civil-rights battles already won and turn ourselves to the more complex and currently more relevant questions of economic policy? Economics may seem a far cry from Black-Jewish relations, but finding viable economic answers will be more helpful to poor Blacks, and to Black-white, let alone Black-Jewish, relations than a thousand and one nights of Black-Jewish dialogue.

There are other for instances in which fraternity can be served, but which require the shedding of once appropriate but no longer centrally pertinent attitudes. Forced racial segregation is wrong. But does it follow that indiscriminate forced busing to achieve color integration is necessarily right? Should not alliances that fought segregation in education now turn their attention to being allies on the quality of education? After all, no less an authority than James S. Coleman has found that it is a "mistaken belief" that Black students learn better in integrated classrooms.

In some places "law and order" was used as a cover for police brutalization of Black activists seeking their due rights as Americans. Does it follow that a concern with law and order is necessarily racist? Statistics reveal that Blacks dominate the lists as victims of lawlessness—at the hands of Blacks. Should not alliances that fought police brutality now turn their efforts to support of law and order? And will not both Black and white citizenry be the resultant beneficiaries?

And if these illustrations of future agendas are suggested for the consideration of Jews and Blacks, we have at least one suggestion for Blacks.

Blacks have frequently, sometimes eloquently, sometimes angrily, cried out for attention to that which, deep down, anguishes their "soul." The advances of the past two decades suggest that whites and certainly Jews have heard and have been, if not totally, certainly substantially, even if clumsily, responsive. Laws evidence this, court decisions underscore it, attitudinal surveys support it.

We would like to suggest that Blacks, understandably preoccupied with the Black agenda, pause and listen closely to what anguishes other hearts, other "souls." We are none of us single-dimensioned. We are all of us with the capacity in both mind and heart to hear and to be responsive to the calls of others—or at least, minimally, of neighbors and friends. We would like to see motions introduced, resolutions passed, delegations sent to Washington by mainstream Black organizations in behalf of—yes, we'll say it plainly—a Jewish agenda. Let us widen and deepen our candor. Jewish organizations, profoundly concerned as they are with the Jewish agenda—Israel, anti-Semitism, Jewish identity, assimilation, the needs of our elderly and

of our young—somehow have not been so preoccupied, so exclusively self-referent that we have not found the time, the
empathy, the conviction to speak out and act against racism.

And while the future of Jewish responses to the Black community will inexorably be a continuation of our past commitment to equal rights and to our past support for those in need,
and while this means that we will do what is right because it
is right, still it would be warming to read a ringing denunciation
by a mainline Black organization of the racism implicit in the
new quota system. Time was when the late Roy Wilkins, the
NAACP's leader, did just that. And if Black short-term interests are viewed by Black leaders as being inextricably inter-
twined with the new quota system and if *realpolitik* in Black
organizational life renders such candor politically hazardous,
there are other signals from mainline Black organizations that
would make for welcome news. Loud, clear, repeated condemnations of the United Nations' offenses against the Jewish people; loud, clear, repeated contradictions of the National Council
of Churches' skewed reports on the Middle East; delegations to
Washington supportive of Israel's security. After all, friendship
no less than love, should be requited.

9

A Measure of Violence

ON AN OTHERWISE uneventful Sunday afternoon, the routine of house chores the same as the Sunday before and the Sunday before that one too, we received a phone call that the Anti-Defamation League's building in New York's United Nations Plaza had been bombed. It was the kind of unexpected expected which Caribbean islanders must experience when the hurricane suddenly strikes, Californians when the earth suddenly trembles. Bombings have become commonplace, at least those we read about. But the explosion, up close, surprises, always will. We caught a taxi and in overly long minutes came to within three blocks of a sea of shattered glass. There, because of one-way streets moving the other way, we got out and walked hurriedly to our building. As we wound our way through the thickening throng, it occurred to me that maybe we were not the target, that perhaps the intended target was Turkey's Mission to the United Nations, directly across the street from ADL. And as the Turks came to mind, I thought maybe the target was really the Chase Manhattan Bank, our ground-floor tenant. No sooner did I think Chase Manhattan than the Trilateral Commission, also a tenant, also a possible bomb target, crowded my suspicions. That the bomb, detonated in a car alongside the Turkish mission, parked parallel with ADL, was, according to the police, intended for the Turks is not quite the point of my recollection however. The point is that in the fleeting, overflowing second of my excited searching for "whos," fully four potential victims came to mind, each one a qualified target. Four, count them, four, their nationalities diverse, their preoccupations unrelated, all cheek by jowl on a pinhead of real estate, and each of them secretly tried, found hatefully guilty and sentenced to death by bombing. That this Sunday was the Turks', another the Jews', still another a bank's, does not vitiate the generalization: It simply suggests that we wait a while, a short while, and your turn will come too.

Ours is a time in which we expect the worst and it happens. And, melancholy thought, as we grow more accustomed to violence, as violence assumes the normalcy of the Ganges' flooding, our indignation lessens and our acceptance of it grows. Indeed, bomb a synagogue in Paris, or a Jewish Community Center in Brussels, commit your terrorism repeatedly, brutally, defiantly, and all the while you are relentlessly terrorizing worshippers or walkers-by, insist that you are practicing Liberation, and soon the repulsed witnesses who abhorred you will discover culpability in the victim. That's when terrorism becomes validated.

During the racially turbulent 1960s, we had a friend who was a militant radical. He was also brilliant and perverse. "You must bear in mind," he once admonished me, "these people have been locked into poverty for generations, as if it were an inheritance or a curse or something, while on their TV sets the good life is sung and for all they know, lived by everyone but themselves. Wouldn't it bug you, too? Hungry, poor, they're without any education that's worth a damn, just like their fathers and mothers were before them, and they know damn well that their own kids, no matter the crap from the Urban Coalition, are also going to be functional dummies. Add the frustration of political powerlessness and economic powerlessness . . ."

I interrupted him and unwound my own litany—that a society that tolerates violence is a society headed for anarchy, and besides the Black isn't the world's first poverty-ridden, inadequately educated and powerless human, and what's more, even today he doesn't have an exclusive on these conditions, and if every group with a legitimate bitch emulated the Black Panthers . . ."

"Who's talking about the Black Panthers? I was talking about the mountain boys in the North Carolina Ku Klux Klan."

On other occasions in those years, he had said much the same thing rationalizing Black Panther violence. The charm that distinguished him from the period's sentimentalist radicals was in the fact that his mercilessness was not strained. He was for the misbegotten engaging in guerilla warfare regardless of their race, color or creed.

But our erstwhile friend aside:

He had described several objective conditions—poverty, lack of education, powerlessness, and I, Pavlovian, word-associated Black. Most of you reading his interrupted statement did too, despite the same conditions applying to the rank and file of the Ku Klux Klan. So our point is us.

In those years we were far less equivocal about Mississippi violence than about ghetto violence, and our failing lay in our hypocrisy. Because Mississippi is distant, we saw clearly brutish men victimizing innocent men. Being sane people, we held them morally accountable. In the nearby Black slums, an altogether different stimulus to our guilt and on our haplessness, we complicatedly see not men but Blacks, not lynching but "acting out their anguish," not on men but on other Blacks or whites, and we transform both brute and brutalized from the he or she of them into sociological types. It's as if they were, unlike Klansmen, nonpeople and consequently, unlike Klansmen, not morally responsible. So it is that white brutes are depraved but Black ones deprived.

During the middle fifties, not long after the United States Supreme Court desegregated the public schools, we attended a Ku Klux Klan meeting. We drove some six hours north and west out of Miami, past the Cork Screw Swamp, up beyond Tampa to a cow pasture in a place called Inverness. The usual clearing, the usual platform and row of chairs for robed "dignitaries," the huge wooden cross, and set in a deep purple sky, a yellow, postcard moon.

"God stamped ugliness on the face of the Jew for the same reason he put rattlers on a snake." Cheers and whoops, and from the audience seated in their automobiles, appreciative horn-honking.

"Nigger, he black on the outside, white on the inside. Jew, he white on the outside, black on the inside." More cheers, more whoops, more horn-honking.

After it was all over we joined our car to a line that snaked across the pasture onto a state road and drove south toward Tampa. Shortly one of those ubiquitous roadside signs, EATS, appeared and we broke file, as did several other cars, for a coffee break.

Inside we sat down facing each other on the wall side of a table for four. In no time, two Klansmen sat down alongside of us, facing each other, and for all appearances, we were a congenial foursome. The waitress came along. "What'll you have?" We all ordered coffee.

The two of us talked artificially about the distance to Tampa; our companions about the "speaking" they had just attended. When the coffee arrived, the man at my side turned to me, his leather-tanned outdoor face in friendly repose. "Would you pass the sugar, friend?"

"Sure," and smiling back, I did.

"Thank you."

"You're welcome."

I thought of an hour ago, the calumnies of Jews, the brutish and primitive whoops and hollers they evoked; and here we were pleasing, thank-youing, and you're-welcoming each other.

Of course, the Klansman didn't know that we were Jewish, but on another related occasion in a courthouse in Miami with an American Nazi party member, we found ourselves arriving at the same door at the same time. He knew who I was and I knew who he was. We both stopped to let each other in, not in mock courtesy but in reflex-reaction politeness. He held the door for me and I automatically said, "Thank you," and he, "You're welcome."

Interesting that chivalry in America is associated with the Southland; in Asia, politeness with Japanese; and in Europe with the Germans. Sadism, too.

The red-neck Klan of the 1950s has given way to the blue-collar Klan of the 1980s. The Klan then, the vanguard embodiment of truculent resistance to desegregation, counted on the implied sanction and approbation of scores of sheriffs, dozens of mayors, some governors and the covering fire of White Citizens Councils positioned throughout the South. Today's Klan is politically powerless. Approximately 75% of its membership is under thirty years of age. In recent years, the memory of its night-riding forays still lingering in Black memories, its vitriolic rhetoric still echoing in Jewish memories, the Klan has been rediscovered by the media, its rate of growth recorded, broadcast and feared over in print and on TV tubes. And indeed, in the past several years Klan membership has almost doubled. But the actual numbers are no less significant than the percentages. Surely, the alarming news of the rate of Klan growth is put in perspective and ought to be calmed by the fact that in 1978 Klan membership was estimated at 7000 members and in 1981 at 10,500 members. Nor are they a unified cadre of 10,500. The grand total is inclusive of a handful of competing Klans. In a population of 240,000,000 and in a nation war-splotched with burgeoning religious cults and leveraged political cults, the Klans are trailing also-rans. Indeed, the media attention paid them is an advertisement, a windfall to their paltry treasuries.

The Klan today is to be found where it always, albeit in richer abundance, was. In small and middle-sized towns. "Drive through a small or medium size Southern town," David Chalmers, author of *Hooded America,* has observed, "Look at the men you see leaning on the gas pumps or chatting at the barber shop. Find out their trades, and you'll know where the Klan has traditionally drawn its human strength." While klaverns function in such metropolitan areas as Dallas, Denver, New Orleans, Houston and San Diego, the Klansman is likely to be a resident of a nearby small community and typically more native to Tupelo than to Denver. Curiously, in our liberated age, Klansperson may be a more fitting term than Klansman. An estimated third of Klan membership consists of women. Moreover, ecumenism has seeped into the once hermetically sealed order of Anglo-Saxon Protestants. The Grand Dragon of the Invisible Empire in Connecticut is a Roman Catholic of Italian descent. Two cheers for religious tolerance?

Latter-day Klan themes are adaptively current. Its devils are still, however, the old ones—Blacks, Jews, foreigners. In speeches and in pamphlets it exploits legitimately controversial

issues—busing, crime, inflation, the energy crisis, permissive-
ness in sex and movies, immigration from Indochina and
Cuba—beveling and sanding their complexity with simplistic
racial and religious hate. Interestingly, the ADL's Irwin Suall,
a foremost authority on terrorist organizations, has maintained
that the "commonly held notion that the Klan thrives when
unemployment runs high is of doubtful validity. The Klan's two
peak periods in the present century, the 1920s and 1960s, were
notable as decades of prosperity and high employment. What
these periods had in common was a breakdown of traditional
moral values as our society accelerated its transition from
predominantly white, Protestant, rurally-based origins to become a cosmopolitan complex of diverse races, religions and
cultures."

If Suall's is a sociological overview, Studs Terkel has pro-
vided a journalistic close-up. In his *American Dreams; Lost and
Found,* he interviewed one C. P. Ellis, a former North Carolina
Klansman turned union official.

The first night I went with the fellas, they knocked on the door
and gave the signal. They sent some robed Klansman to talk to
me and give me some instructions. I was led into a large meeting
room, and this was the time of my life! It was thrilling. Four
robed Klansmen led me into the hall. The lights were dim, and
the only thing you could see was an illumined cross. I knelt
before it and made certain vows. We promised to uphold the
purity of the white race, fight Communism, and protect white
womanhood.

After I had taken my oath, there was loud applause goin'
throughout the buildin', musta been at least 400 people there. For
this little ol' C. P. Ellis.

It disturbs me when people who do not really know what it's
all about are so very critical of Klansmen. The majority of 'em
are low-income whites, people who really don't have a part in
something. They have been shut out as well as the blacks. Some
are not very well educated either. Just like myself. We had a lot

of support from doctors and lawyers and police officers.

Maybe they've had bitter experiences in this life and they had to hate somebody. So the natural person to hate would be the black person. He's beginnin' to come up, he's beginnin' to learn to read and start votin' and run for political office. Here are white people who are supposed to be superior to them, and we're shut out.

I sometimes think that God's disproportionately generous gifting of Jews with brimming empathy was His way of slyly meting punishment to us in the form of vulnerability. There is implied sympathy in our recounting the monologue of our radical friend, and our sympathetic quotation from Terkel belies once again the disarming "understanding" I experienced with the Nazi I "liked." But the fact is that while it is admittedly not rational either to overestimate the Klan's current strength or to view Klansmen as B-movie stereotypical heavies, underestimating them—no matter they are few and no matter they are the troubled children of attractive Norman Rockwell mothers and fathers—is dangerous to our health and our lives. Understanding may be broadening; but disarming, too.

In the past several years a smattering of crimes committed by Klansmen, gleaned from a bulging bill of particulars as long as their perpetrators' hate is durable, should dissipate social-worker "understanding." The smattering:

Three Maryland Klansmen convicted of an attempted bombing of synagogue.

Five Klansmen indicted for shotgun and semiautomatic weapons shootings at a Black man in Detroit.

Thirteen Klansmen convicted in Alabama for firing rifles at the homes of Blacks and of racially mixed couples.

In Alabama, a dozen members of the Klan's Youth Corps set fire to a school bus, protesting school desegregation.

In Mississippi, Black schoolchildren were tear-gassed by classmates identified as members of the Junior KKK.

In California, the Klan has distributed a manual which the *Saturday Review* described as a "manual for murder (providing) specific information for the home manufacture of bombs, grenades, and other devices for killing and maiming people."

Two Klansmen and a neo-Nazi were found guilty in Tennessee for plotting to blow up a synagogue, a television transmission tower and Jewish-owned businesses.

In California, three Klansmen were convicted of conspiracy to murder the West Coast leader of the Jewish Defense League.

Imperial Wizard Bill Wilkinson, given to publicly displaying weapons, boasted, "These guns ain't for killing rabbits; they're to waste people. We're not going to start anything, but if anyone does, we're ready to defend ourselves."

In Alabama, in a confrontation with the Southern Christian Leadership Conference, some thirty shots were fired. Four persons, two white, two Black, were wounded. Only a Black was convicted.

In California, two Klansmen were found guilty of shooting into the homes of Mexican Americans.

In Alabama, a Klansman was convicted on charges stemming from his having held a knife to the throats of Vietnamese refugees, warning them to leave their jobs and threatening to kill them if they informed on him.

In Tennessee, three Klansmen were arrested for wounding four Black women with shotgun blasts.

On and on, shootings, bombings, intimidations, never random, always premeditated, the bull's eye the race or religion of the target.

The most widely publicized Klan action in recent years was the 1979 Greensboro, North Carolina, bloody and lethal confrontation with the Workers Viewpoint Organization, now known as the Communist Workers Party; orientation: Maoist. When the shooting was over, four self-identified Communists lay dead; a fifth died in the hospital. Nine Communists and one Klansman were wounded. For all of the horror implicit in an armed civilian convoy of vehicles, rendezvousing, turning ignition keys at zero hour, proceeding along public highways with their loaded at-the-ready weapons, cruising by, one can assume, naive McDonald's, apple-pie Howard Johnson's and friendly Fill-er-up signs to visit sudden death upon adversary demonstrators, this action was both different and differently instructive.

The Communists had billed their rally as a "Death to the Klan" demonstration. While in numbers, like the Klan, small, the Communists, unlike the Klan, were educated; many were professionals. But for all their differences in formal education, their social syntax shared common values. Bill Wilkinson's boast that "These guns ain't for killing rabbits; they're to waste people" is of a stripe with the Communist Workers Party member who after the massacre observed, "Talk is only a guide to action. There has to be some fighting, some bloodshed. We want as many comrades and friends alive as possible, but some will be killed." Like so many of the underground Weathermen and of the German Baader-Meinhof gang and the Italian Red Brigades, these terrorists, unlike the Klan, are the offspring of well-to-do families. Ironically, however, as noted by the *Greensboro Record*'s editorial page editor, Terry Eastland, the blue-collar Klansmen "are the same sort of people the Communist Workers party would organize in the mills; they are the sort of people the CWP believes will suffer first as capitalism kicks into its final spasms, and the revolution begins."

One, the Communists, professes hate for an Amerika that isn't; the other, the Klansmen, professes love for an America that isn't. Like Kenneth Goff, whose transition from communism to right-wing extremism was made in one small step, the murderous antagonists of the bad day in Greensboro were closer to each other than they were to their professed ideals.

In the past several years a new and possibly more serious— read: lethal—form of Klan activity has surfaced. In clandestine training camps in Alabama, California, North Carolina and

Texas, Klan and Klan-like groups have launched paramilitary training programs. Sometimes self-described as "defense" or "survival" courses, they are sponsored by armed and avowed haters of Blacks, Jews and foreigners. In Alabama Bill Wilkinson's Invisible Empire, Knights of the KKK, sponsors target practice with M-16 rifles, courses on guerilla-warfare tactics and search-and-destroy missions. Reference has been made to the California Klan's distribution of manuals of instruction in terrorism. In North Carolina the paramilitary training courses have taken place on property owned by a former Green Beret, leader of the Carolina Knights of the KKK. In Texas, itself a hyperbole, guerilla-warfare instructor, Louis Beam, Grand Dragon of the Texas KKK, has declared, "We'll set up our own state here and announce to all non-Whites that they have twenty-four hours to leave. Lots of them won't believe it or won't believe us when we say we'll get rid of them, so we'll have to exterminate a lot of them the first time around."

We have been discussing made-in-America terrorists and their ism's prototype, the Ku Klux Klan. We have noted their fractional proportion of the American people, and their recounted exploits testify to the distance removed they are from our nation's mainstream. Distance or no, however, and no matter their numbers are relative handfuls, they are capable of murder, provenly so. Moreover, the teaching of terrorism can be reasonably assumed to be the seeding of terrorism. Still, for all that Klansmen today are far more aberrational than representational, scattered 1980 elections foreclose certitude that the Ku Klux Klan's future is behind it.

In the Democratic party's 1980 congressional primary race in California's populous Forty-third District, which includes San Diego, Klan leader Tom Metzger polled 37% of the votes, a plurality sufficient to designate him as the party's standard bearer. While his Republican Party opponent subsequently handily trounced him, Metzger, without disavowing his Klan affiliation, polled better than 35,000 votes.

In North Carolina, Harold Covington, leader of the neo-Nazi National States Rights Party, running in the Republican primary for state attorney general, roundly condemned by the state's press and community leaders, nonetheless polled 43% of the election returns, approximately 56,000 votes.

In Michigan's Fifteenth District which includes blue-collar Dearborn, Gerald Carlson, an avowed racist and onetime Klansman and neo-Nazi, defeated his Republican Party primary opponent by a 55% to 45% margin. In later losing to his Democratic Party opponent, he nonetheless received 31% of the vote, or close to 54,000 affirmations from the electorate.

Other blatant bigots sought office: J. B. Stoner, the Georgia veteran racist and anti-Semite and Lyndon LaRouche, onetime Trotskyite turned anti-Semitic propagandist; both polled pittance votes in their respective assaults on the United States Senate and the presidency. But what were the mind-frames of the 35,000 men and women in the San Diego area, the 56,000 Americans across the continent in North Carolina, the 54,000 Midwesterners in Michigan, who cast their ballots for Klansmen and a neo-Nazi, the three, boastful racists and anti-Semites? Were they votes prompted more by disfavor for the opposition than by approbation for their candidate? Were they the expression of perverse political black humor? Whatever the meld of explanations, disenchantment with incumbents, intended messages to our political parties to provide us with more viable candidates, approval of specific planks in the bigots' platforms on the economy or on troubling local issues, one hard fact glistens coldly. Anti-Semitism and racism, not your garden variety of prejudice but the deadly bigotry of the Ku Klux Klan, was not a put-off for this hefty sampling of the electorate, their civic responsibility mockingly evidenced in their having exercised their franchise as Americans.

As there is a symbiosis between men who bite dogs and prowling, never quite satiated newsmen, so is there one between the Ku Klux Klan and the media. Georgian Roy Blount, Jr., author of *Crackers,* tells it this way. "For access to most surefire story subjects, you have to wade through agents, secretaries and aides who wonder exactly what kind of story you have in mind and how much time you'll need. But the Ku Klux Klan, these days, is easy. They will put on their robes for you and light crosses for you and take you out to the woods and show you their guns and maneuvers, and they will come out with startling quotes. They will even give you reason to believe that you might, with luck, get caught up in a shoot-out between them and the Communists."

Dean Calbreath, writing in the *Columbia Journalism Review,* quotes from the horse's mouth, an official in the Invisible (but not mute) Empire, Knights of the Ku Klux Klan: "We used the press. We lied and did anything we could to make reporters happy. We intentionally staged things just to get coverage."

In recent years, the KKK, .00004% of our population, has been "exposed" by the Associated Press, by *Time* and *Newsweek,* by *Playboy* and *Penthouse,* by the *New York Times,* by Sunday supplements, and its leaders invited on television by "Today," "Tomorrow" and "Good Morning, America."

We have quotation-marked the word exposed in deference to Don Black, an Imperial Wizard of the Knights of the Ku Klux Klan who has another view of the free publicity. After all, he should know. Asked how he felt about a broadly carried profile of the Klan, he confessed to being "flattered and impressed." With reason. During the two weeks in which his Knights were the subject of exposure in the *Nashville Tennessean,* he received a score of communications asking how to join up.

Calbreath also spent time with Jeff Murray, another functionary in the Invisible Empire. Murray, an actor of sorts as well as a critic of sorts, complained, "I'd always get the same standard questions. Almost every reporter asks the same thing, almost like they're robots or something. They always want to know how many members we have, what the cross-lighting means, how are we organizing. We always gave 'em good answers."

Good answers simply meant, by Murray's admission, fabricated numbers, a blown image of numbers and klaverns the Klan simply did not have. But in news, bigger is better, and so both the Klan and the media, feeding on each other, nourish each other.

The manner in which criminal activity is reported helps condition our receptivity to it and to its perpetrators. As a boy, I preferred to identify with the tough, law-defiant James Cagney rather than with the goody-good policeman or priest, Pat O'Brien. That's boys and that's Hollywood. However, growing up, even if not growing wiser, we tend to sublimate the outlaw in us, prefer to be viewed as law abiding, and are gratified by community approbation. The Klan presents a difficult and socially suggestible problem for the news media. As we have seen, one man's exposure is another's welcome advertisement. His very publicity is his felt approbation. And even if it were possible to report violence without, by any objective standard, romanticizing it, still there would be those titillated by it, self-goaded to emulate it. In Europe, where the television drama, "Holocaust," was well received, it nonetheless triggered a spurt of anti-Semitic desecrations.

Still, there is room for improvement of Klan coverage. Equipped to cover court cases, thousand-page, highly technical budgets, state legislatures, Washington, D.C., let alone the Super Bowl and World Series, all because of matchingly expert journalists, reporting the Klan is left to relative innocents. They write engaging color stories of cross burnings now become exotic media events; they interview Klan leaders articulate in the expression of social resentments, but are themselves without the expertise to refute lies or to hold murky theories to the light. The stories carry themselves, sometimes shocking, sometimes amusing but rarely as befits a label on bottled poison—instructive. What is required for worthy standards of journalism, let alone to clearly describe the evil banality of the Klan, is investigative journalism which examines the links and the ideological kinship between domestic terrorism that poses as patriotic and terrorism abroad that is steeped in hate for America. To be sure, even this caliber of reportage will not impact the strays in our society who are more the product of their own abnormal psychology than they are social protestors, but it would surely impress itself on persons who like those legion voters in North Carolina, in Michigan, in San Diego, were not repelled, did not read the small print as they voted yes to the Ku Klux Klan's candidate.

The violent bigots among us make do, no matter that night riding and lynch parties are receding history, catharses enjoyed by their racist progenitors, kicks denied them. The progress we have made in getting along with each other has not blighted brutish racism, but stunted it. No small thing that—at least for its classic victims. Today's Klansmen are a pale, even sorry version of the once dread and influential Knights of the Ku Klux Klan. But few and despised though they are, they *are,* and so long as they exist, intimidation and murder are their constant consorts. It is not likely that we will ever be free of irrational, welling hate, but the very decline of the Klan suggests society's capacity to isolate and contain social groups in which racists in their very communion rouse and activate each other.

The most effective way of aborting illegal Klan actions is through infiltration. Stopping them at the pass makes for more than a good Western; it makes for effective police work. Time was when at a Klan rally or klavern meeting, the FBI was an involved presence. In the wake of Watergate, its surefootedness lost, sensitive to criticisms charging it with *agent provocateur* roles, the bureau drastically cut back its undercover infiltrations. In doing so, the nation's foremost law-enforcement agency sabotaged both law and order. It did so by (1) unilaterally disarming itself, and functionally, the nation, of vital intelligence affecting millions of citizens, (2) freeing of inhibition an emboldened and demonstrably homicidal Ku Klux Klan, no longer concerned that their actions are being monitored, possibly by one of their own, and (3) consequently increasing the vulnerability of the Klan's defenseless targets.

An overly zealous police may exceed the law, but a handcuffed police saps the law. Had the FBI infiltrated the North Carolina Klan, as it would have in the blemished reign of J. Edgar Hoover, Greensboro likely would have been aborted, and the Communists to whom the Bureau is anathema would, ironically, still be Red rather than dead.

If the law's role vis à vis violence is to abort or, failing that, to punish its practitioners, education's role is to inoculate us against ourselves becoming its carriers and to sharpen our moral indignation against its operants. Recently, responsive to the increase in Klan activity, the National Education Association published an instructional kit titled, "Violence, the Ku Klux Klan and the Struggle for Equality" to meet the pedagogical needs of its concerned teachers. The loftiness of its intentions, alas, were not met by the level of its performance. Given, however, the dominant place in American education occupied by the NEA, and the tens of thousands of teachers whose daytime wards number in the millions, and who are using the kit, its failings may be instructive for future efforts.

Predictably and usefully the teaching guide includes a history of the Klan including its record of violence, an updated listing of contemporary Klan malpractices as well as relevant historical documents. Surprisingly and counterproductively it contributes to the polarization of Americans by purporting to Black children that because of white racism, Blacks have made no significant progress in the past score of years and that there is little hope of future progress. America, our preeminent association of teachers maintains, is a racist society of which the Ku Klux Klan is typical. The following are excerpted from the curriculum:

> . . . The Klan seeks to protect . . . the special privileges and benefits available to whites in a society structured around white supremacy.
> The violent nature of the Klan feeds on a climate of general social acceptance of racism.
> It is important to remember that the Klan is only the tip of the iceberg, the most visible and obvious manifestation of the entrenched racism in our society.

After using selective economic statistics to prove that the gap between Blacks and whites has widened rather than narrowed, the NEA endorses racial quotas and moving right along, identifies opposition to quotas with racism and the Klan.

The teaching lesson that the Klan fattens on a "climate of social acceptance of racism" and that it is merely "the tip of the iceberg" of "entrenched racism in our society" is flawed teaching on several counts. (1) It is factually wrong. (2) It absolves Klansmen of responsibility for their malfeasances. (3) It meanly stereotypes whites. (4) It stirs frustration in Blacks and, for some, vindicates dropping out.

(1) The declarative statements concerning the alleged entrenched racism of our country run into and collapse before the Civil Rights Act of 1964, the Voting Rights Act of 1965, *Brown* v. *Board of Education* and the long row of subsequent decisions which freed Blacks of the pernicious "separate but equal" doctrine. These landmark turnabouts in our race relations, expressions of the Congress of the United States and the United States

Supreme Court, make dubious the NEA's flat assertions concerning our "social acceptance of racism" and racism's "entrenched" qualities. To ignore the progress they represent is to suggest a questionable preference for dwelling on old grievances rather than moving forward from realized gains.

(2) If the Klan is only the "tip of the iceberg," it can't really help itself, can it? Our problem then is not so much the Klan as it is our society. But ours is a society which has scorned and repudiated the Klan. Its numbers and its influence are virtually nil. Still, the NEA would have our children taught that the Klan is endemic to our people, their parents. We suspect that the authors of this significant teaching kit reveal a fundamental distaste not so much for the Klan whose existence, after all, they rationalize, as for our society, which, rather than the Klan, they have placed in the dock.

(3) The United States is described as "a society structured around white supremacy." Once it was, but at last look the Congress, the Supreme Court, the various state legislatures which have long since outlawed racial discrimination, are predominately white. So is approximately 90% of their constituencies. It is no less mischievous to generalize about whites than about Blacks. Moreover, it is a pedagogically unsound curriculum which precludes white children from identifying with white good-guy role models. Blanket assertions of unmitigated white culpability for sins, psychic and legislative penance for which is in payment, qualifies more as preaching than as teaching.

(4) By painting a picture of unremitting oppression of Blacks and failing to adequately limn the recent sea changes in civil rights, the NEA implies drastic options for Black children of resignation or rebellion. These are options which Martin Luther King and Hubert Humphrey, Roy Wilkins and President Lyndon Johnson, the NAACP, Urban League and human-rights organizations which successfully captained the civil-

rights revolution eschewed in vindicated preference for reliance
on law and public opinion. With law and with supportive public
opinion, Martin Luther King's "dream" became animated, its
promise of full citizenship even now maturing. The alternative
of what's-the-use despair, a not unlikely reaction to the teachers' bleak assessment, can well dissipate the dream, its place to
be wrested by personal and social nightmares. Propaganda can
take root, but that doesn't make of it education.

Effective police work is suited to frustrating already-in-place
Klansmen. But police work is a shield; no more. Education can
at one and the same time inoculate us against our own baser
natures and in doing so thin racism's future ranks. Because the
educational establishment is so dominant a factor in our culture, because the Klan, for all that it is historically in a recessive
period, has the potential for rising again, multiplying its terror,
the success of our educational efforts is of vital importance. At
this point, however, the NEA gets commendation for its declared intentions and our hope that it will do more homework
in American history before taking on the Ku Klux Klan. To do
so counterproductively is not much better, if better at all, than
doing nothing.

The Jewish perception of the Klan is a more dimensioned
portrait of the beholder than of the beheld. The fear of being
imperiled and a commitment to the ogre's freedom would seem
to be incongruous, too incompatible for most people; certainly
for Jews whose ogres have been real, their flesh heated, their
blood cold. But Jews, for better or worse, though just like most
people, also aren't. In a 1981 survey of Jews in the San Francisco area, its Jewish Community Relations Council found that
the Jews' long and simultaneously held apprehensions concerning Nazis and the Ku Klux Klan and their affinity for civil
liberties remain in balanced place.

Nine out of ten polled agreed that "anti-Semitic acts are

increasing in the United States." Eighty-four percent were of the opinion that "anti-Semitic organizations are growing in the United States." Sixty-three percent believe that the Ku Klux Klan "is a major threat to the Jews." And yet, 93% agreed with the proposition that "it is good for the Jews that the Constitution protects everyone's right to free speech, whether we like what they say or not"!

Asked to "strongly agree," "somewhat agree," "somewhat disagree" or "strongly disagree," with the affirmation that neo-Nazi and KKK meetings should be broken up by private citizens, 82% disagreed, and 56% did so "strongly." Moreover, no matter that 90% were of the opinion that anti-Semitic acts are on the increase and 84% that anti-Semitic organizations are growing in strength, a strong 60% opposed "a law against the public expression of anti-Semitism."

How supremely rational. We seem at one and the same time to be indulging our nervous suspicions while holding fast to our civil-liberties blanket that while it shelters our enemies, secures us as well. The Constitution, we seem to be saying, is a safer harbor than anti-Semitism is a killer storm. Earl Raab, however, expresses a less romantic, perhaps more flattering, perhaps less flattering, view. "If Jews *really* believed that the Nazis were a serious threat at this time, fewer would be so strongly opposed to breaking up their meetings. Jews engaged rather freely in the breaking up of Nazi meetings in the United States in the 1930s, when, of course, they *were* fully perceived as a real and present danger."

If the Klan's violence is a familiar handiwork, darkly reminiscent of long nights of fear, and is, for suggesting the past, a spur to our forebodings, we have become conscious of a new violence, more surprising than frightening. Anti-Semitic vandalisms. In 1978, the ADL reported 49 cases. In 1979 the attacks against Jewish institutions rose to 120. In 1980 the reported cases zoomed to 377 and by 1981, that last figure, itself triple its predecessor, more than doubled. We are talking of cases reported to the ADL. However, surveys reveal that only a fraction of such depredations are formally brought to the League's attention. But it is neither the fact nor the nature of the vandalisms that are puzzling—to manifested anti-Semitism, one's conditioned response is, so what else is new?—rather is it that in the large majority of instances in which the culprits have been apprehended they turn out to be youths—or shall we say in their tender youth? To be sure, crime is up too: muggings, rapes, murders; and inhibitions are down: film violence as entertainment, the commonplace currency of pornography, the over-the-counter availability of divorce complete with disposable families. So why not an upward trajectory for anti-Semitism, not as old as Cain, but as violence the durability of which—given its age, one might say the venerability of which—matches and exceeds most.

The phenomenon we are discussing excuses acts of vandalism or assaults against Jews, the motivation for which is theft or free-floating aggression. The included cases, physical assaults, cross burnings on Jewish-owned property, swastika and anti-Semitic graffiti on Jewish property, are ones in which Jew hatred has been the visitor's calling card.

Two-thirds of the 1981 nationwide total of vandalisms are accounted for by four states, New York, California, New Jersey and Massachusetts. Illinois and Florida are right behind.

Data reveal that in addition to being young teenagers the junior anti-Semites are mostly white, from middle-class neighborhoods, and in New York, according to a New York Police Department source, usually from a Roman Catholic family.

In the immediately preceding two short paragraphs, two long-standing popular wisdoms have been jostled. Religious bigotry and inferior education have been long coupled. But New York, California, New Jersey and Massachusetts boast the nation's better educational systems. Bigotry has long been attributed to the deprivations of poverty. These haters, however, are from middle-class homes.

But there is a third curiosity in the statistics of juvenile marauding against Jews which puts in question the old saw that getting to know each other is an antidote to prejudice. The states the leaders in this melancholy hit parade are those with major Jewish populations, places presumably in which the cliché, After you get to know him, you'll like him, would prove out. But not so. Anti-Semitic vandalisms have sprouted where Jewish and gentile youths are, if not on the same wavelength, side by side in school.

As long ago as 1975, Charles Glock, Robert Wuthnow, Jane Allyn Piliavin and Metta Spencer in their study, "Adolescent Prejudice," saw it coming. They surveyed gentile adolescents in three communities, one of which had a 43% Jewish school population, another, a 23% Jewish school population, and the third, .5%. The significant finding was that the greater the Jewish numbers, the more negative the gentile youths' anti-Jewish stereotypes; the fewer the Jews, the lesser the measure of gentile animus. Given the high-scoring academic performance of the Jewish students, Mark Twain's thesis of Austrians' resentful envy of Jews echoes down the high-school corridors of New York, California, New Jersey and Massachusetts. This envy factor, blended with parental shaping of our prejudices, was highlighted in a Long Island, New York, high-school incident in 1981. The school paper published a Valentine's Day message in the form of an advertisement. The love note read: "To the princesses. It's been a GAS knowing Yews. Meet us in the showers." The heart-shaped message, appropriate to romantic Valentine's Day, also included a Star of David, lest any reader who was not familiar with the derogatory term *Jewish American Princess* miss the point. The capital letters for gas and the reference to "showers," the Nazi's method for wholesale

extermination of Jews, was self-explanatory. Following protests
and school-administration apologies, the mother of one of the
ad's sponsors told *Newsday* that her son had "suffered the
most."

"My son has suffered mentally from this. If those girls keep
flaunting their wealth, what can you expect?"

As in the instance of Klan and neo-Nazi activities and the
media's exaggeration of the measure and imminence of their
social impact, so is the social significance of these vandalisms,
outrageous though individually they are, often exaggerated in
their very discussion. Nor is the distortion attributable solely to
the media, which after all is simply the messenger. The swastika, the burning cross, painted hate messages to Jews to "get
out," abrade aching wounds not yet scar-tissue protected. Our
memory, more so than press clippings, is our seismograph. Still,
the figures, no matter they shock, without proportions are misleading truths. The doubling, tripling or quadrupling of 1 is a
far cry from the doubling, tripling or quadrupling of 100,000.
And while the rate of growth of anti-Semitic vandalisms is
ample reason for concern, some 900 instances in a population
of 240,000,000 does not suggest budding pogroms. It is also
both comforting and discomforting that in the several years of
ADL's monitoring of anti-Semitic vandalisms they seem overwhelmingly to be the acts of loners or duets, sometimes triads,
rather than the planned forays of organized hate organizations.
Comforting, because youthful, individual, *ad hoc* actions are
more an expression of individual psychopathy, while organized
hate-group actions would be evidence of a broader, deeper social malaise. Discomforting, because our image of a bigot is the
mean-eyed, cruel-lipped Klansman, or the genteel guardian of
the "Christians only" executive suite, and hardly the kid next
door with the freckled face and the apple cheeks.

In executive session the ADL has worried about the wisdom of releasing its data on anti-Semitic vandalisms. Beyond our awareness that the shock of our arithmetic is more newsworthy than our cushioning dicta—the relative size of the American population and the overall rise in violent crime—there has been another nagging argument against releasing the information. Does one in making public the extent of the dramatic and provocative depredations further advertise violence? Are we ourselves by broadcasting successfully executed anti-Semitic acts triggering new ones, setting in motion a self-fulfilling prophecy? These are not easily negated arguments. In opting to override them, in the decision to release the information, it is not so much an evidence that the propublicizing arguments have clearly prevailed as it is an indication that in weighing the arguments, the go-ahead-and-release-the-data arguments, netted out, seem, admittedly subjectively, to be more compelling. Essentially these arguments are that a Jewish organization charged with the security of its people would be hard pressed to justify having hidden burgeoning truths. There is an essence of liability in refusing to see an unpleasant truth. To see it and to hide it converts that liability into culpability. Also, the proverb of the squeaking door and its being favored with lubricating oil argues for making the bad news public. And indeed, in 1981 eight states—Arizona, California, Maryland, New Jersey, New York, Oregon, Rhode Island and Washington—have enacted statutes specifically aimed at racial and religious vandalisms. Nor is the ugly phenomenon restricted to Jews. Testifying before the subcommittee on criminal justice of the Judiciary Committee of the U.S. House of Representatives in 1981, William Reynolds, chief of the civil-rights division of the Justice Department, informed the legislators: "There are repeated instances of Black families terrorized by crosses set ablaze and of immigrants and refugees assaulted because of their race or national origin." And Governor Hughes of Maryland, testifying before the same committee, candidly told its members, "Our first tendency was not to speak out, not to give legitimacy to these abhorrent acts. There has been, over the past year, however, a growing consensus that silence condones."

What is needed now that state legislatures have bestirred themselves is responsive judiciary action. When Johnny sees that Jimmy is scot-free, punished if punished at all by the requirement to write an essay on brotherhood as chastisement for defiling a synagogue or intimidating Black neighbors, he understands that society does not seriously revile criminal hate. Absent credible punishment, Johnny is a candidate for imitative behavior. Indeed, Jimmy is a candidate for recidivism. In another but not unrelated context, New York's Mayor Koch has told the story of his addressing a meeting of senior citizens and telling them of a judge of his acquaintance who had been mugged. Subsequently, the judge convened a press conference and declared that the mugging would in no way affect his judicial decisions in sentencing muggers. At this point in the mayor's story he was interrupted by an elderly lady who called out: "Then mug him again."

Our point is that there are theorists and disciplines properly concerned with abstract philosophies of crime and punishment and justice and properly concerned with the dynamics of criminal behavior, but our violence-ridden times are ripe for considering as a priority the defense of the victim. The victim's defense, more so than conjectural explanations of criminal behavior, is vital to the very defense of our values and societal security. A first step in this direction would be the exaction of a felt price from the culprit, both as a deterrent to him, minimally operative for the length of his sentence, and as a clear message to would-be imitators, that vandalism simply isn't worth the advertised price.

Given the evidences of juvenile anti-Semitism, given the evidences of adult anti-Semitism, at least one lesson seems certain: We outgrow our youth sooner than we do our prejudices.

Taking us beneath the act itself of bigoted violence, deeper, finely deeper into the very seed of contemporary anti-Semitism, Nikos Kazantzakis in his *Report to Greco* wrote a volume in a paragraph. Recalling his young boyhood, he wrote:

> The sound of certain words excited me terribly—it was fear I felt most often, not joy. Especially Hebrew words, for I knew from my grandmother that on Good Friday the Jews took Christian children and tossed them into a trough lined with spikes and drank their blood. Often times it seemed to me that a Hebrew word from the Old Testament was a spike lined trough and that someone wanted to throw me in.

A Greek boy and his nightmare. A million boys, millions of boys, each of them and all of them nightmared by Jews. Towheaded German children, blond Polish children, chubby Austrian children, all of them growing older, all of them nightmare-haunted. Suddenly they are men, boys grown older, but still men and their fear has turned to resentment, and muscled now and shrewder, they have available recourse more fitting manhood than their grandmother's protecting bosom.

Imagine! The anti-Semitic graffiti, no, the very crematoria, were committed in self-defense! They are an old score finally settled.

And they tell us Jews are too sensitive.

10

Petrodollars and Durrenmatt's Whore

As SHOULD BE by now evident, neither anti-Semitism nor Jews have rid themselves of each other. And, as we have earlier remarked, the anti-Semite doesn't really require our presence to indulge his passion. We might have changed our name or our nose, might be in the ovens or in Israel; it doesn't really matter to him. In a kind of masturbation turgid with hate, his climax requires only the dream of us. For Jews, however, reacting to anti-Semitism is somewhat more complicated. Victims, that very status evidence that they are outnumbered, outgunned, reach in desperation for rational responses, but alas logic is a less wieldy weapon than bully muscle. To react at all or not to react? When does our response magnify the anti-Semite's volume? When does our silence, either strategied or fearful, for leaving a canard unchallenged give it the appearance of substance; for leaving it unchecked, an open field? But these are long-lived, familiar considerations. There are newer, more involved conundrums facing us today.

It is our contention that Jews today face greater jeopardy from quarters which though innocent of bigotry, nonetheless pose us greater danger than do our long time, easily recognizable, anti-Semitic nemeses. Unchallenged and unchecked, these issues in surface appearance Semitically neutral, can hurt Jews and resisted as need be, can loose once again classical anti-Semitism. It's already happening. Prominent among these seemingly a-Semitic issues are (1) oil and our economy's reliance on recycling home massively expended petrodollars; (2) neo-isolationism and the lure, as distinguished from the reality, of peace; (3) attempts to tamper with our democratic system toward the end of institutionalizing group rights in favor of individual rights.

These issues and their often not unfriendly proponents are more mischievous for Jews than our familiar enemies because full-time anti-Semites are today small-time retailers of worn wares. The Klansmen and the neo-Nazis are today no more than socially scrawny imitations of their once politically meaningful forebears, while uptown, the very fact of whispered anti-Semitism is testimony to its low estate. But foreign policy, as it is shaped by oil and by petrodollars, has wholesale implications for American Jews and—to paraphrase the classical lexicon of anti-Semites—for international Jewry. Moreover, the issues of which we speak, because they are more subtly nuanced than scowling anti-Semitism, because among their propounders are nice people, their moderate contentions in pastel distinction from Black and white anti-Semitica have a lulling quality, divide and confuse Jews whose barricades are practiced to withstand frontal attacks.

The Reagan administration's United States Senate victory in the AWACS debate of 1981 was a textbook illustration of how an essentially a-Semitic issue, as reasonable on its face as Dr. Jekyll, turned quickly wrathful, assuming the mien of Dr. Hyde. The question before the Senate was whether to sell or not to sell to Saudi Arabia sophisticated Airborne Warning and Control Systems, sidewinder missiles and sundry enhancements for F-15 fighter planes.

Several weeks before the vote I received an invitation to luncheon with a senior administration official. The conversation, following appetizers and niceties, was about the AWACS issue. We talked round and round, his views the predictable expression of his responsibilities; mine, no less predictably, the expression of my responsibilities. It was an amiable standoff. Later, driving me to Washington's National Airport, the conversation now about this and that, I reverted to it, suggesting that it was my feeling that had an impartial eavesdropper overheard our respective arguments on the desirability of supplying the Saudis with the AWACS, he might well have decided that the call was a close one. The official agreed that it was indeed a close call. Pursuing what I sensed was a useful opening, I evenly offered, "You know, we were both somewhat hypocritical." And I explained that my own arguments that the Saudis would not be placated by AWACS, would not be beguiled to the point of making peace were pure speculation, convenient to my bottom-line opposition to the sale, but no more than speculation. "And your prognosis," I continued, "that the Saudis would be converted by the sale is also speculation, guesswork to buttress your bottom-line position." Chuckling, he again agreed.

"So tell me," I asked, "if the merits make for a near draw, and we're both self-servingly guessing the Saudis' response, why is the administration pushing its case so hard?"

We had arrived at the airport and his response, as matter of fact as small talk between friends, was, save for Thanks for the ride and See you, the curtain line: "Nate, do you know how much money eight and a half *billion* dollars is?"

Stripped of side issues, arching over the conflicting interests of the debate's *dramatis personae,* the core question before the Senate was: Would the AWACS and F-15 enhancements render Israel, our most credible ally in the Middle East, more vulnerable to its enemies, or would it in securing American interests in the Persian Gulf also thereby serve Israel's long-range interests? By a narrow fifty-two to forty-eight vote the sale carried. Presumably then, the Senate was affirming the administration's argument that the sale furthered American interests in the Persian Gulf and over a period of time would be good for Israel as well. Perhaps. Perhaps too and alternatively, the Senate's vote was more a reflection of the lobbying influence of the issue's contending special interest groups than it was of an august deliberative body pondering preconditions of war and peace.

Israel and its supporters in the American Jewish community were prominent in the long jockeying for position with the Senate. They were concerned with the consequences for Israeli security from a dramatically upgraded improvement in Saudi weaponry. Recalling Crown Prince Fahd's January, 1981, rallying call for Arabs and Moslems to mount "a persistent and long drawn-out *jihad*" (holy war) against Israel, followed in April by Sheik Ahmed Yamani's flat-out appraisal of the Soviet Union as a "potential danger" but Israel as "an actual danger," they were skeptical of administration assurances that the Saudis were moderates. Besides, they worriedly maintained, Saudi moderation was belied by its infusion of hundreds of millions of dollars into PLO arms budgets. As for the United States' need to monitor movements and actions in the Persian Gulf not otherwise detectable, both Israel and its American lobbyists pointed to the four AWACS, American manned, currently patrolling the desert empire's skies. Why not keep them in place, they argued.

To assume that the forty-eight senators who voted against the sale or the three-hundred-and-some Congressmen who also voted against it were a measure of either Prime Minister Begin's persuasiveness or the American Jewish community's influence would be to flatter both. Jewish opposition to the sale was augmented by an odd couple. Defense-minded senators, apprehensive lest the Iranian scenario in which the Ayatollah Khomeini reaped the military harvest sown by the Shah be replayed in Saudi Arabia, coupled with senators who, consistent with their previous opposition to the sale of arms to Israel in the conviction that an arms race was a precursor to war, opposed this sale as well. In short, Jews, split personalities historically preeminent in peace movements but contemporaneously an embattled and battling David, ironically were joined by an aviary of hawks and doves.

By a margin of two to one, the American press agreed with them.

Squaring off against the Israeli lobby was the Saudi lobby, albeit President Reagan's admonition that American foreign policy should not be dictated by any foreign power was generally interpreted as intended for Israeli mulling. The interests of both nations were politically natural. They were pursuing their national interests, else what's a government for? In its arguments supportive of Israel, the American Jewish community, whether ably or inadequately, whether wisely or mistakenly, was declaring its foreboding that the sale would offset Israel's military edge, invite, again, war. Said otherwise, lobbying American Jews were propelled by their troubled love. Not so the Saudis' American surrogates. The aerodynamics industry, the oil industry, the military industrial complex all understood how much $8.5 billion is. As in the case of an ages-old software industry, they were doing it for the money. Joseph Pulitzer IV, writing for the *St. Louis Post-Dispatch* during the debate, reported a White House denial that it was coordinating industrial support for the sale because, the spokesman admitted, the companies "haven't needed much pushing. It's simply a matter of dollars and cents."

As the Senate readied itself for a vote, Mobil, in a blitz of full-page advertisements, cofeatured greed and candor:

> There is more to Saudi Arabia than oil. Saudi Arabia means trade, jobs, and favorable implications for the U.S. balance of payments. Consider these facts:
> More than *700 American companies* are now doing business with Saudi Arabia.
> The enterprises involved extend to *42 states,* to businesses large and small—contractors, subcontractors, suppliers.

The ad went on to say that, not including oil interests, American businesses hold work contracts with Saudia Arabia well in excess of $35 billion, and that these contracts involve a wide and diverse range of enterprises, including weather stations, chains of supermarkets, construction of pertochemical and tire manufacturing plants, shipbuilding and hospitals.

And if Jews made no bones about their promptings as lobbyists—fear for Israel's safety—the military industrial complex was no less guileless. In bold, black letters, the Mobil ads declared: "Saudi Arabia: far more than oil . . . $35 billion in business for U.S. firms." As a subtheme to their devotion to Israel, the Jews had stressed American self-interests in the Middle East. The subtheme of the corporate giants' paeans to profit bespoke arms plants jobs, balance of trade figures, the firmness of the United States dollar abroad, the reduction in per AWACS cost to the United States military in the consummation of the Saudi sale. In the vote, hard facts about ranges and microgadgetry, about wingspans and balance of payments were more resonant than importunings that the Saudis meant what they said about a *jihad* against Israel. Salesmen—their clients arms merchants, their reward commissions—prevailed over Jews, their keepers their brothers, their reward that they tried hard.

To this point the AWACS case history is an account of an a-Semitic issue—AWACS, like oil, is neither anti- nor philo-Semitic—which impacts Jewish interests far more seriously than garden-variety anti-Semitism. But our proposition also maintained that resisted, Semitically neutral issues "can loose once again classical anti-Semitism."

Its jab was from a bare fist, its punch was delivered in a velvet glove.

Richard Nixon publicly chastised Israel and American Jews for their lobbying efforts. They alone were foiling American interests. No matter the adversaries in the debate numbered the proverbial cast of thousands, including Arab sheiks, hundreds of American companies doing or aspiring to do business in Saudi Arabia, lobbyists working for princely retainers, Nixon saw only the specter of Jews. His crude appeal to latent anti-Semitism fired. Senators as diversely divided in their constituencies and their political philosophies as Texas' John Tower, Oregon's Mark Hatfield and New York's Daniel Patrick Moynihan reported a rising tide of anti-Semitism in the debate. New York Senator Alphonse D'Amato spoke of the "incredible, terrible, unbelievable letters he was receiving; David Durenberger, the senator from Minnesota, said, "I have never experienced anything like this in my life, in terms of basic prejudice." But it was anti-Semitism's velvet glove that provided the points for the administration's victory.

It was as cunning as it was persuasive. It simply maintained that it would be better for Jews to lose than to win. It was, in Moynihan's view, "the principal strategy used" to convert senators opposed to the sale on its merits nonetheless to vote its passage. "We were told—by some of the most eminent figures in American public life—that the defeat of the AWACS would soon or late bring forth a violent anti-Semitic reaction and that as none of us would wish to be responsible for that, it was clearly our duty to vote for the sale of arms to a nation which, among other things, had once called for a holy war against Israel and an effort to 'cleanse Jerusalem of the Jews.' " This threat of impending anti-Semitism was suggestive of a chapter in a Mafia manual on how to make money from "protection." Nice people give in to protection and nice senators staved off anti-Semitism by submitting to it.

The Saudis were, of course, no less entitled to lobby their interests than was Israel. The military industrial complex, no matter profit its spur, was no less entitled to lobby its interests than Jews, alarmed faith their spur. The administration was patently justified in pursuing its strategy in quest of peace through mollifying Saudis, no matter its opposition's reservations. But anti-Semitism had rudely burst into the forum, foul had been called by Republican and Democratic senators, by supporters and opponents of the sale, and the president said nothing. Anti-Semitism in the White House? No. Simply that the perceived advantages—the high-roll gamble on the Saudis, huge profits, and given the issue's development, presidential face—mattered more than interests vital to the beleaguered Jewish state, more than anti-Semitism against Americans.

The Jewish stake in the AWACS debate aside—it was, after all, influenced by remembered Jewish devastations and by apprehensive forebodings both more relevant to personal psychology than to military science—the debate's dynamics do not augur well for future confrontations on issues affecting Jewish interests. Jews lost this debate despite powerful allies whose arguments that the sale was inimicable to American interests were based on the demonstrated unreliability of Saudi Arabia as an American ally and the acknowledged instability of its very government. When in the foreseeable future the Saudis press for a PLO state or for the bisection of Jerusalem, the price of oil and the recycling of petrodollars their leverage—issues not as readily definable as impinging on American security interests as

the controversial AWACS debate—how will Israel fare then?
And how readily will anti-Semitism, its bared teeth and its
gloved fist, be used? For surely the American Jewish community, by and large, will not, on these issues, acquiescently maintain silence.

   Governments are not given to acknowledging that their
kneeling is a genuflection. They would have it that they are
groveling because they are looking for something. In matters
related to Middle East oil, for lost peace. So it is that neither
President Reagan nor President Carter, in whose administration the sale of AWACS and F-15 enhancements was conceived, spoke openly of balance of payments, of recycling
petrodollars and like workaday mundane matters. Rather their
sales talk was of the beneficence of peace, of their administration's commitment to it, and for a mighty nation bordered by
Canada and Mexico, patronizingly, of the requirement of Israel
to chance further sacrifices for peace. A government's moral
capitulation requires that its shame be masked in the guise of
high moral purpose. American Jews, however, will assuredly
continue to resist policies which threaten Israel's security. It is
at this point that old-fashioned anti-Semitism can meld with
a-Semitic actions themselves infectious of Jewish interests. In
their political dissent, Jews may then see themselves charged by
sundry spokesmen as having dual loyalties. Richard Nixon's
reemergence in national discourse bore the seed of this accusa-
tion; the currency given "Begin vs. Reagan" as a slogan purporting to encapsulate the diverse issues in the AWACS debate
foretold the charge's still handy availability. And if administrations dissemble by feigning patriotic fervor to camouflage
political cowardice, the Mobils and the arms merchants, their
constituencies single-minded stockholders rather than a mul-
tipurposed electorate, speak more forthrightly. How distant
from the Mobil advertisements linking jobs to assuagement of

the Saudis is the implication that Jews are insensitive to unemployment, favor Israel over the American worker?

The case history, continued.

Shortly after the Senate vote I shared a platform with Secretary of Defense Caspar Weinberger and former President Gerald Ford. The occasion, a testimonial dinner in which the three of us were featured speakers, presented me with an opportunity to indulge candor without fear of interruptions. After all, dinner guests at New York's Plaza Hotel are more often sedate than irate, and besides, the speaking format, one following the other rather than a roundtable discussion, foreclosed punching in clinches.

In my remarks I stipulated that a vote against the AWACS sale was no less an expression of Americanism than a vote for the sale, and that a vote favoring the sale was on its face no more suggestive of being anti-Israel or anti-Jewish than a vote against the sale. My evenhandedness thusly established, I ratcheted feeling up a notch by deploring the injection into the debate of "nonrelevant, even mean-spirited innuendo." Bearing down now on my point, very much conscious of Weinberger's stewardship of the sale and of Ford's indebtedness to Nixon, I continued, "When a former president of the United States, even as Prince Bandar of Saudi Arabia was lavishly lobbying Washington, attributes opposition to the sale solely to Prime Minister Begin and to American Jews, this tack, plainly said, pulls the cork, lets loose the genie of anti-Semitism and its crony, dual loyalty." Next, Weinberger more than Nixon in my craw and in my mind, the former, after all being "in," the latter "out," I delivered my oratorically couched message: "The prospect of anti-Semitism will not silence American Jews. We have learned too well, in too many lands and in too many times, that hiding in silence simply doesn't work. *Sha sha* is a historically discredited strategy for Jews. We will not voluntarily surrender the freedom of speech for which we have so long struggled. To do so would serve neither democracy nor ourselves."

End of account of indignant forensic performance; beginning of surprise turn in story.

My seat on the dais was next to Ford's. When I completed my remarks and resumed my place, the former president turned to me and inquired, "You meant Nixon?" Mildly amused, I answered, "Of course." Amused because there being only three living former presidents, himself one of them, and only Nixon having been reported as making the statement to which I had alluded, that he should feel prompted to ask the question.

The next morning the press and television having broadcast my remarks, I received several calls making identical inquiries. The first call's thrust suffices for this story. My caller inquired whether in my remarks concerning a former president I was talking of President Ford, and what was his reaction. Surprised, I answered, "No. Nixon. In fact Ford asked me about it too. What on earth makes you think it was Ford?" The answer—this call was from Boston, later corroborating calls came from Washington, D.C., and Los Angeles—was that days before the Senate vote a Republican senator opposed to the sale, while meeting with several opponents of the sale, was interrupted by a message that he was wanted on the phone. He left and minutes later, returning to the group, told them the call was from Gerald Ford soliciting his vote for the sale. Then, as the phrase goes, more in sorrow than in anger, that Jerry had urged him not to let the Jews win on this.

Suddenly Ford's curiosity the night before simply casual, now rang cagily defensive. He had probed me not so much to have me reveal Nixon's culpability as in my doing so, to assure himself that his was concealed.

President Ford, Mr. Nice Guy, is not an anti-Semite. To classify him as one would drain the term of its toxic meaning. But to grant this does not obviate the nearness of anti-Semitism to the skin of our discourse. The stakes were high. So high, that all the stops of political horse trading were pulled, all the levers of party loyalty were leaned on, perquisites and punishments, the stock of a party in office were respectively promised and threatened. Tactical anti-Semitism was too.

President Nixon is a tape-exposed anti-Semite. Gerald Ford's lifelong decency is well known. In the clutch of this highly staked issue, however, the villain publicly exhibited his anti-Semitism, the good guy, publicly eschewing it, privately dipped his toe in it.

In Friedrich Durrenmatt's story, "The Visit," a wealthy whore comes to town and offers its good townspeople an enormous fortune. The *quo* for her *quid* is that they kill one of their number, a popular fellow whom she happens to hate. Appalled and repelled by her hideous proposal, the villagers categorically refuse. The whore, a patient sort, lets her offer stand. At first slowly, but soon with gathering momentum, the lure of the fortune's appeal grows as inversely the marked man's popularity wanes. Shortly the burghers, so recently protective of their townsman, turn on him. His being alive, wedge that it is between them and the riches in their offing, assumes the appearance of intransigent selfishness. So for the common good, they kill him.

Before the Yom Kippur War of 1973, before the OPEC cartel's quantum jump in the price of oil, before the cascading outflow of dollars, francs, pounds, marks, lira and yen from industrial powers to Arab sheikdoms, before the urgent requirement of them to tourniquet their bleeding treasuries and to recycle their gushing money through sales and proffered investment opportunities to Arab powers, the West's foreign policy in the Middle East reflected its disapproval of bellicose Arab dictatorships while manifesting sympathy for the beleaguered democracy in their midst, Israel.

After 1973, with the visitation of Arab petrodiplomacy, the Durrenmatt syndrome came into play.

By 1981 the Treasury Department's estimates counted $57.5 billion of recycled Arab OPEC investments in the United States. The Federal Reserve System estimated an additional $29.3 billion invested in foreign branches of United States banks. Arab oil dollars returning as investments to the United States through camouflaged money centers in the Netherlands Antilles, British Virgin Islands, the Bahamas, Grand Cayman and Panama, raise these Croesus figures to at least $100 billion.

Before 1973 American military sales to Saudi Arabia amounted to $300 million. By 1981, even prior to the AWACS sale, Saudi orders for American military weapons and supplies totalled $21 billion, seven and one half times the size of pending Israeli orders. The more the Saudis spent and invested, the more our eyes beheld them as being "moderate."

The lion's share of Britain's, France's, West Germany's, Italy's and Japan's oil is supplied by the Arab members of OPEC. Their respective pounds, francs, marks, lira and yen in payment for their fuel have hemorrhaged their treasuries and spurred their competition with each other and with the United States for Arab favor, investments and arms markets.

Post-1973 in the course of seeking balm for its economy's Saudi-inflicted wounds, West Germany's Chancellor Helmut Schmidt—unlike Mobil's capitalist board members, a Socialist—suddenly discovered Saudi Arabia's policies to be "moderate and moderating" and West Germany's "friendship" with the Saudi oligarchy as "based not only on moral grounds but also on certain parallel interests." This accommodating assessment followed Sheik Yamani's stipulation that the Jewish state, not the Soviet Union, was Saudi Arabia's main enemy.

Greece, long oil-dependent on the Persian Gulf, anxious also for Arab backing in its disputes with Turkey, an issue devoid of any relationship whatsoever to anti-Semitism, has under its new Socialist government upgraded the diplomatic status of the PLO. Toasting the archetype of twentieth-century terrorism, Prime Minister Andreas Papandreous, legatee of the "glory that was Greece," addressed him: "You, brother Yasir Arafat, are the epitome of popular struggles for freedom and independence."

The reverberations of the oil embargo and its subsequent soaring oil prices rocked the foundations of Japan's economy. Seventy percent of Japan's fuel imports are from the Middle East. Moreover, Japanese estimates project the archipelago as becoming the world's thirstiest importer of oil in the years ahead. On the other side of her oil ledger, with the onset of petroeconomics, more than fifty Japanese concerns are involved in a single Saudi undertaking, the construction of the industrial city of Jubail. Billions of dollars are involved. And so with smiling complaisance, in courteously hissed amenities pitched for Saudi ears, and with nary an anti-Semite from the Ryukus to Hokkaido, Japan's foreign ministry welcomed Arafat. "We regard the PLO as an important organization. We don't regard them as a bunch of terrorists."

Since 1973 the governments of England, France, the Netherlands, Italy, indeed, the European Economic Community partners have grown increasingly solicitous of the Arab nations while simultaneously they have distanced themselves from the erstwhile object of their favor, Israel. The lure of the Arabs: oil and the promise of profits. The repellent of Israel: not Jews as such, no, not at all, but that the state of Israel, collective Jewry's religious and psychic anchor, is simply in the way of the lure.

The European Economic Community professes the motive of merely seeking to stave off a renewed Middle Eastern war. To that declared end it has formally called for the PLO to be part of the Middle East peace process. No matter EEC member France has turned a deaf ear to the national aspirations of the Alsatians, Basques, Bretons and Corsicans; no matter EEC member Spain has refused autonomy to the Valencians and the Galicians, let alone rebuffed the separatist movements of the Basques and the Catalans; no matter EEC member Great Britain has incorporated the national movements of Northern Ireland, Scotland and Wales and there are more tranquil silences on the West Bank's front than in Belfast's streets; no matter EEC member Belgium has turned deaf ears to demands for autonomy by its Flemings and Walloons; the EEC prescribes self-determination and a sovereign state for the Palestinians whose PLO in its very charter commits it to the murder of Israel.

Belle France beds with the cruel Iraqi government, liaisons with the mad Libyan government and Tories and Socialists, monarchies and democracies, old Allies and the Axis of old wait in line for seconds, while all lecture Israel on her manners. If, on some tomorrow morning, Israel is again attacked, but this time more awesomely in its consequences, by Arab-purchased, made-in-France, or made-in-America, or made-in-West Germany tanks and planes, for their not being a participant in the *jihad,* the West's hands will be cleaner than Durrenmatt's townsmen's, but with the guilt nonetheless which civilized mankind reserves for murder's accomplices. To be sure, there are gradations of guilt for homicide. Intent counts and our intentions of record are to further the prospects of peace. But alas, there are no gradations in death, no extenuating circumstances to modify the duration of its sentence on the grounds that the accomplice really, honest-injun, likes Jews and intended only to make a buck.

11

Peace, the United Nations and Jews

JEWS PRIDE THEMSELVES as being the People of the Book, an honorific, if frequency of practiced orthodoxy is accepted in evidence, more an inherited one than an earned one. What we unquestionably are is a people of words. There are so few of us, not 1% of the world's population, and yet we are so visible, so audible, so ubiquitous a presence. Perhaps Darwin explains why. Perhaps so long outnumbered and not infrequently hunted, so long dispersed and wandering, chronically short of balances to power, words have been our quills, talons, fangs, our not so secret weapons of survival, and in a process of natural selection, we have survived because words have served us as fleetness has the deer, as his shell the turtle.

Because we are a people of words, words, words—the accused tend to explain, explain, explain—we have, tropismically, sought refuge in peace movements. Wars and national tensions

245

have ever discomforted Jews, so often scapegoated by both sides. Indeed and ironically, even during World War II, a war launched by history's grizzliest anti-Semite, surveys of the American people, history's longest assembly-line producers of popular democracy, revealed high levels of anti-Semitism even among Nazism's challengers. So it is that when the war ended, when the ovens cooled, when the concentration camps' survivors began their hesitant, enfeebled journey back to the living, Jews—especially Jews—longingly welcomed the United Nations. It would make peace through talking, not warring, and talking was a demilitarized zone; it was Jewish turf.

And talk it has. But for Jewry and for peace, communicating more the chill of political danger than the warmth of a social hearth. On issues throbbing with human pathos it has even been mute. The United Nations' euphemistically titled Human Rights Commission has never uttered a word about Soviet anti-Semitism; it has been silent in the face of national and religious repression by Syria and by Iraq; it has been functionally indifferent to the slaughter of hundreds of thousands of political dissidents by the Indonesian dictatorship; it said nothing when Libya invaded Chad; it said naught to encourage Poland's Solidarity movement; its records are devoid of a brief in defense of Andre Sakharov; it has failed to protest the Communist genocide in Cambodia; India's oppression of millions of Untouchables goes unremarked; it ignored Uganda's racist expulsion of scores of thousands of Asians, let alone Idi Amin's mass murders of his countrymen; the genocide practiced upon the Ibos by Nigeria, by the Pakistanis against the Bengalis, by the Burundis against the Hutus were accompanied by blood-curdling screams the United Nations pretended not to hear, resulted in steaming rivers of blood it pretended not to see.

But still there are the words. For Jews, long of counsel for the United Nations against the John Birch Society's bill of particulars, the U.N.'s verbal assault on November 10, 1975, the thirtieth anniversary of the Nazis' defeat, was a stunning sneak attack. On that day the General Assembly in formal resolution declared Zionism to be a form of racism. A British critic, Gorondwy Rees, was present for the linguistic mugging. Later, he was to describe it in historical perspective:

> There were ghosts haunting the Third Committee that day, the ghosts of Hitler and Goebbels and Julius Streicher, grinning with delight to hear not only Israel, but Jews as such, denounced in language which would have provoked hysterical applause at any Nuremberg rally . . .
>
> And there were other ghosts also at the debate, the ghosts of the 6,000,000 dead in . . . (the) extermination camps, listening to the same voices which had cheered and jeered and abused them as they made their way to the gas chambers. For the fundamental thesis advanced by the supporters of the resolution, and approved by the majority of the Third Committee, was that to be a Jew, and to be proud of it, and to be determined to preserve the right to be a Jew was to be an enemy of the human race.

In 1975 the inversion of the meaning of words was so blatant that thirty-five nations, their revulsion their conscience, cast their dissenting votes against the resolution which also condemned Zionism as a threat to world peace. By 1979 the Durrenmatt syndrome with no less sway in the world peace organization than among its constituent members, a like resolution evoked negative votes from only four countries, the United States, Canada and Australia alongside the defendant, Israel. In 1975 the European community voted against the resolution; in 1979 it abstained. In 1975 half of Black Africa refused its support for the resolution and five states braved a vote against it; in 1979 Black Africa supported the resolution.

Because international lip service continues to picture the United Nations as mankind's best hope for peace, its resolutions carry weighty propaganda value. The Soviet Union, not altogether insensitive to its image as anti-Semitic, by citing the authority of the United Nations can thereby launder its bigotry. Thus, in *Pionerskaya Pravda,* a weekly publication for children between the ages of nine and fourteen, it can maintain:

> Zionists try to penetrate all spheres of public life, as well as ideology, science and trade. Even Levi jeans contribute to their operations; the revenue obtained from the sale of these pants are used by the firm to help the Zionists.
>
> Most of the largest monopolies in the manufacture of arms are controlled by Jewish bankers. Business made on blood brings them enormous profits. Bombs and missiles explode in Lebanon—the bankers Lazards and Leibs are making money. Thugs in Afghanistan torment schoolchildren with gases—the bundles of dollars are multiplying in the safes of the Lehmans and Guggenheims. It is clear that Zionism's principal enemy—is peace on earth.
>
> The United Nations described Zionism as a form of racism and racial discrimination. More and more people today are beginning to realize that Zionism is present-day fascism.

Echoing the Soviet Union, providing stereo sound for the United Nations broadcasts, the so-called nonaligned nations in solemn session in Havana, in 1979, declared:

> The heads of state or government reaffirmed that racism, including zionism [*sic*], racial discrimination, and especially apartheid constitute crimes against humanity and represented violations of the United Nations Charter and of the Universal Declaration of Human Rights.

A detailed recapitulation of the United Nations' long list of anti-Israel votes, of the unrefuted anti-Semitica echoing in its chambers, would only add redundancy unnecessary to our stipulated premise that the peace-commissioned United Nations has become an arena for vicious assaults on Jewish interests. Still, one vote stands out, one vote surpasses even its

Zionism/racism equation. In 1980 the Security Council approved a resolution blandly identified as 465. In it, Israel was declared to be in "flagrant violation of the Fourth Geneva Convention." Now, the Fourth Geneva Convention is a 1949 treaty designed by the Allied Powers of World War II to codify the atrocities of the Nazis, as in their behavior at Auschwitz, to the end that such barbarities would thenceforth be internationally illegal. Not since the Convention's adoption had any nation been declared guilty of its violation—until the United Nations, including then United States Ambassador Donald McHenry, in solemn convocation declared Israel guilty.

Senator Moynihan, himself a former American ambassador to the United Nations, commenting incredulously on the publicly convened kangaroo court, observed: ". . . according to Resolution 465, Israel is an outlaw state, guilty of war crimes. Not the Vietnamese invaders of Cambodia, or the Soviets in Afghanistan. Israel!"

In 1980 the Security Council met seventy-seven times. In thirty-eight of these sessions, but one short of half its deliberative sessions, its needle stuck on Israel and the Middle East. It adopted eighteen resolutions, fully half of which were condemnatory of Israel. In the United Nations, Israel is a *de facto* as well as a *de jure* pariah—not the Soviet Union, not Cuba, not Libya—and is excluded from every one of its bodies other than the General Assembly. Even regional U.N. bodies as, for example, the Economic Commission of Western Asia, designed to include all the areas in the region, excludes Israel.

Nor is Israel the sole whipping boy in the United Nations' theater of scapegoat propaganda. In 1981 ninety-three member nations professing nonalignment produced a document maintaining that the United States is a threat to world peace and prosperity. Only the United States. It accused the United States of "aggression" for having downed two Libyan planes, no matter Colonel Qaddafi's admission that the Libyan planes had opened fire. The nonaligned nations "condemned" America for our "hostility" to the "inalienable rights" of Palestinian Arabs and for our links with Israel. They expressed their dismay with the arms race but singled out one weapon for criticism, the American neutron bomb. They made no reference to already deployed Soviet missiles in Europe. In fact, the Soviet bloc was not even mentioned in the document other than as victims of American machinations. Included in the twenty-one page guilty verdict against the United States was a condemnation of us for refusing to grant independence to Puerto Rico. No mention was made of the well-known fact that Puerto Ricans themselves have repeatedly voted to reject this available option. In 1978 on one of several previous occasions in which the United States was put down for its relationship with Puerto Rico, the vote of the General Assembly's Decolonization Committee was unanimous. Ten voted guilty; no votes to the contrary. The sheer—unmitigated, ordinarily a term used in exaggeration, in this instance is apt—hypocrisy of the vote is evident in the contrary desire of Puerto Ricans but even more so in the identity of the ten advocates of freedom. The Soviet Union, Iraq, Syria, Cuba, China, Bulgaria, Tanzania, Afghanistan, Chile and Czechoslavakia, all dictatorships.

The tint of rose in the lens of our expectations for the nascent United Nations is long faded. Like the love-nurtured infant grown matured and sardonic stranger, our then dreams for our seed have turned to fear of what we have wrought. The United Nations, a war-ravaged and weary world's hope for peace, is today an amalgam of 156 states, 75% of which are totalitarian or authoritarian regimes. It has failed to abort wars; it has failed to deliver peace. It has covered the social acne of dictatorships with the rouge of words; it has exaggerated the pores of democracies with distorting words. In the anguished eyes of Alexander Solzhenitsyn, "It is not a United Nations but a United Governments, in which those freely elected and those imposed by force and those which seized power by arms are all on a par. Through the mercenary bias of the majority, the U.N. jealously worries about the freedom of some peoples and pays no attention to the freedom of others."

"Is it good for the Jews?" is the refrain of vulnerable Jews the world over, worried on cue to changes in governments, changes in their policies. As a boy when mama worried it aloud in reaction to this or that world development, I reacted impatiently. Youth tends to universalism and my mother's self-reference threatened to delimit the bounds of my broader identification. Older now, she is wiser then. Jews have tended to care more for mankind than the world has cared for them. Surely this has been the case with the United Nations. William F. Buckley, Jr., once an American delegate to the United Nations, put it succinctly when looking back he characterized the U.N. as "the most concentrated assembly of anti-Semitism surely since Hitler's Germany."

But the child is indeed father to the man and if as adult Jews we have concluded that this United Nations ought be abandoned by the United States—because it is an amphitheater for the Esperanto of anti-Semitism—we nonetheless continue to hear universalism's promptings. Consequently we are tolerating audience to the question, Granted that the U.N. is bad for Jews, but is it good for America?

Seventy-one of the 156 member states of the United Nations contribute .01% of the $2.5 billion annual budget of the U.N. and its sundry specialized agencies. Another fifteen countries pay .02% each. More than half of the member nations together pay 1.75% of the total budget. Money-bloated Saudi Arabia, its surpluses in the billions of dollars, pays the U.N. the same amount as Israel, whose deficits are in the billions, .25% of the organization's budget. The Soviet Union, fountainhead of the anti-American diatribes that characterize U.N. rhetoric, provides under 12% of U.N. wherewithal while the United States, receptacle for the free flowing vitriol, contributes 25% of the budget.

If rational discourse and the bona fide intentions of its participants are prerequisites for the maintaining of peace, they have not been in evidence at the United Nations. Quite the contrary, the record bulges with calumnies of America as oppressor, while the U.N.'s budget mockingly portrays a suckered United States. The Reagan Administration has indicated that in 1983 United States contributions to the U.N. will be frozen. That's a beginning, a promising glimmer that we are recouping national pride. To be sure, cuts in U.N. funding can create undesired results. Who, with equanimity, can witness curtailed funds for programs to better the lives of children, of refugees? But is not this possibility the responsibility of the member nations of the U.N. no less than of Jews and of Americans? For Jews to stifle their objections to the U.N.—in the form of sharply cut American contributions and failing a U.N. turnabout, calling for withdrawal—for fear that a humanitarian program will resultantly suffer is tantamount to being voluntarily held hostage by political extortionists, of passively accepting anti-Jewish assaults. For Americans, continued membership or at the least, failure to avail ourselves of the political leverage in drastically cutting our contributions, provides putative respectability to a forum in which our enemies debase us while simultaneously we ourselves haplessly underwrite the platform for their defamations.

To be sure, the fact of peace far outweighs in treasure the coinage of abuse. And if the United Nations were to serve peace, defamation is a relatively small and affordable price. But no matter that here and there, sometimes real, sometimes tenuous, peace has happened, the United Nations has been an irrelevant bystander rather than a facilitating participant. It has no role in the groping courtship of the United States and China; it was irrelevant to the European security settlement; similarly in Middle East disengagement agreements; similarly in the

Zimbabwe settlement; similarly in the Egyptian-Israeli peace treaty. Indeed, it is an observable fact that when nations earnestly seek resolution of differences, they practice bilateral diplomacy while shunning the U.N.; when nations pursue propaganda advantages they turn to the United Nations.

Alas for Jews, it is not a demilitarized zone: it is a staging center and a dangerous place. As for the United States, we entered it in search of peace, and found instead its despoilers. Joining was an expression of our hope; disabused, leaving would be an affirmation of our national pride.

The dream of nations united for peace offered the idealized prospect that political ecumenism would prevail over bellicose nationalism. But just as utopian communes have ever been vulnerable to the pride and the prejudice of their individual members, their communal founding ideals now their burial markers on history's landscape, so is the United Nations vulnerable. Presumably united for peace the United Nations simply isn't united and peace remains elusive. Nor should we be united nations. Some members have resorted to force in order to retain their hegemony—the Soviet Union, as in Czechoslavakia, Hungary, Afghanistan and Poland, let alone internally. Some intend war—Arab powers, as in their wars waged and wars still vowed against Israel. Their U.N. attestations of peace have muffled their preparations for war, and war waged, returning to the U.N. as to a masked ball, they appear as aggrieved victims. Uniting one's nation with company of this sort is akin to playing the piano downstairs and allowing as how you really don't know what the couples upstairs are doing.

Earlier we suggested that the essentially a-Semitic "neo-isolationism and the lure, as distinguished from the reality of peace," undermines Jewish interests. The United Nations is an easy example. There are more advanced lessons which American Jews are learning about war and peace and the Jewish quotient.

The Palm Beach setting for the Anti-Defamation League's winter executive-committee meeting was familiar. The Breakers Hotel, still the reigning and gracious dowager queen of Florida hostelries; the breeze swept palm fronds, tirelessly bowing and nodding their welcome; the murmuring of the lapping breakers, assuringly comforting winter's emigres; all, as always they have been.

But there was a difference this February of 1980. It was in the sessions of the venerable Jewish organization, and it had more to do with Afghanistan and the Soviet Union, with Israel and the United States than with warming Palm Beach or with chilling anti-Semitism. At that meeting, decisively moving afield from Jewish establishment organizations, the ADL called upon President Carter and the Congress to adopt a sharply increased military budget so as to more credibly deny expansionist threats to world peace. The discussion preceding the resolution seemed more suggestive of a conservative defense organization than of a Jewish human-rights agency. What kind of talk was this—of missiles and of warheads, of navies and of conscription—for nice Jewish men and women?

In fact, American Jewish organizations have not been strangers to issues of war and peace. Again and again they have called upon Washington to bolster Israel against its enemies—with armaments. But if Jews have been percipient that planes and tanks are indispensable ingredients of peace for Israel, at home we have generally opted for butter over guns.

But not this time.

Why?

There were at least two givens underlying the discussion, propelling us in this unfamiliar-for-Jews direction.

1. Recognition that the *realpolitik* stakes in the Middle East are neither Jews nor Palestinians but oil, and whether the United States and the Soviet Union respectively can feel assured that

their long range leverage in the area is secure. Jews, their awareness an expression of their experience, know well that the Soviet
Union is a purposeful persecutor of Jews and an opportunistic
enemy of Israel, while the United States has been Jewry's warm
water harbor and Israel's staunchest friend.

2. The ruthless Soviet violation of Afghanistan; its arming and
encouragement of the PLO; its lavishing of arms upon Syria,
Libya, Iraq; its stockpiling of sophisticated weaponry in South
Yemen; its capacity to land within twenty-four hours divisions
of troops in Saudi Arabia. All this and more, constituting potentially serious threats to vital American interests in the Middle
East and, as a corollary, real-world, grave threats to Israel.

Discussion was unusually sober, words carefully chosen, like
steps taken through unfamiliar, perhaps mined fields. Even the
orators, those who with their compelling advocacy or thunder-
ing rebuttals spice Jewish organizational life, spoke softly,
thoughtfully, in a kind of undeclared mutual understanding
that this time the issue itself was amply dramatic. Ambassador
Max Kampelman bridged the distance between misgiving Jewish doves and hesitant Jewish hawks by quoting Admiral Elmo
Zumwalt, former Chief of Naval Operations, on the Yom Kippur War: "I know of no competent authority in the business at
the time who did not share my view that had we gone to war
with the Soviet Union in that confrontation, the U.S. Navy
would have been defeated." Kampelman added that the dispar-
ity between the Soviet and American navies was now even
larger.

Perhaps, however, the comment most representative of the
prevailing mood, itself the organizational crystallization of the
ambivalent Jewish mind-frame toward questions of guns vs.
butter, was one participant's declared intention to vote for the
resolution while confessing to a discomfort with it. His support
for escalating our military budget was even voiced; his caution
against incipient jingoism, pop patriotism and political styles

alien to our Jewish traditions, however, was moving. And so in a sun-drenched hall on the Gold Coast of Florida, a micro recasting of an ancient and unyielding enigma took form, one faced daily in macro proportions by Israel. Guns or butter? Would voting for the weapons of war contribute to peace? Or would voting against increased arms expenditures actually increase war's likelihood?

Kenneth Bialkin, then chairman of the League's executive committee, sensing the room's mix of conflicting emotions, perhaps himself their churning vessel, called for a hand vote, one easier, more precisely counted than are voices. It might as well have been a voice vote. More apologetically than resolutely, but unanimously nonetheless, American Jews broke rank with themselves, opted for guns.

In Holland, in West Germany, in Italy, throughout Western Europe hundreds of thousands of marchers have protested the proposed American deployment of missiles, which if ever delivered would be postmarked "USSR." The demonstrators are neither anti-Semitic nor anti-Israel. Indeed, it is not demonstrable that they are anti-American in the biased sense of the term. They are propelled by fear of war, by their yearning for peace. They have not, however, demonstrated against already-in-place Soviet missiles aimed westward at their and our freedoms. Failing to protest Soviet missiles, and indeed without the influence on Soviet strategic policies which they politically bring to bear on their own governments, they are reminiscent of our America First movement in the predawn of World War II. And as the consequence of American isolationism was to slow American preparedness against Nazism, in effect shielding aggressive tyranny from resisting democracy, so do these latter-day neo-isolationists tilt the balance of power in favor of the politically predatory Soviets and away from the United States. The fortunes of Jewish interests, if not quite the fate of Israel, being subsumed under the struggle between the Soviet Union and the United States, the demonstrators for peace augur casualties for Jews.

The isolationists of the early 1940s cannot fairly be described as either necessarily anti-Semitic or pro-Nazi but their advocacy of "peace" provided the German American Bund with lulling harmony for its Nazi propaganda. And so, today. Even as well-motivated marchers—mothers and children, students, lovers, war remembering veterans—demonstrate against American missile placements and their own homeland's military preparedness, others, their allegiance the updated counterpart of the Bundists, propagandize the Soviet cause. Illustrative is Italy's dread Red Brigade. Within weeks of a massive demonstration for peace, within days of terrorists having kidnapped U.S. General James Lee Dozier, the Red Brigade issued a communique in behalf of the "organization of Communist combat." It called for "War on imperialist war! War on NATO! War on the strategic centers of the American military machine!" They, too, did not refer to Soviet missiles pointed at Western Europe. They, too, did not refer to Soviet occupation armies, in Afghanistan or poised over Poland. Their propaganda, because it is transparent, because its auspices are those of a terrorist band, is discounted by the general public. But the peaceable demonstrators, themselves ordinary people, no matter the drummers to which they march are different, would lead us to and leave us vulnerable in, the same duck's pond.

We are not suggesting collusion between the substantially numbered decriers of increased defense budgets and an enhanced American military presence in Western Europe and the bands of like-opinioned radical Left terrorists. There isn't, as by and large there wasn't a conspiratorial relationship between rank-and-file isolationists and our German American Bund or between the membership of fellow-traveling American Communist-front organizations and the American Communist

Party's leadership. We are maintaining, however, that the political consequences of an American military capacity which is inadequate to deterring the Soviet Union's, whether brought about by anti-Jewish terrorists in Europe or by a-Semitic petitioners for peace here or abroad, saps American influence. For Jews, for whom a militarily credible United States is their Middle East political leverage, a peace decreed by American military impotence will render them enfeebled keepers of their Israeli brothers.

Shortly after President Reagan's last-minute AWACS touchdown in the United States Senate, the administration's ball carriers were rested and relieved by a defensive squad. The victory secured, the Republican pols, the professional politicians whose seismographs register the voting impulses of ethnic groups and ideological constituencies, were fielded. Now was fence-mending time and a group of Jewish organizational leaders, some resentful, some flattered, and all respectful, were invited to the White House to be mended with. Likely the president neither made nor lost friends. Those among us who had favored his election and those who didn't could, upon leaving, feel vindicated in the views with which we arrived. For myself, however, the Frank-Merriwell-grown-older earnestness which I find attractive in President Reagan troubled me. Sincerely, movingly, he explained his search for peace using as his divining rod "moderate" Saudi Arabia. "Saudi Arabia is the key to this. It is the key to peace in the Middle East, and only when there is peace will Israel be secure."

It troubled me because President Reagan understands that history is devoid of evidence in which a nation having achieved military superiority has not transmuted it into foreign policy advantage. That insight, whether scholarly or intuitive, guides him in the double-pronged management of our own foreign policy and our defense budget. But in his propounded peace-making formula for the Middle East, he withholds its application from Israel, a state far more vulnerable to its contiguous enemies than are our fifty to our distant adversary.

Saudi Arabia's moderation looms larger in President Reagan's beholding eye, as it did in President Carter's, than in its actions. Immediately following the Senate's enabling vote on the AWACS sale and well before our visit with the president, the Saudis ratcheted still higher the price of oil and declared their intention to reduce its production. The president, however, did not don a rueful smile and amend his publicly embarrassed view of their moderation. Weeks later, the administration revealed that Colonel Qaddafi had dispatched killers to the United States with the thriller-movie mission of assassinating our president and our leaders. Even as our borders were being policed to abort the hit-squad's contract, Saudi Arabia reestablished diplomatic relations with Libya. The president of the United States pretended not to notice lest acknowledging Saudi immoderation and the royal family's mocking indifference to our servility, our blueprint for "peace"—they, its keystone—be revealed as a house of cards.

What Western Europe maintains openly, our State Department leaks. Middle Eastern "peace" is in the offing if only Israel would take risks to facilitate its coming. If peace can be defined as the absence of war, however, Israel has, if not enjoyed, assuredly nonetheless suffered peace with its neighbors for a decade. But war has engaged Iran and Iraq, with Arab and Moslem Jordan supporting Arab and Moslem Iraq, and Arab and Moslem Syria supporting Moslem Iran; Arab and Moslem Libya has been at dagger points with Arab and Moslem Egypt; South and North Yemen and their Arab and Moslem populations have had at each other; similarly Arab and Moslem Algeria and Morocco. Throughout the Persian Gulf, unstable, feudal and repressive regimes are engaged in power struggles in which Shiites hate Sunnis, Sunnis hate Alawites, Christians hate Moslems and as in a round dance, now turning counter-clockwise, Sunnis hate Shiites; Alawites, Sunnis; Moslems, Christians. But only Israel is scolded to make sacrifices for "peace," to cede to its despoilers the territories that are its shield and in four wars its neighbors' avenue of attack. Only Israel is politically jostled to make sacrifices for "peace" because in the *realpolitik* of our interests, both intramurally war-dead Arabs and strategically imperiled Israelis are of small account to us. Why? Because it is not really Middle East peace as such which prompts our diplomacy—else why our political indifference to warring Arabs against Arabs, to Israel's validated fear of still another *jihad?* Arab threats of oil withheld, of investments withheld or withdrawn, of hinted retaliatory flirtations with the Soviets are what ultimately count in the world of bottom-line politics, and so Socialist prime ministers and capitalist presidents urge selective peace, and because she has neither oil nor surplus funds, Israel is in the dock. There is an old Yiddish expression which has it that we speak to our daughter whom we can take for granted, really intending to be heard by our daughter-in-law. Western democracies reproach Israel, publicly lecture her to make peace, really intending to be heard by and to appease the Arabs whom we cannot take for granted.

Warlike actions can serve peace; indecisive peace can explode in war. When Israel granted pacifist supplications and the faithfuls' prayers for surcease of nuclear proliferation by preemptively laying waste Iraq's atomic-bomb factory, she was roundly condemned as an aggressor. But Israel's action, no matter it dismayed—or so they alleged—Western supplicants of the Persian Gulf, served peace. At the very least, peace between herself and a now chastised Iraq. An Iraq confident, even if mistakenly so, in its military prowess was patently a war maker. It had attacked Moslem Iran; in possession of the bomb, why not Jewish Israel? Should Israel have waited to find out? Perhaps

Neville Chamberlain would have. But would Winston Churchill, Charles de Gaulle, Franklin D. Roosevelt or Harry Truman? Even the United States, whose president had campaigned for his office in the no-nonsense syntax of John Wayne, joined in the censure of Israel whose violation of "peace" was that she had cut the cattle rustlers off at the pass. A United Nations genuinely concerned with nuclear nonproliferation and peace would have held France accountable for providing truculent Iraq with a nuclear capacity, not Israel who lessened the chances for nuclear war.

The hypocrisy of Western protestations of concern for peace and of abhorrence of war was further bared when Israel bombed PLO command posts unconscionably situated in residential Beirut. Governments, determined pursuers of terrorists in their own midst, would not, however, abide Israel's retaliation against its terrorizers. No matter that the PLO has trained the Italian Red Brigades, the Japanese Red Army, the Argentinian Montoneros, German and Turkish terrorists, Western Europe and the United States joined with Arab, Communist and Third World nations in condemnations of Israel's retaliatory strike. The raid had resulted in the death of innocent civilians. But Israel did not situate the PLO command post in urban Beirut. The PLO did. And Israelis, not Londoners, Parisians, Los Angeleans or New Yorkers were being mutilated and murdered by the PLO. In striking back at the PLO, in spurning her imposed role as passive victim for fear that in retaliating innocents would suffer, Israel's bombs served peace—again, at the least, its own. But again its critics, their economies rather than their lives hostage to Arabs, inveighed against her, intending their sanctimony to be heard as indignation in the Persian Gulf's oil-producing states.

The gelling outline for peace in the Middle East is a death trap for Israel. She is being maneuvered by sincere friends, Western governments themselves acknowledgedly levered by

Israel's most influential enemy, Saudi Arabia, to "negotiate" a "comprehensive peace." The terms *negotiate* and *peace* have in common with *motherhood* the characteristic of being unexceptional. Israel, cornered in the public-relations cul de sac of "peace," apprehensively, with wanting conviction, agrees, conditioning her amenability on being recognized by her adversaries. Recognition would presumably evidence the authenticity of Arab moderation. In the not unlikely event that the Saudis may yet, calculatedly, technically proffer recognition, the ensuing negotiations are destined to become an impassable mine field for Israel. What Israel must reciprocate for the promise of peace are its protective fences—real estate captured in wars unleashed through it against her. The Arabs would thereby receive through negotiation what in war they have failed to regain. Mightier now, they would be repositioned in box 1, from which their previous attacks were launched. In return, Israel would receive a Saudi and/or a Jordanian and/or a Syrian and certainly a PLO word of honor (no Arab power would participate in even a hollow peace with Israel without PLO sanction, lest the PLO unleash its terrorism against it). Their words of honor would be pledged by the then current ruling king, general or Moslem fundamentalist, and would, of course, have the enduring value of the life expectancy of Middle Eastern despot kings, generals and fanatical fundamentalists.

If in such negotiations Israel's concessions were deemed insufficiently accommodating, she would thereby prove her alleged intransigence. In this scenario the United States, in consideration or "friendship" for whom the Saudis would have agreed to negotiate, would be aggrieved. "After all we've done for you!" In this eventuality, the extent of United States disappointment in Israel would be conditioned by the Saudis, their price for oil, the numbers of barrels per day they produce, their American investments and imports, all being sleeved cards in the "negotiations" stacked deck.

Meanwhile, back at the ranch of American public opinion, American Jews, their conditioned reflex—explaining to gentiles—will be at it again, this time trying to explain why imposed peace really means war. And once again, the precedent having been established in the AWACS debate, we will be reading more about the "single-issue Jewish lobby" than about the Arabs' business partners, senior among whom are the oil companies and the military industrial complex of exporters to the Gulf States. This time, however, purists for peace, happenstance allies of Jews in the AWACS controversy, will be in opposition. It is not that they opposed AWACS because they loved Jews more and Arabs less but that their comprehension of peace being limited to the absence of war, and AWACS and enhanced F-15s being weapons of war, they opposed the sale. And so now, Jews being heard to argue against "peace," peace advocates not loving them less nor Arabs more, will join with market-sensitive corporate vendors of advanced technology—each in his own rationale to mollify Israel's enemies. Jewish arguments will be only faintly heard that no matter Arab remonstrations, the Golan Heights and the West Bank retained are more certain guarantors of peace than Arabs emboldened rather than satiated by their repossession.

Throughout this scenario, alas already unfolding, the role of anti-Semitism will be that of a walk-on. As in the prototype AWACS instance, Jewish interests will essentially be competing with Semitically neutral interests, among their propounders even our friends. War the Arabs' threatened card, admonitions to Israel to "take risks for peace" will pepper State Department briefings and garnish editorial columns. For Jews, themselves not immune to the hunger for peace, it will be well to remember that the last people for whom it was insisted that they "take risks for peace" now are resident in Southeast Asian "reeducation camps" or lie decomposing at the bottom of the South China Sea.

12

Affirmative Action's Negatives

WE HAVE DISCUSSED oil and its spawn of petrodollars and how they impact on Jewish interest no matter anti-Semitism has little more than a supporting role; similarly neo-isolationism and peace as a cloak for war and as a mortification of Jewish interest, though anti-Semitism is no more than an aside. There is another source of danger to Jewish interests and to their sheltering democracy, and it too is essentially free of anti-Semitism. It is the institutionalization during the past two decades of group rights at cost to individual rights.

It would seem an anomaly in the evolvement of Jewish defense strategies for Jews who have so long been bowed by the burden of group responsibility to be suspicious of group rights. Surely, group rights decreed by a benignly intentioned democratic society is an antidote for wronged individuals suffering the sting of group prejudice. Or so it would seem. The fact of the matter, however, is that quota systems—the crystallization of group rights—their birth in exclusionary discrimination, their rebirth in inclusionary recompense for past wrongs, continue to wrong both individuals and groups. Only the victims have been changed. Where yesteryear's mean-spirited quota systems arbitrarily barred doors to Blacks, Jews, Roman Catholics (notably those of Mediterranean stock) and other darker, less fashionable breeds, today's compensatory quota systems have opened the door to Blacks and selected minorities, their pigmentation now their password. But a quota system, no matter its subjective promptings, remains a quota system, granting advantage or withholding opportunity from a boy or a girl, from a student, a professor, a mechanic or an apprentice for no more reason than his parents' race. In short, just like the old quota system did.

As Mendelssohn did at the whimsical pleasure of Frederick the Great, so have succeeding generations of Jews broken free of the confines of group prejudice. But the difference between his and their freedom roads is nothing less than the difference between freedom the prize of fortuitous happenstance and freedom one's birthright under law. When the state blindfolded itself to their creed, Jews became unshackled, freed by right rather than by favor. The in-tandem fortunes of Jews and the sponsors of individual rights, their host democracies, quickly flourished. The Jewish bloom is plainly evident in their achievements in the social, economic and political worlds of Western democracies. And their good times have been reciprocated, as evidenced in the arts, the sciences, the economies of these nations and the disproportionate contributions to them by their fractional Jewish populations.

A reversion to state prescribed rights, no matter intended as inclusionary quotas, and no matter based on race rather than religion, establishes a precedent serviceable tomorrow in ways our yesterdays have taught us are anathema to Jews, depreciative of democracy.

During the early 1970s I had occasion to visit the office of the president of a New England university. Arriving, I found the corridor leading to his office occupied by some forty students lounging, sprawling this way and that, forming an obstacle course blocking entry to his office. They were white students and in some intuitive ways—perhaps their dress, perhaps their seeming ambivalence—I gathered, in puzzlement, that they were not the period's ubiquitous protesting radicals. Donning a look of firmness of purpose, moderating it with self-conscious affability in the form of "Excuse me" and "Sorry," I stepped over and around legs, torsos and heads, weaving and wending my way to the president. "Hey, Mr. Perlmutter, you gonna ask him to come out and talk to us?" I recognized the sitter-in, a nodding acquaintance, so asked him what in the world was going on. The answer was at least as instructive as the university's course in Political Science 101. The students occupying the corridor, I learned, were all of either Italian or Irish extraction. They were aware of the school's quota of financial assistance to the "underprivileged," which, they complained, really meant for Blacks only. Their contention was that in the Boston area not only were the Irish and the Italians the largest ethnic groups, outnumbering Blacks by far but that they were also, demonstrably, the area's most numerous poor. And so they wanted their proportionate share of the quota "due" them from the school's set-aside funds.

They were logical. If racial quotas, whether practiced straightforwardly or under cover of euphemism, are sanctioned, why not quotas on ethnicity? And if on ethnicity, why not on religion? The racial precedent established, its logic assumes a life of its own. On that day the populous Italian and Irish students were reacting to the disproportionate presence of Blacks as beneficiaries of the university's favors. But pursue their argument, retaining their and the university's mutually agreed upon premise that individual rights are a derivative of group identification, and what potential does it augur for Jews—2.7% of the American population?

The mischief in state-sanctioned precedents, Monday opportunistically compensatory, Thursday at the disposal of a less compassionate government, opportunistically punitive, was foreseen by George Washington in his farewell address: "The precedent must always overbalance in permanent evil any partial or transient benefit which the use can at any time yield."

How and where did we make our U-turn? The culture of white supremacy had been legally grounded in racist statutes themselves secured by Supreme Court decisions upholding the doctrine of separate but equal. In 1954, however, *Brown* v. *Board of Education of Topeka* shattered racism's legal foundation. In sounding legal segregation's death knell, the U.S. Supreme Court finally exalted individual rights over group prejudice. But soon, even as tardily we grew sensitized to the cruelty in our past racial policies, we fell back upon group discrimination, now punishing white Peter as a palliative for the pain we inflicted on Black Paul. It happened so quickly, so quietly. In the 1960s construction workers in Philadelphia were ordered to institute a racial quota so that Blacks might gain a leg up in an industry their absence from which clearly evidenced their purposeful exclusion. It was widely heralded as the Philadelphia Plan. At the time few who would later protest student and faculty quotas objected. Construction workers are predominantly limitedly educated, white ethnics. They abound in the Middle American bush but are rarely found nesting in sociology departments. And so the alarm was unsounded; quotas affecting laborers, people with linoleum on their living-room floors, were gorings involving Archie Bunker's oxen. Besides, while admittedly a racial quota system, wasn't it, after all, a long overdue correction for centuries of discrimination? Jewish organizations, practiced petitioners against the quota system,

were also uncharacteristically quiet. Racial justice, maybe mis-
guidedly, but surely long overdue was being served; objection
seemed a carping stance, even impolitic.

The failure of timely liberal responses to an awakened and
stirring quota system was attributable to other factors as well.
A Constitution tampered with is less pitiable than are victims
of discrimination and therefore deemed less in need of our
ministrations; our guilt feelings mesmerized our reasoning; our
frustrated ignorance of just how else *do* you make quick restitu-
tion for long wronged minorities sedated our future fears. And
there was something else that paved the way for the quota
system's return.

The old quota system had been routed in times during which
we celebrated the inviolability of individual rights. Human-
rights organizations, clerical leaders, liberal politicians, concerned academicians using political stumps, pulpits, billboard
posters, jingles, invoking God and our founding fathers convinced Americans to accept the precept that each of us should
be judged on our individual merits "regardless of race, color or
creed." The effort succeeded. Not only were the civil-rights
laws handily passed but discrimination based on race, color or
creed actually became gauche. Racial tolerance emerged from
the closet; racial prejudice was confined to it.

Still something was lingeringly wrong. Equal rights of access
to places of public accommodation, falling racial restrictions in
housing, employment and education did not produce the
changes envisioned in the struggle for their attainment. Equal
opportunity, the civil-rights movement's battle cry, achieved, it
gave way to an insistence upon equality of results, a quicker fix.
Virtually overnight we dismounted Individual Merit, chucking
its banner of "regardless of race, color or creed" and bestrode
Group Identity, raising its banner of "because of race and
color." No longer were our civic selves our own persons, the
core identity of each of us and the only identity a democratic

state can safely recognize, but we became Blacks or Whites, Minorities or Others. What had been a part of our identities somehow became its core—so declared by the state. From this perception of our group identity, it was an open field run to group rights and inexorably—given the motivation of its hungry pursuers and the political languor common to "haves"—to racial quotas as a means of realizing group benefits.

That reverse discrimination has been arbitrarily punitive of individual whites is self-evident; that it has been a placebo for Blacks has yet to be widely acknowledged. The economist Thomas Sowell, senior fellow at the Hoover Institution, points out that before racial "goals and timetables" for employment were mandated in 1971, Puerto Rican family income was 60% of the national average. By 1981, quotas a decade in place, it had fallen to 50%. Black family income as a percentage of white family income is lower today than it was in 1969. Moreover, the rate of economic improvement for Blacks, following the institutionalization of quotas, is slower than it was in the equal-opportunity phase of the civil-rights movement. Sowell attributes this surprise in part to quota-generated pressure on employers to favor the exceptionally qualified Blacks while at the same time disfavoring the more numerous averagely qualified minority members. The disincentive results from employer fears that if the average or less than average job seeker is hired and is subsequently passed over for promotion or is deemed expendable, the ensuing litigation—racism the charge—becomes a predictable and burdensome cost of operation. Citing a study of 50,000 academics, he found that Black faculty members who had completed their Ph.D.s and had published were earning more than whites with similar qualifications. Conversely, Black faculty members who had yet to attain their doctorates and had not yet published earned less than their counterparts. His conclusion that reverse discrimination has artifically increased demand for the exceptionally qualified Black while artifically decreasing demand for the more numerous nearer-to-average Black for fear of subsequent legal harassment was confirmed by a Black administrator: "I have no time to spend at EEOC (Equal Employment Opportunities Commission) or in the courts."

The effect of recycled racial preference on a blameless generation of whites aside, does it have the redeeming virtue of materially helping the minority community? Sowell, the dominant scholar in the field, observes:

> Quotas and preferences have been tried in a number of countries. Nowhere has any racial or ethnic group risen from poverty to prosperity by these methods, though many have done so by all sorts of other methods. The Chinese in Southeast Asia, Italians in Argentina, Germans in Brazil, Japanese in the United States, and Jews in various European countries have begun in poverty and ended in affluence while avoiding politics. Where preferential treatment has been tried, it has not merely failed to achieve its object but has torn countries apart with internal strife . . . After ten years, it is time to ask what affirmative action has achieved for the disadvantaged, and what it has done to this country.

Karl Marx once observed that history repeats itself, first as tragedy, then as farce. And so with reverse racism.

One Robert Edward Lee, a Maryland civil servant, changed his name to Roberto Eduardo Leon in order to qualify for preferential treatment for promotion. Under county law if he and other white Anglo Saxon engineers were competing for promotion and were considered to be equally competent, his new Hispanic identification would qualify him for the prize.

A court-appointed desegregation administrator ordered Cleveland highschool principals and coaches to recruit white athletes to play on the school system's predominantly Black basketball teams, and to place Black athletes on the largely white baseball teams. Basketball teams, he ruled, should be at least 20% white and baseball teams at least 50% Black.

Alan Campbell, a former Dean of the Maxwell School of Public Administration and a onetime chairman of the U.S. Civil Service Commission, solemnly declared the Professional Administrative Career Examination employed by the civil service to be "a fully validated instrument for efficiently examining a very large number of applicants from whom high quality candidates are selected for important entry level positions." Later, as director of the Federal Office of Personnel Management in the Carter Administration, he eliminated the examination. Its sudden failing? Though "validated" for "efficiently" predicting performance, requisite numbers of minority members failed to pass it.

The Los Angeles Unified School District determined to apprise itself of the ethnic identity of its employees. Requiring verification of racial or ethnic ancestry unto the grandparents' generation, it set about defining Hispanics. Asserting that a Hispanic was a "person of Mexican . . . Central American, South American or other Spanish origin," it proceeded to qualify its definition by declaring that a teacher would not be included in the Hispanic designation if he or she is of "Brazilian, Portuguese, or Sephardic Jewish origin," no matter the teacher's Spanish surname or having been reared in a Spanish culture.

A New York City qualifying test for policemen determined simple-level reading comprehension and dealt exclusively with police procedures. Of those who passed, 15% had identified themselves as Black or Hispanic. This arithmetic convinced a New York Federal District Court judge to find the test to be "conscious and deliberate" discrimination. He ordered that 50% of the police hired by the city must be Black or Hispanic.

The U.S. State Department in 1980 waived written examinations, but for minority candidates only.

Florida's Dade Community College terminated a white faculty member and retained a Black faculty member in the course of reducing staff. It justified its decision on the grounds that the white music teacher failed to meet the "needs" of Black students. In reaction, 150 students including Hispanic and Black students petitioned the school for the reinstatement of the white teacher. It seems that the dismissed white was the school's only double-reed woodwind instructor and the retained Black, a keyboard teacher.

In a 1980 meeting with Alan Campbell, then Director of the U.S. Office of Personnel Management, my colleague, trying to convey the absurd lengths to which racial preferences had run, told of the New York bank whose white employees by and large reported to work promptly at 9:00 A.M., but whose minority workers, in disproportionate numbers, straggled in at 9:30. The vice-president in charge of these matters convened the employees and lectured them on the importance of timeliness, warning that continued tardiness would be grounds for dismissal. Shortly thereafter he received a visit from an equal-employment-opportunity official who suggested that after duly considering the facts it was decided that the bank would be well advised to reflect its "cultural accommodation" by recasting its work hours. Whites should continue to report at 9:00; minority members to report at 9:30. If tardiness persisted, then the case would be given further consideration.

Having told this story, a true one, the director did not smile. Instead he pensively suggested to us that sensitivity to cultural differences was essential if ever we were to mature into a compassionate society.

The farcical results of fiats equating race to competence, worthiness and privilege do not always amuse. Sometimes they are both mean and demeaning. In a 1980 case involving the U.S. Small Business Administration, the programmed divisiveness of racial *newthink* embarrassingly bared the hypocrisy of its proponents. Perhaps equally troubling, at least to me, it introduced me to my own hypocrisy.

The Small Business Administration had rejected an application from Hasidic Jews for designation as "a socially and economically disadvantaged group" which would entitle them to federal aid provided minority-owned businesses. In their petition the ultraorthodox Jews maintained that their businesses are often shunned by outsiders because they "speak halting and broken English compounded by a thick accent" and have unusual dress such as black frock coats, broad-brimmed hats, and white collarless shirts. They told of their odd hairstyles and religious customs which "contribute to an overall image of strangeness and complement the other visible differences that set them apart from the rest of the population."

The application, submitted in behalf of approximately 150,000 Hasidim, considered in the context of other pertinent data, prompted the Small Business Administration to formally observe that "the evidence of prejudice and discrimination experienced by Hasidim is overwhelming and essentially unrefuted." Further, the bureaucrats found that the "cultural bias imposed by the larger society upon the Hasidim" was evident in suffered employment discrimination and in financing of Hasidic businesses. Thusly finding, the SBA proceeded to rule against the application. In explanation of its decision, a conclusion tortuously antithetical to its own premises, SBA held that "it would be abuse of discretion" in the absence of "express congressional direction to render a decision which might establish an impermissible religious classification." Congress, it seems, had restricted financial lifebelts for use only by "traditional minority groups."

The Anti-Defamation League of B'nai B'rith protested the decision. Indignation and its lubricating prose flowed tumultuously in my missive to the Small Business Administration.

This remnant of East European Jewry that miraculously escaped the furnaces of gas chambers of the Holocaust is being told by SBA that it is not a "traditional minority." One cannot but wonder how many thousands of years of slavery, expulsion, inquisition, ghettoization, pogroms and genocide it takes to qualify as a "traditional minority" in the eyes of the SBA.

The Anti-Defamation League has consistently and vigorously devoted itself to safeguarding the First Amendment to the Constitution of the United States. It is against this background that we believe the SBA has erred in its decision. The application did not request aid to a synagogue; it did not request aid to a religious school; it did not request aid to a religious publishing house; it did not request aid for religious purposes. The application requested aid to a socially disadvantaged minority group for secular purposes. The disadvantaged status of the Hasidic people derives directly from the manner in which they exercise their religious freedom. Consequently, to deny them the benefits of a federal program designed to assist the disadvantaged—which demonstrably they are—on the grounds of their religion, is to discriminate against them because of their religion.

It is not relevant to the telling of this story that individual Hasidim qualifying for SBA assistance are entitled to it and that the SBA provides such help. What is relevant is that as in the Orwellian state in which all men are equal except that some are more equal than others, so with affirmative-action programs for minorities, or, well, some minorities.

Significantly, the Hasidim drew support from the Black community. Ohio's Congressman Louis Stokes found the SBA opinion to be "contradictory" and "out of touch with the essence of the request." Brooklyn's Congresswoman Shirley Chisholm urged the SBA to reconsider its decision. But Sowell's foreboding about the divisive effects of racial preference were stoked by Maryland's Congressman Parren Mitchell, who in opposing the Hasidim's application said simply, "I might be sympathetic toward the economic conditions of the Hasidic Jews . . . but there's a limited pie."

And my own hypocrisy? Many Hasidim are poor and strug-
gling, but Hasidim should not by definition of their group identity receive government aid. No more than Blacks, Hispanics
or whoever. There are rich persons and poor persons and it's
the individual's own qualifications, characteristics and actions
which in each instance should determine his rights and his
responsibilities under law. Else a rich Hispanic's bite of the pie
deprives a poor white, a rich Hasid's a poor Black. Notwithstanding, I table-thumped for the Hasidim's group application.
Of course, I was being inconsistent. But if hypocrisy can be pled
guilty with mitigating circumstances, I submit that state-sanctioned racial preferences tool group competitiveness and programmed my protest. The law was drawn for "minorities" as
a constitutional euphemism for its real and illicit intention—to
favor some minorities. To stand aside, to not avail oneself of
what the law actually says, to submit compliantly to what it
surreptitiously means, is to shelter the lie, to nourish its roots.
Moreover, the pie, as crassly but accurately described by Mitchell, is just so big. My demurring, declining the law's putative
tenderings, might satisfy my principles, but it would be sore
solace to Hasidim who in their long and harried history have
ever been reminded by the state that they indeed are a minority,
uncared for and vulnerable. Comes now a benign state, tells
them they are not a minority, but that nevertheless they must
remain uncared for and vulnerable. I forgive myself, would do
it again—but only for so long as my country's laws, dissem-
bling, arbitrarily, statutorily forsake me.

Before the passage of the civil-rights laws, in times in which
our lenses were coated with group prejudice, minority persons
were invisible to us. Seeing a Black, we saw the reflection of
our own stereotypes, his individuality unseen, unregistering,
unfelt. And so today with the white applicant for the job
whose quota is filled. His whiteness defines him, as in years

past the Black's color did him. Joseph Califano, the former secretary of health, education and welfare, recalling a 1979 cabinet meeting in *Governing America,* communicates the essential cynicism of racial vision in which some flesh-and-blood persons are arbitrarily ruled invisible, others arbitrarily exempt from sentencing. "Carter wanted us also to fill out personnel evaluations of each of our key staff members. Hamilton Jordan would distribute some 'tough forms' to fill out on each one. He wanted us to review the work of our subordinates and 'get rid of all those who are incompetent, except minorities and women.' No woman or minority member could be fired; their situations were to be discussed with the White House, the President said."

This cynicism, embroidered and extended as it has been, is anything but an unqualified boon to its purported beneficiaries. Submission to demands that medical staffs of hospitals be racially reflective of the community is an example of how Blacks, long short-sticked by white racists, are now the like victims of white patronization. Provision to the minority poor and the minority sick of medical assistance, a distinguishing characteristic of which is approved color rather than demonstrated excellence, is a cruel hoax—played by do-good whites on a field of hapless minorities. The privileged bureaucrats who grant these demands assuredly will avail themselves of medical services regardless of their doctor's race, while the ghetto is assigned medical services because of the doctor's race. As if race medicates . . . or can teach . . . or can run a railroad.

But beyond group rights' depersonalization of our individuality, beyond the false pregnancy it is for minority opportunities, its lethal element is reserved for democratic government, the very source and sustenance of our individual freedoms. In 1975 the constitutional scholar, the late Alexander Bickel, said it this way:

The lesson of the great decisions of the Supreme Court and the lesson of contemporary history have been the same for at least a generation; discrimination on the basis of race is illegal, immoral, unconstitutional, inherently wrong, and destructive of democratic society. Now this is to be unlearned and we are told that this is not a matter of fundamental principle but only a matter of whose ox is gored. Those for whom racial equality was demanded are to be more equal than others. Having found support in the Constitution for equality, they now claim support for inequality under the same Constitution. Yet a racial quota derogates the human dignity and individuality of all to whom it is applied; it is invidious in principle as well as in practice. Moreover, it can as easily be turned against those it purports to help. The history of the racial quota is a history of subjugation, not beneficence. Its evil lies not in its name but in its effect; a quota is a divider of society, a creator of castes, and it is all the worse for its racial base, especially in a society desperately striving for an equality that will make race irrelevant.

13

If I Am Not for Myself . . .

IN OUR PUBLIC discourse, in our social gatherings, we are so self-referent, we Jews. I sometimes wonder what it's like being an Episcopalian. What do they talk about?

But of course, this book is about Jews and for all that here and there we have smilingly deprecated our temperature-taking tic, all the while we have ourselves been doing just that—taking our temperature, diagnosing our dis-ease. And our conclusion has been in the well-worn Jewish tradition of on-the-one-hand . . . but on-the-other-hand.

Educationally, socially, economically we have in one, two and three generations journeyed light years. But for all the distance in time and space between us and Sholem Aleichem's Tevya, like him, we worry. He worried about gentiles and about the tsar, and sought solace in his *shul* where he prayed, "Next year in Jerusalem." And he worried about his children, Juda-

278

ism's relay runners, and would they hold fast his faith's baton.
We have made our accommodation with our gentiles and they
with us—well, by and large; individually we are equal share-
holders with the Daughters and the Sons of the Revolution in
our president and at least quadrennially he pays us heed; and
for the so-disposed among us our prayer "Next year in Jerusalem" is redeemable today simply for the asking at El Al or at
TWA. But even light years leave some things unchanged. We,
too, worry about our children, our relay runners in Judaism.
Impressions these, on the lens of our experience, but evident too
in empirical data.

In 1981 the Council of Jewish Federations and Welfare
Funds and the United Jewish Appeal published a survey which
probed the views of young Jews (for Jews, the least procreative
progenitors among America's ethnic groups, mid-thirties is
young) on their weighting of Jewish communal problems, their
felt priorities for communal activities and their notion of a
"good Jew." The responses, no matter the respondents were
communal activists and consequently likely well off, arrived or
arriving, suggested an elemental concern with survival—Jewish
survival. Nearly 85% of the demographically and sociologically
representative sample worry about Jewish security, while a like
percentage regard assimilation as the greatest threat to Jewish
survival.

Asked to rank in the order of their importance eighteen
problems facing the American Jewish community, these young
men and women born after World War II and raised in the
benign social clime of the United States, nonetheless self-por-
traitured apprehension. The five topmost concerns expressed
were: the conflict between Israel and its neighbors (97% voted
"very serious," 3% "moderately serious"); the treatment of
Jews in the Soviet Union (88% and 12%); the high rate of
intermarriage (72% and 21%); the alienation of youth from
Jewish life (72% and 18%); anti-Semitism in the United States

(54% and 32%). Their topmost priorities for communal action followed suit. Foremost was the need "to provide financial support for Israel," followed by support for "Jewish education and culture," "social and welfare services for Jews in need," "to defend Jews against anti-Semitism and discrimination," and "to provide political support for Israel." The survival issues thusly given priority, they were trailed by a range of action goals in support of religious institutions, of increased participation in Jewish life, for the promotion of unity among American Jews, etc.

The survey's attempt to elicit from its respondents their concept of what makes for a "good Jew" was structured around twenty-one descriptive phrases. If the top-ranked five make for an instructive insight into the opinions of young Jewish leadership, the five lowest-ranked definitions are no less revealing. In the order of deemed importance, the following emerged as the most essential requisites of being a good Jew: accept being a Jew and not try to hide it; lead an ethical and moral life; marry within the Jewish faith; support Israel; contribute to Jewish philanthropies. The five characteristics deemed least essential were: attend weekly services; observe the dietary laws; have mostly Jewish friends; be a liberal on political and economic issues; give Jewish candidates for political office preference.

The data mirror a first-things-first realism. The prominence accorded the Jews of Israel and of the Soviet Union suggests both the long-lived injunction that we are indeed our brother's keeper—at least when he's in trouble—and the psychic saliency of Israel to American Jews. Both adumbrate our nudging fears for Jewish survival, and no matter, too, the storm watch is neither in New York nor Beverly Hills, but in distant Jerusalem and in alien Moscow. Intermarriage, Jewish education as an antidote to the alienation of Jewish youth, anti-Semitism, are our rankling domestic concerns, our perceived threats to the viability if not quite the survival of Jewish life. Given the rela-

tively lower priority accorded religious observances, it would
appear that survivalism—spiritually melancholy, but curiously
life-sustaining juice that it is—more than faith itself nourishes
us.

How to hold safe our Jewish interests in a land—ironically—more hospitable to us than to anti-Semitism? And irony
compounded because we are hostage not as Jews to anti-Semi-
ties but as Jewish standers-by to arguments not of our making.
And then, and then . . . how as a community to remain Jewishly
viable?

We have discussed a-Semitic issues, the resolution of which,
one way or another impact our Jewish interests. Among these
issues are ones in which many Jews have been strangers to,
sometimes prosecutors against, their own interests. For instance, if America has been good for Jews, as demonstrably it
has, and if the Soviet Union has been bad for Jews, as demonstrably it has, and if the two Goliaths are locked in a power
struggle, as demonstrably they are, the U.S. military budget is
decidedly a Jewish issue. Alas, organizationally, our defense
reflexes jerk more responsively to a seasonal carol in a hinter-
land public school. Moreover, are congressmen who vote
against funding our military capacity while issuing press releases championing increased military aid to Israel quite the
allies they purport to be? Our references to the Third World
have suggested Jewish love unrequited, disabused. Long the
beneficiaries of Jewish empathy, itself an expression of our own
national oppression, much of the Third World today represents
a Jewish problem, albeit they are without Jewish populations.
Of what avail our support of national independence or of insur-
gent forces in authoritarian Third World countries if the
successor governments through their United Nations delegates
gang up on Jews? We have suggested the the electoral college,
established with Jews no more in mind than Martians, is

nonetheless a vital Jewish issue. As is compensatory group rights. As are peace plans which still the short-term future but which agitate Israel's days-after-tomorrow. And the international brotherhood of the dollar is a Jewish issue, as witness the Semitically neutral sales of sophisticated weaponry to Israel's sworn killers.

There are other issues, secular and political, their seed without Jewish content, their development without a Jewish component, but whichever way they are resolved impact Jews as Jews. With other Americans, Jews have anguished over the West's dependency on OPEC oil and more latterly over our economy's thralldom to recycling petrodollars. With the onset in 1973 of oil-leveraged diplomacy, the direction of American foreign policy veered—from Israel toward Saudi Arabia. In the light of this forsaking change in American foreign policy, in view of its promptings, the Reagan Administration's commitment to the development of nuclear power is a *de facto* Jewish issue. Notable physicists favor the rapid development of nuclear power plants as a safe and effective substitute source of energy; peace professing movements and environmentalists do not. The issue's pros and cons are without a trace of a Jewish accent; they resonate, however, with implications more fundamental to Jewish interests than State Department policies, themselves in substantial measure a corollary of our energy dependence.

We must deepen and broaden our definition of Jewish issues. We must overcome our ambivalence in being perceived as an ethnic voting bloc. Is it reasonably imaginable that if there were no Jewish lobby there would be no oil lobby, no Saudi Arabian influence on American foreign policy in the Middle East? We have, alas, been disingenuous about our "Jewish power." Here and there we have advantageously utilized our voting strength and being observed, have pled, "Who me?" Our disavowals are attributable to Jewish self-consciousness, itself the consequence of feared visibility before hostile eyes. As if having special interests was in some way an admission of faulted patriotism. But, of course, observers of American voting patterns have known for some time that there is a Jewish voting pattern and the very impression of our power has been a source of it. Besides, why the shyness? Jews have been voting for candidates whose political platforms they deem compassionate of the needy, caring of the underdog, and which are critical of such socially baneful conditions as racism, discrimination and ultranationalism.

   This voting pattern has seen Jews vote against Jewish candidates and in favor of non-Jewish candidates when the former were viewed as less liberal than the latter. Moreover, Jewish voting singularly among ethnic voting patterns has been supportive of political platforms frequently at odds with the economic interests of the relatively comfortable Jewish community. All this by way of contending that there is, indeed, a Jewish vote and that it reflects favorably on our civic-mindedness. But we are affirming something else, too. That Jews must reexamine their voting impulses. Does the candidate with soothing words for Israel have an understanding of the implications for Israel's security in an inadequate American defense budget? Which candidate is the surer guarantor of peace, the candidate whose heart and whose rhetoric affirms it, or the candidate who confrontationally signals his preparedness to defend it?

   The 1980 presidential elections witnessed a change in Jewish voting patterns which may, with the passage of time, be looked back upon as having been a watershed. For decades we have been considered as being "safely" in the Democratic fold. Even in 1972, when in the Nixon-McGovern race fewer Jews voted for the Democratic Party's candidate than had been the case in modern times, that candidate, nonetheless, received 65% of our vote. Had George McGovern done nearly as well with the rest of the country, he—rather than Richard Nixon—would have ridden 1972's landslide. But in 1980 President Carter received

45% of the Jewish vote, a radical sea change in Jewish voting. Without commenting on the respective qualities of Messrs. Reagan and Carter, this stunning shift in our voting patterns, whether it be an aberration or a precursor of real change, is, we believe, a positive contribution to our interests. It suggests that in 1984 the Republican Party need no longer write off the Jewish community; conversely, that the Democratic Party may no longer take us for granted. To be sure, Jews constitute but 2.7% of the U.S. population. However, our actual percentage of the total vote approximates 5% and while even 5% is itself a small figure, given our deployment in the major states and the electoral college system, the 1980 Jewish voting distribution augurs well for both Democratic and Republican future attentiveness. At least, quadrennially.

Are we suggesting that liberals are no longer our trustworthy allies and that conservatives are?

Hardly. But to the extent that liberals support state-sanctioned racist criteria for participation in either the public or the private sector, they diminish us, diminish democracy. To the extent that in their sympathy for those who do not enjoy self-rule they are indifferent to the military-strategic implications for the United States and for Israel of a self-rule that is dictatorial or faces toward the Soviets, they are our and democracy's trappers.

On the other hand, it was Kaiser Aluminum which conceived and implemented the racial quota system sanctioned by the U.S. Supreme Court in the Weber case. Their conservative, rugged individualism crumbled before the prospect of losing government contracts in retaliation for refusing to practice reverse racial discrimination. Academic institutions thought to be the fountainhead of intellectual elitism and the merit system have indulged racial preference lest they lose government grants. Industrialists, the villainous archetypes of *Pravda* cartoons, vie with each other to sell their wares to *Pravda*'s bosses, and in consumating their sales, nourish communism, their and Jewry's nemesis.

If liberal political ideology lists its ship portside, conservative greed lists its starboard. Jewish interests are secure in neither vessel. The liberal agenda and ours are no longer coincident and at times not even parallel, while, alas, commonality with the conservative agenda is as sound as rhetoric. If here and there, liberals or conservatives are potential allies, the alliance should evolve *ad hoc,* when our interests coincide, and we ought not mistake liaisons of convenience for lasting marriage. Just as the liberal agenda has been forming and reforming in response to its ideology and to its political opportunism, and the conservative agenda in response to the self-interests of its business-minded patrons, so must the Jewish agenda look to Jewish interests. Happily, or at least fortuitously, Jewish interests are in harmony with democracy's professions—the supremacy of the person rather than of his race or class and the security of the democratic system vis-à-vis totalitarianism. Group rights effectively mean government intercession in behalf of their realization. In a popular democracy, that means the courtship by politicians of the largest and/or most leveraged groups. Therein lurks the danger of quotas to all minorities. And accommodations to the Soviets and their client states which strengthen the Communist sphere of influence, renders democratic America relatively weaker, thereby exposing Jews to dangers, the auguries of which are even now painfully evident from the gulags of the Soviet Union west to the kangaroo court that is the United Nations.

Twenty-odd years ago I used to tell this story for laughs, but the truth is that I derived from it a kind of star-spangled pride.

We were living in Miami Beach when Castro took over Cuba. When the refugees began pouring into Miami our daughter was a thirteen-year-old junior-high-school student. One dinner

time, in response to my serviceable, if uninspired, parental conversation opener: "How was school today?" she replied that
there were now over forty Cuban children in her school.

"Really?"

"Yes, and they have such funny names, Menendes, Morales,
Gonzales . . ." She paused, and then, thoughtfully, "but some
of them have American names . . . Goldstein, Schwartz."

My audiences, largely first-generation American, had personal memories of the sometime burden of a Jewish name in
years past. Their laughter was in response to our daughter's
innocence, but their pleasure was in the recognition that for all
that our sons and daughters are less harriedly Jewish than we
were, they are also more relaxedly American. And although the
story was about the innocence of a child, my intended message
was of folksy melting pots and of an America that has been
good.

America has indeed been good, but the innocence was mine.
So nervously American were we that in gladness that our children were not, I missed the real point of my own story. That
the other side of the coin of homogenization may be dilution.

Coming and going, our generation of first-generation Jews
knew itself. Coming, reared in traditional Jewish homes, dispatched to school, released to the streets, Mama's cautioning
instructions to behave communicated in Yiddish, how not
know you are Jewish? And going, entering a school world
overseen by Misses Harringtons and Mulvaneys, how not but
know you are different, you are Jewish? And later, the gentile's
confirmation of your Jewishness, his emphasis marker, discrimination. Mordant thought: Being Jewish was easier when
it was hard to be a Jew. Our parents' religiosity and their island
lives, whether in apartness imposed or in self-segregation, were
open-valved conduits for transmitting their Jewish identity to
us. Our own religiosity diluted, easy riders on the American
mainland, we have been constricted conduits to our children of

our parents' legacy. And for Jewish identity, for the politics of Jewish interests, it has had a cost. In the Boston area during the late 1960s and early 1970s Jewish students were mainstays among the disaffected youth protesting the Vietnam War, racism, poverty. Good. But the issues of Soviet Jewry and of Israel brought out another, a smaller platoon of Jewish students. A less universalist student, students who were identified—often patronizingly—as their university's Kosher Kitchen Line. We are not suggesting that participation in or leadership of public or others' causes is not a praiseworthy activity for young Jews. We are suggesting that the relatively few Jewish youth who were educatedly Jewish were the sparkplugs in issues affecting all Jews, while many universalist Jewish youth were indifferent to their relationship to Goldstein, to Schwartz. And if these are personal observations, such research as has been conducted on Jewish identification suggests a strong correlation between the degree of an adult's Jewish identification and the intensity of Jewish education experienced during the child he or she was.

But to suggest, as we are, that Jewish education is a sophisticated weapon in the arsenal of our defense, that to prevail in our political engagements but to fail as a "Jewishly viable" community is a Pyrrhic victory, is neither novel nor controversial. Jewish education has been championed, its shortening embrace deplored with the sonorous repetitiveness of rote sermons. And for all that in principle broadening and deepening Jewish education is unexceptionable to Jewry, in practice we have often and regularly checkmated its advance.

For instance, for many years bills have been introduced in the congress which would provide parents with a modest tax deduction for each child enrolled in a private elementary or secondary school. The 1981 version cosponsored by Senator Daniel Moynihan, long a dominant advocate of Jewish issues, and Senator Robert Packwood, leader of the anti-AWACS forces, pegs the deduction at $250 per student. Still, as in the instances of previous similar bills, major Jewish organizations have registered their opposition to its passage. A coalition of Orthodox Jewish organizations favors the bill.

The opposition to tax exemptions for private-school students is based on apprehension lest the wall separating church and state be breached; on concern that by siphoning off monies that might otherwise be available to public schools, deprived public schools would lose students; on fear that eased financial burdens on parents of private-school students may encourage public-school parents to withdraw their offspring from integrated schools thereby fostering racial and religious divisions; and on worry that tax exemptions may presage state meddling in private-school affairs.

Proponents of tax credits as a means of lightening inflation's burden on private schools maintain that the tax credit is for the parent, not the school, and consequently that the relevant amendment is the Sixteenth, granting Congress the power to tax, and not the First, separating church and state; that asserting deprivation to the public schools is not the same as proving it, and besides, more viable private schools are likely to encourage public schools to be more competitive; that private schools are not necessarily racially segregated schools and moreover that racial divisiveness is more apparent in public schools than in private schools; and that if state meddling in private schools takes the form of minimum requirements for teacher certification and curricula and for compulsory attendance, it warrants welcome rather than fear.

American Jews, overwhelmingly graduates of the public-school system, their success testimony to the efficacy of public-school education, or at least the public schools that were, are among its vanguard defenders. It is likely that the American Jewish Committee, the American Jewish Congress, the Anti-Defamation League of B'nai B'rith, the Union of American Hebrew Congregations, the Central Conference of American

Rabbis, the National Council of Jewish Women, all on record as opposed to tax credits, and not the Orthodox congregations, speak for the majority of Jews on this issue. But if American Jews have a debt to the public schools, how, in acquitting it, acquit as well our responsiblity to nourish Jewish education? It is disingenuous to simply offer Jewish education rhetorical good wishes. The economic dynamics of private education inexorably propel parents to send their children to public schools—not because they're better but because they're so much cheaper. But as Charles Silberman has observed, "The more acculturated American Jews become, in fact the more important formal Jewish education becomes as an instrument of Jewish survival." For Jews, the American public-school system their secular launching pad, Jewish education their banked deposit on their children's Jewish identity, the tension in the options is discomforting. The least we can do, however, is to reevaluate the urban public schools of today, determine whether they are in fact those we gratefully remember, and to ponder the consequences for our tomorrows of vaunting Jewish education while simultaneously frustrating its affordable availability.

Jews, liberals, people concerned with public education hailed *Equality of Educational Opportunity,* James Coleman's seminal 1966 massive study buttressing the educational utility of desegregation. Not so the limp greeting for his follow-up study. Published in 1981, Coleman offered impressive evidence that students in Catholic and other private secondary schools outperformed their public-school counterparts even with statistical controls for family and class differences. Private-school students were found to study harder and longer, to present fewer discplinary problems, to enroll for more advanced courses and to have lower rates of absenteeism than public-school students. In terms of our academic strategies, given these findings and their high auspices, from whom and for whom are we saving public schools? And for children trapped in deficient public schools, would not assistance to their financially strapped parents give them a better chance at the educational opportunities we capitalized on yesteryear?

But returning to the Jewish *qua* Jewish component, the premise that the adult's Jewish sense of identity is the offshoot of the child's Jewish education is incontrovertible. Moreover, while approximately one-third of American Jews never attend religious services, as many as 90% at some time in their lives belong to a Jewish organization. Indeed, it is an observable fact that as religious observance has weakened, Jewish organizational identification has remained relatively strong. Who are the members? Middle-aged persons who in their youth were reared in "Jewish homes," educated in after-public-school-hours Hebrew schools. But after-public-school-hours private schools are diminishing ranks. The Jewish home, its declining sacramentalism, its Yiddish dying even as our grandparents are, is increasingly the residence of Joneses, no matter our names end with a witz or a bloom. So it has befallen the Jewish school to be our surrogate teacher of Judaism, the hired sower of our children's Jewish learning. But alas, our private schools are in need and their financial ailments blight the propagation of Judaism. Are our memoried public schools with all their currently glaring deficiencies so meaningful to us that we must bar eased access to Jewish schools, stop at the pass future identification with Jewish life, the organizations of which are our meeting grounds and our political unions? And beyond the fiber that Jewish identity is for Jewish involvement, there is the matter of Jewish mental health. Earl Raab's study of Jews in the San Francisco area, *The Foreboding Syndrome,* found a higher insecurity among those who do not belong to any Jewish organization, but a significantly lower sense of insecurity among those identified as Jewish organizational board and committee members.

The rising rate of intermarriage and the levels of our assimilation are inversely related to our sense of Jewish identity. Be-

cause intermarriage is read as a measure for the loss of Jewish
identity and the loss threatens our social and religious cohesive-
ness, Jews have long been worriedly counting their fallouts.
Between 1900 and 1920 some 2% of Jews who married, inter-
married. Between 1940 and 1960 the rate climbed threefold to
6%. In the years 1960 to 1965 the percentage of intermarriages
soared to 17%. In 1980 the Rabbinical Council of America
reported a 50% intermarriage rate in some sections of the
United States, and a lesser but "shockingly high" rate in areas
with large Jewish populations. Bertram Gold, executive vice-
president of the American Jewish Committee, has revealed the
committee's findings that in most intermarriages "there is little
Jewish practice in the home, and little is done to provide positive Jewish experiences and Jewish education for the children."
To be sure, most Jews who intermarry identify themselves as
Jews and some involve their children in Jewish religious practices, but the momentum of seeded assimilation is building. Nor
is the seepage all into the segment of the population which
responds "None" when asked to identify their religious preference. Rabbi James Rudin, coauthor with Marcia Rudin of
Prison or Paradise?, has estimated that young Jews seeking
some form of identity constitute 25% to 30% of cult membership.

Jews are not alone in their high rates of exogamy. American
hyphenated Greeks, Puerto Ricans, Mexicans, Poles, Czechoslovakians, Italians are undergoing high levels of intermarriage.
But there are differences. They have higher birthrates than
Jews; Jews are the oldest mean-aged ethnic group in America;
the Jewish birthrate barely matches its mortality rate; all this
within two generations of our having lost fully one-third of our
numbers in Hitler's war against us. In Argentina, where anti-
Semitism seems endemic, the number of practicing Jews has
declined from 500,000 to 300,000 in the last generation. The
decline, ironically, is not attributed so much to anti-Semitism

per se as to assimilation—itself the product of weakening Jewish educational institutions.

Moses Mendelssohn's daughter converted to Catholicism;
her sons were baptized. Abraham, his son, raised his own children as Christians, explaining that he was concerned for their
social "adjustment." What does watered Jewish identity augur
for us today? Beyond our concern with Jewish survival, no
matter it is vulnerable to the charge of bathos, in the words of
Philip Perlmutter, director of Boston Jewish Community
Council, "If (the) trends continue, America will become one
big, dull glob of people who won't even know they had a grandmother." Tax credits, tutition grants, while admittedly more
complex issues than tax credits for insulating and winterizing
our homes, are surely no less insistent on our attention. They
will not winterize Judaism, but they may bring a warming
trend.

Rabbi Joachim Prinz has commented on the contradiction he
perceives in the Jewish psyche. "The apparent inability of the
Jews to understand or predict their own catastrophes. The
Jews, whose history consists of one tragedy after another, have
yet to be prepared for any one of them. Clemenceau, who as a
young man witnessed the most notorious of anti-Jewish trials,
the affair of Alfred Dreyfus, is supposed to have remarked that
'only the defendant did not understand' the Jewish implications
of the trial . . . This sort of blindness has been true throughout
Jewish history."

Rabbi Joseph Soloveichik teaches us that there are two cove-
nants that bind Jews together: the covenant of suffering and the
covenant from Sinai.

We have—or I think we have, or, at least, for the while I
think we have—learned from our suffering. If, as Rabbi Prinz
has suggested, we have been blind throughout the ages, our eyes
are seeing now. The Holocaust, infernal Lourdes, made us
sighted. Jewish sensitivity, Jewish nervousness, Jewish over-

reaction, Jewish neuroses, whatever else they may suggest mean too that our ancient covenant of suffering is our renewed compact to live. But to do battle, even successful battle, with Jew haters or those insensitive or indifferent to our Jewish interests while ourselves sieves for our legacied Jewish identity, is to default on our convenant with Sinai, to hollow our victory.

Moshe Dayan, musing on the dual challenge Jews have always faced—of having to fight their oppressors and simultaneously to fight for the preservation of their Jewish identity—would of an evening read poetry aloud with his wife. Nathan Alterman's "The Battle for Granada" was a poem he found especially poignant. In it, Samuel the governor, a thirteenth-century leader of the Jewish community of Spain and the Berber king's commander of Granada's army, is addressed by another Spanish officer:

> . . . for apart from the military campaigns of Granada
> you have another war
> a war of your own
> an unending war.
> It is the war of your people,
> whose shepherd you are.
> It is the war of your language
> whose hosts you command.
> It is the war of your son,
> whose teacher you are,
> to teach him the writing of antiquity . . .

Index

294